Musings and Meanings

Musings and Meanings

Hermeneutical Ripples...

Edited by
Nishant Alphonse Irudayadason

Christian World Imprints(TM)
&
Jnana-Deepa Vidyapeeth

First Published in 2016 by

Christian World Imprints(TM)
Christian Publishing & Books from India
H-12 Bali Nagar, **New Delhi-110015**
info@christianworldimprints.com
www.ChristianWorldImprints.com
Phone: +91 11 25465925

&

Jnana-Deepa Vidyapeeth
Ramwadi, Nagar Road, **Pune-411014**
jdvoffice@jdv.edu.in
www.jdv.edu.in
Phone: +91 20 41036111

ISBN: 978-93-5148-163-8 (HB) ISBN: 978-93-5148-164-5 (PB)

Cataloging in Publication Data--DK
Courtesy: D.K. Agencies (P) Ltd. <docinfo@dkagencies.com>

Musings and meanings : Hermeneutical Ripples... / edited by Nishant Alphonse Irudayadason.
pages cm
"... outcome of the international conference hosted in honor of two eminent veteran scholars Richard De Smet and Jean de Marneffe of the Faculty of Philosophy at Jnana-Deepa Vidyapeeth, Pune in January 2014 ..."--Editorial.
Includes bibliographical references.
ISBN 9789351481638 (HB)
ISBN 9789351481645 (PB)

1. Hermeneutics--Congresses. 2. Hermeneutics--Religious aspects--Christianity--Congresses. I. Irudayadason, Nishant Alphonse, 1971- editor. II. Jnana-Deepa Vidyapeeth, publisher.

BD241.M87 2016 DDC 121.686 23

Printed in India.

Editorial

Defined generally as the art of understanding, hermeneutics appears distinct from semiotics that is considered a science equipped with a rigorously determined method. Hermeneutics is defined as an art because the rules it sets out cannot in turn be reduced to rules, or because there are no rules for the application of rules.[1] This, according to Gadamer does not exclude the possibility of discerning in the phenomenon of hermeneutics an "experience of truth." Before him, Heidegger also emphasized the constant aspiration of hermeneutics to universality; Schleiermacher already tried to make it the theory and methodology of all kinds of interpretation.

Without intending to oppose hermeneutics and structuralism, Paul Ricœur defines in his essay "Structure and Hermeneutics" these two approaches:

> Structuralism is part of science, and I do not at present see any more rigorous or more fruitful approach than the structuralist method at the level of comprehension which is its own. The interpretation of symbols is worthy of being called a hermeneutics only insofar as it is a part of self-understanding and of the understanding of being; outside this effort of appropriate meaning, it is nothing. In this sense, hermeneutics is a philosophical discipline. To the extent to which the aim of structuralism is to put at a distance, to objectify, to separate out from the personal equation of the investigator the structure of an institution, a myth, a rite, to the same extent hermeneutics buries itself in what could be called "the hermeneutic circle" of understanding and of believing, which qualifies it as science and qualifies it as meditating thought. [...] If hermeneutics is a phase of the appropriation of meaning, a stage between abstract and concrete reflection, if hermeneutics is thought recovering meaning suspended within a system of symbols, it can encounter the work of structural anthropology only as its support not as its contrast. One appropriates only what has first been held at a distance and examined."[2]

It is worth recalling that before the constitution of philosophical hermeneutics by Schleiermacher and Dilthey, the problem of understanding was first raised in the context of exegesis and classical philology. Posed in philosophical terms, the problem of understanding had to be addressed in the context of the twentieth century phenomenology. Therefore, the question of understanding arises within a larger problematic of existence as a whole. For Heidegger, who developed the ontology of understanding, understanding no longer appears as a mode of knowledge, but as a mode of Being. To avoid remaining a prisoner of language, the analysis should go beyond the narrow linguistic plan to lead into ontology. In turn, Gadamer, in the Introduction to his book *Truth and Method*, began to narrow the field of hermeneutics by taking the experience of art as the starting point. Identifying the transmission of "truth" inaccessible by other means as unique to art, he postulates the possibility of hermeneutics as a particular mode of knowledge, the meeting point of all sciences of the mind, beyond their methodical consciousness: "The hermeneutics developed here is not, therefore, a methodology of the human sciences, but an attempt to understand what the human sciences truly are, beyond their methodological self-consciousness, and what connects them with the totality of our experience of world."[3] Thus, Gadamer seems to be trying to develop a value neutral or ideological free theory of how human beings understand and interpret reality, garnering it universality in the process.

Whereas literary science focuses on writing techniques, the transmission methods of significance to reveal the mechanism of the literary text, hermeneutics introduces Being in an endeavor to self-understanding and understanding of others. The need for appropriation in the literal sense of hermeneutics responds to the demands of objectivity of literary theory.

However, as Paul Ricœur points out, to get there we must overcome the otherness of cultural codes: "the very work of interpretation reveals a profound intention, that of overcoming distance and cultural differences and of matching the reader to a text which has become foreign, thereby incorporating its meaning into the present comprehension a man is able to have of himself."[4] For hermeneuts, there is a genuine adherence through knowledge to the otherness proven and overcome, that is to say, from a distance. For Ricœur, distanciation incorporated by the hermeneutical experience represents the condition of all understanding.

This edited work titled "Musings and Meanings: Hermeneutical Ripples..." is the outcome of the international conference hosted in honor of two eminent veteran scholars Richard De Smet and Jean de Marneffe of the Faculty of Philosophy at Jnana-Deepa Vidyapeeth, Pune in January 2014 to dwell extensively on the art of understanding from both the Eastern and the Western perspectives. All the scholarly essays in this edited work critically engage with contemporary theories of cross-cultural understanding and the discourse on the stranger. This work therefore is attempt to formulate a cross-cultural interpretation that incorporates the ambivalence of boundaries, the enabling dimension of essentialism and acknowledges the role that fore-meanings and fore-structures have on cross-cultural understanding.

I am indebted to many persons who have contributed to the success of this international conference and the publication of this book. I wish to thank all the scholars both from India and abroad for their contribution to this book. A brief description of all the contributors is given at the end of this book. A special word of gratitude is due to Prof. James Ponniah, the former Dean of the Faculty of Philosophy and Prof. Kuruvilla Pandikattu, the present Dean as well as all the staff and students both former and present of Jnana-Deepa Vidyapeeth. I am hopeful that this work will give fresh insights on hermeneutics and will contribute to further research on this theme.

Nishant Alphonse Irudayadason
Jnana-Deepa Vidyapeeth
Pune-411014

Notes

1 "L'herméneutique est comme un art parce que les règles qu'elle énonce ne peuvent pas à leur tour être ramenées à des règles, ou parce qu'il n'y a pas de règles pour l'application des règles." Christian Berner, *La Philosophie de Schleiermacher* (Paris: Les Editions du Cerf, 1995), 49.

2 Paul Ricœur, Structure and Hermeneutics," in *The Conflict of Interpretations: Essays in Hermeneutics*, ed. Don Ihde (Evanston: Northwestern University Press, 1974), 30.

3 Hans-Georg Gadamer, *Truth and Method*, trans. Joel Weinsheimer and Donald G. Marshall, Second Revised Edition (London: Continuum, 1989), xxii.

4 Paul Ricœur, Existence and Hermeneutics," in *The Conflict of Interpretations: Essays in Hermeneutics*, ed. Don Ihde (Evanston: Northwestern University Press, 1974), 4.

Contents

Chapter 1

Navigating Cross-Hermeneutical Currents
A Subaltern Perspective

Felix Wilfred
Professor Emeritus, University of Madras, Chennai

In his presidential address to the Indian nation on the eve of the 65th Republic day, Shri Pranab Mukherjee spoke of "populist anarchy," and thus made a veiled attack on Delhi Chief Minister A. Kejiriwal's street protests. Kejiriwal responded with a simple proposal: "Let's have a debate on the subject." This very invitation testifies not only to the polysemy of the word "anarchy," but also to the possible perspectives, sometimes contradictory, on any act. In this "populist anarchy" accusation, the questions would be as follows: what exactly constitutes anarchy? Would political activism, a *dharna* by the ruling Chief minister, be seen as unconstitutional? Can an agitationist against corruption be considered as a harbinger of political disorder and confusion?

My second example refers to one of the seven fundamental rights recognised by the Indian Constitution, namely, the *Right to Life*. This right was traditionally interpreted in a liberal vein: the state guarantees one's security as a citizen. But Justice Krishna Iyer gave it a new hermeneutics, and thus expanded its meaning. Moving beyond the narrow perspective of a right to mere existence, Iyer's interpretation pushed the frontiers of understanding of this right to include all those essentials that make life liveable. Hence, right to life is not simply about providing security to one's life; rather it should be read as the right to all those provisions indispensable for a dignified human life. The new interpretation means that the state should protect an individual's right to live near the place of work; malnutrition of children would become a violation, as would the suicide of indebted farmers.

The above examples not only point to the polysemy of words, the plurality of possible interpretations and the conflicts of interpretations, but also emphasize the way hermeneutics affects life and the experiences of everyday life. Hermeneutics is therefore a vital issue touching upon all areas of the life of people and society.

I do not intend to cover all areas and questions regarding hermeneutics. Nor do I plan to construct a discourse on the Western versus Eastern hermeneutical traditions, for, as postcolonial studies have shown, the reality is much more complex, and such simple contrasts are best avoided. What I intend to do is to examine how both these traditions could converge in enlightening the life of the world, of humanity.

For this, I approach the question of hermeneutics from a conscious bias, namely, from the perspective of the subalterns. Therefore, my reflections will focus on the implications of the various issues and questions of hermeneutics on the life of the subalterns. This is possible and necessary. To speak on hermeneutics from the subaltern perspective implies trying to bring out the social and political implications in every act of interpretation. It is an attempt to bring into conversation the hermeneutics of East and West with focus on the cause of the subalterns, and to see how a dialogue between these two traditions would contribute to this project.

Feminist studies, postcolonial theories, and postmodernism tend to reject the contrasting of the subjective and the objective, and question the concept of objective truth. The last serious attempt to dichotomize the subjective and the objective was by Emilio Betti, whose very ideological moorings lie in the radical difference between subjectivism and objectivism.[1] As such, Betti's objectivism made him a vehement opponent of the hermeneutical views of Hans-Georg Gadamer modeled on '*horizontverschmelzung*' (fusion of horizons), and the dialogical structure of understanding. Like Betti, E. D. Hirsch opposes the philosophical position of Gadamer on the impossibility of arriving at an objectively determinable meaning. For Hirsch, the meaning is already determined and it never changes. A defender of objectivism, Hirsch redefined hermeneutics as the logic of validation.This position is far from the truth. What we can realistically aspire for is as Amartya Sen stated, a "*positional objectivity*" resulting from what feminist theorists would say a "*standpoint epistemology*." This is the perspective from which I will be reflecting.[2] For, such a perspective is the one that helps us most to understand and interpret the reality and experience of the subalterns.

Convergence of Indian *Dhvani* and Western Hermeneutics

Heideggerian hermeneutics is not merely a method, nor is it a tool. Nor does it limit itself to being an epistemological question of understanding and the conditions for its possibility. It also goes beyond the classical Greek and Western metaphysics of being as an ontic reality with its own nature and essence, or metaphysics of presence. For Heidegger, the manifestation of being itself is a hermeneutical act. It is in interpretation that being comes to be and reveals itself (*aletheia* – truth as manifestation of being), for which, of course, language is very important, as the second Heideggerian efforts will show. However, interpretation is not so much about bringing out the meaning of a text (*Auslegung*), as bringing to manifestation the being. It is not so much about *meaning* (*Bedeutung*) as about *significance* (*Bedeutsamkeit*). Heideggerian hermeneutics is about the significance and meaning of human existence, an interpretation of *Dasein* – being-in-the-world. Ultimately, for Heidegger, human understanding of existence is hermeneutics.

I see here reflections of the Indian concept of *dhvani*, and I think that there could be a fruitful encounter between the *dhvani* theory of Anandavardhana and the existential hermeneutics of Heidegger, and to some extent with the anthropological hermeneutics of Paul Ricœur. *Dhvani* is not the primary meaning of a text, but is its very breath and soul; it is the experience of being drawn into the vortex of the suggested (secondary/implied) meaning of the text, moving beyond its literal meaning. The text evokes this significance, something like in the Heideggerian view of the interpretation of the self and its transformation that happens by *standing under* (understanding) the text.

In Indian philosophy, *dhvani* (literally 'sound') is a hermeneutics of poetics. The word derives from *dhvan* 'to reverberate,' signaling the power of the *dhvani* poetry to echo endlessly within those hearers or readers capable of merging with its soul. The meaning of *dhvani* is 'suggestion,' 'resonance,' and refers to the implied and evoked meaning behind a text. It is the suggested meaning of the text, the disclosed meaning behind the stated, literal meaning. This implied meaning most often escapes the reader at the first encounter, and it is only in the subsequent readings that it is revealed. The grammarian Patanjali explained *dhvani* thus: a word has two facets, the *sphota* – a permanent and invariable element of the articulated sound, and *dhvani* – the actualized, variable element of the sound. But it was Anandavardhana, who developed the hermeneutical theory of *dhvani* in his *Dhvanyaloka*. In doing so, he let Indian linguistics move beyond the realm of mere semantics to the realm of poetics. The different Indian schools of thought did not accept the theory of *dhvani* and the implied, suggested meaning it represented. The opposition was strongest in the Nyaya and Mimamsa schools, whichlay emphasis on the grammar and structure of a text, especially that of poetry; it did not recognize the evocative role of a text.

Here are three examples of *dhvani*. The first one refers to a seemingly banal experience in day-to-day life. As dusk approaches, a grandmother says, "It is already getting dark."[3] The distinct phonetic, syntactic and semantic features of the phrase "it is getting dark" is fixed, and the sentence signifies the setting sun and the fast approaching night, but the suggested meaning of the utterance varies. The differences in the meaning of this phrase depend directly on the context, the speaker's intention, the hearer's disposition, and so forth. Thus, the simple evocation of the grandmother "it is getting dark" triggers various existential responses from those around, the father, the mother, and the child. For the father, it is time to get the cattle home; for the mother, it is time to light the lamp; and for the child, a warning to finish the homework. In another context, the same sentence would imply the time for tryst with one's beloved. The phrase is experienced differently according to one's situatedness, one's existence as father, mother, child, or beloved. In fact, the suggested meanings are infinite. Likewise, a text becomes polysemous in relation to one's singular existential condition, and it could perhaps even be pointless to assign a universal meaning to any text for that matter.

The second example refers to the reading experiences that most of us have had. A book that held us spellbound as children has lost its magic when we return to it as an adult. Alternatively, a book that seemed simple, when read as a child, brings out clusters of meaning that we never suspected it had, when read at a later stage of life. It is as if meanings lay glued in secret layers behind the words, with each reading revealing more hidden meaning. The text has not finished speaking to us. In the first experience, the text that held us enthralled as a child does not speak to us as before; does not evoke sentiments or feelings in us as it did earlier, because we neither perceive nor receive it as we once did. In the second reading experience, we have allowed the soul of the text touch us by sensing, and receiving what lay beyond the literal meaning of the printed words that we had not hitherto perceived.

My last example is from *Dhvanyaloka* of Anandávardhana, and is a *vastu-dhvani*:

> "Mother-in-law lies there, lost in sleep; and I here;
> You should mark these before it is dark,
> O traveler, blinded by night
> Tumble not into our beds aright"[4]

In the above verse, the speaker, a married woman, is in fact, contrarily to the denoted meaning of her words, extends an invitation to the passing traveler. The idea (*vastu*) is suggested, and not voiced. Her real needs and desires lie veiled, but resonate alone with the traveler alert to the suggested meaning behind her words.

Dhvani is, therefore, neither a matter of moving beyond literal sense to metaphorical meaning, nor finding a *sensus plenior*. *Dhvani* is the soul to the body of a text. This is also the hermeneutics of Heidegger.

Both these traditions – *dhvani* and Heideggerian hermeneutics – invite us to explore a further aspect with reference to the *collective dimension of human existence*. Society, or a group, is not merely an aggregate of individuals. There is a collective 'we.' Hence, my question is, can we not expand the hermeneutics of Heidegger and *dhvani* by giving a collective and subaltern twist? Interpretation is not simply an understanding of one's being and situatedness, but also interpreting the existence and situatedness of a group as subaltern, as oppressed, marginalized, and excluded. Let me explain the point further.

Texts, symbols, and works of art create a different resonance in Dalits, tribals, women, African-Americans, aboriginals, indigenous peoples etc. They bring out a different *rasa* and emotional response. *Rasa* is the expansion of *dhvani*. Could there be a conversation between Western existentialism and phenomenological hermeneutics and the *dhvani* theory of interpretation, especially in its aspect of *rasa* and emotion? Heidegger's hermeneutics and *dhvani* converge as both of them point towards transformation. Besides this similarity, I think there is one other dimension of *dhvani*, which can help Heidegger's hermeneutics to expand further. I mean the *emotional aspect* or the *rasa* aspect of *dhvani*, which is missing in the Heidggerian hermeneutics. Nevertheless, subsequent developments in hermeneutics in the West after Heidegger, especially the rhetorical criticism, have taken into account this emotional aspect in interpretation. However, this dimension is not sufficiently explored.

A point of bridging between the *dhvani* interpretation and Heideggerian existential hermeneutics could be found in the New Testament, especially in the parables of Jesus. The parables are not meant to be taken literally. Rather, they point to another world of reality to which the listener is invited to respond, not simply through intellectual assent, but with the involvement of one's whole being, and with emotions. It appears to me that the *rhetorical criticism* as a hermeneutical method approximates the *dhvani* interpretation. In *rhetorical criticism,* a text is independent of the author; it exists with semantic autonomy like a work of art, going beyond the origin of the text and the meaning intended by the author. The parables become *metaphors* (different from *simile* where the comparison is explicit), as it evokes, suggests, transforms the listener, the reader. Thus, the parables of the Kingdom evoke and suggest a different reality rather than explain it. In contemporary Christology when *Jesus is spoken of as the metaphor of God*, something profound is being said. It does not give an intellectual explanation of who Jesus is as Chalcedon did, but brings before the reader or the listener a new world of experience.[5] While the historical criticism is limiting, because it confines itself to the meaning of the text as the authorial meaning, a *dhvani* interpretation of a parable like the Good Samaritan, or the father of the prodigal son, has evocative power and eternal fascination on a wide range of audience. They provoke response, so to say, at the gut level.

Furthermore, I find resonance of the *dhvani* concept in the distinction between sense and reference of Paul Ricœur. Let me quote:

> The sense of a text is not behind the text, but in front of it. It is not something hidden, but something disclosed. What has to be understood is not the initial situation of discourse, but what points towards a possible world, thanks to the non-ostensive reference of the text. Understanding has less than ever to do with the author and his situation. It seeks to grasp the world-propositions opened up by the reference of the text. To understand a text is to follow its movements *from sense to reference*: from what it *says* to what it *talks* about.[6]

In Ricœur's thought, the texts or works (*œuvre*) are triggers to the interpretation of existence, a disclosure of a possible world. Moreover, this applies as well in the case of the collective existence of the subalterns. There are texts which served to hide and obscure their true selves (like *manusmriti* in the case of women and outcastes), and there can be texts which bring out the true being of Dalits, women, indigenous peoples, and other marginalized and discriminated against groups. What kind of *dhvani* do classical religious and literary texts, symbols, and signs evoke in the subalterns? Do they, perhaps, suggest a world of oppression and discrimination? If that is the case, what aesthetics and *rasa* experience they could bring to the subalterns?

The above considerations lead me to a second cluster of issues and a new set of reflections.

Text-Constitution and Hermeneutics

Hermeneutics has its origin in the interpretation of classical philology and canonical texts (both judicial documents as well as sacred texts). As such, hermeneutics had the following tasks:

Interpretation: Conflicts in interpretations of classical and sacred texts, due to multiple factors, necessitated an art of interpretation (*ars interpretandi*) to provide rules of exegesis. This was the traditional role of hermeneutics. It was in service of resolving contradictions and settling controversies regarding the correct meaning of a text, for a wrong interpretation would undermine the authority of the sacred texts. In Indian thought, the simplest devise to resolve contradictions in interpretation was to make a distinction between the literal sense (*abhida*) and the figurative, metaphorical sense or metonymy (*lakshana*). In the West, at first, interpretation was concerned with the two fold meanings in a text, the literal, and the allegorical, and to its refinement; in the Middle-Ages this led to the four fold types of interpretations: literal, allegorical, moral and analogical. Those seemingly contradictory passages in the sacred texts were sorted out with the help of these distinctions.

Clarification: Obscure passages in the texts, or aphorisms like the terse *Sutras* required explanations, explications, and further elucidations. In Indian Schools of Thought, this would take the form of commentaries (*bhashya*), and commentaries on the commentaries.

Reconstruction: In some cases, hermeneutics helped in reconstructing the original texts (*Urtext*), which were most often extinct.

The act of choosing a particular text to be considered sacred from myriads of similar texts requires interpretation. In other words, the inclusion (of certain texts as sacred) and the exclusion of other texts from the Canon is a hermeneutical act. The formation of the Canon in which inclusion and exclusion are practiced is a primordial act in which hermeneutics, and the background of the practitioners of hermeneutics, are implicated. The fixing of the New Testament Canon, for example, meant the exclusion of many early Christian literatures like the excellent treatise the *Didache*, or the materials of *Apocrypha*. The case is much more with Indian scriptures.

Thus, hermeneutics not only follows but also precedes the creation of sacred texts. To consider a text as valid and authoritative is itself hermeneutics. Interpreters confer an authoritative character on a text by claiming it to be of divine origin, of having been inspired, and so forth. In its most fundamental(ist) form, inspiration is interpreted as a divine dictation. As s*ruti*, Vedas are considered eternal, not authored by humans – *apauruseya.* It is the source of all revelation and knowledge (the principle of *vedamulatvam*). But before being considered as sacred, there were major conflicts of interpretations with the authority and validity of Vedas being questioned and challenged especially by the *carvaka*, and the *sramana* tradition of which Jainism and Buddhism are a part. The division of *astika* and *nastika* schools is not so much a matter of belief in God or lack of it; rather *astika* and *nastika* have to do primarily with the acceptance and denial of the authority of Vedas.

> The Vedas were not, originally, *scriptures*, for they were written only late in history. They were a fixed text, kept alive by oral recitation as a symbol of the community. Acceptance of the Vedas meant an acceptance of a valid point of reference accepted by the community. In a sense the acceptance of the Vedas seems to have a role similar to the singing of the national hymn, or the recitation of

> the creed in a Christian public worship: it expresses primarily the will of faithfulness to one's tradition, subject always to different interpretations about its significance.[7]

Even among those who accepted the sacred texts as symbol of the community, there were differences in its interpretation, in as much as Mimamsa thought of Vedas as the exclusive authority differing from the position of Nyaya-Vaisesika for whom rituals were not an end in themselves but only means or a preparation to wisdom.

We also need to raise the question of the participation of the subalterns, the marginalized, and the victims in the process of text creation, especially when these texts are the sources for their powerlessness and social marginalization. In other words, we need to raise the question: who creates the text? Who interprets it? To whose advantage are the texts interpreted? Without such critical scrutiny, the claims of sacrality could become counterproductive to the cause of humanization, especially for the cause of the subalterns. This problematic is reflected in the conflict of interpretation based on the questions and concerns of the individuals and communities, which brought forth different versions of the original text, emphasizing different standpoints. Thus, we have not only Valmiki's version of *Ramayana*, but also other adaptations and versions, the best known being the North and South versions. In short, hermeneutics not only interprets texts but also creates a multiplicity of texts and interpolations. The role of the community is, here, very important. I think it is with the process of creating sacred writings through hermeneutics, that the question of orthodoxy and heterodoxy has also come into play. From the perspective of power, often the interpretation of texts by the powerless and from marginalized communities and from their world of experience gets characterized as heterodoxy. To put it differently, the interpretation of orthodoxy and heterodoxy cannot be divorced from the difference in the social world.

Critical Hermeneutics and its Role for the Cause of the Subalterns

Habermas' critique of the hermeneutics of Gadamer needs to be taken seriously. We cannot assume that every interpretation happens successfully and that "understanding persons are willing to submit themselves to the claims of the text and to enter into the traditions which the text represents."[8] For, besides the limits to hermeneutical understanding, there is an ideological, and I may add, a political element in every act of interpretation causing often a systemic distortion in communication. The scope of hermeneutics gets larger now, because its challenge is now not only to interpret, but also to facilitate a process of non-repressive communication. Here, hermeneutics become really a critical intervention as it raises suspicion about a given text or commonly accepted interpretation.

Let me at this point highlight the importance of the "hermeneutics of suspicion" for the subalterns. This critical hermeneutics unmasks and deconstructs the prejudices inherent in the text. A good example would be the deconstruction of the entire Bible, especially the New Testament by feminist theology, and the deconstruction of classical works, including *manusmriti* by Indian feminists.

To substantiate my claim for the need of a critical hermeneutics and its role for the cause of the subalterns, I take an example from the postcolonial, ideologically colored interpretation of the parables by the German biblical scholar Joachim Jeremias. I am referring to his interpretation of the parable of the labourers in the vineyard (Mt 20:1-16). According to Jeremias, the laborers were standing in the marketplace doing nothing, because in the Orient people are lazy, and do not work! [9] The well-known work of the postcolonial thinker Edward Said has many similar examples in his celebrated work *Orienatalism*.[10] Such prejudices are the warp and woof of colonial texts and its knowledge-system. Postcolonial hermeneutics as a critical hermeneutics does many deconstructions.

Critical hermeneutics can relate to an entire system of thought, deconstruct it, and present a counter-perspective. This is what Daya Krishna, one of the great contemporary philosophers of India, did in his *Indian Philosophy: A Counter Perspective*.[11] In fact, Daya's entire writings reflect a counter-perspectival hermeneutics. So, is also, the deconstruction of the myth of *purushasukta* by the Dalits, which is in line with the millennial old deconstructive critique of the *carvakas* and of the *sramana* tradition. Deconstruction is in fact a reconstruction of myths.

The subaltern condition interpreted through postcolonial hermeneutics converges with the Biblical understanding of the poor, and its perspectives on them. In a way, postcolonial hermeneutics goes beyond a liberation hermeneutics interpreted through Marxist theory and analysis. For, in postcolonial hermeneutics, there is not only a class analysis but also analysis based on caste, gender, geography, etc.

We need to direct our attention also to the fact that the Bible itself presents situations and practices in the context of empires and diverse forms of colonialism: Egyptian, Assyrian, Persian, Greek, and so on. One may not understand the Book of Esther, for example, except in the context of Babylonian empire and its colonial practices. The book of Jonah is situated in the context of the Assyrian empire. The New Testament has the backdrop of the imperial Roman rule and domination. The people of Palestine of Jesus' times were under the Roman colonial rule. Such being the case, the Bible itself presents many ambiguous and complex interpretations, sometimes tending to favor the colonial rule and other narrations representing a resistance and revolt against it. *Bible in that sense is an admixture of both colonial ideology and postcolonial theory*, which in fact necessitates that it should be subjected to critical scrutiny, and may not be used solely as an unambiguous text to speak of God, the world and of human beings. It requires not merely the application of historico-critical method and literary criticism, but also a good measure of postcolonial hermeneutics. Such a critical hermeneutics, with its ideological critique and deconstruction, will prepare the ground for the liberation of the subalterns, and help bring out their agency.

The Significance of Structuralist and Poststructuralist Hermeneutics for the Cause of the Subalterns

Indian tradition also has a structuralist approach to language, and to the relationship of various units of a sentence, text etc. especially in the *Purva Mimamsa* school of thought. This traditional heritage is well brought out in modern times by Kunjunni Raja in his *Indian Theories of Meaning.*[12] In the West, with Ferdinand de Saussure, a structural-linguistic approach came about. Both these traditions have many things in common, and they go beyond a genetic, lexicographic, and philological study of language, namely the diachronic approach to language. Both the Indian and Western structuralist tradition have *synchronic* approach to language and its structure.

Structuralism may be accused of being a closed system and self-referential.That is only partly true. On the positive side, however, it brings out the radical relativity in language where the very nature and meaning of any part is entirely dependent on its relationship to other parts and to the whole. What happens in the realm of linguistics serves as a paradigm to interpret society, inter-human relationships, community, and various other areas of our life and action.

Post-structuralism does not take for granted the structures, but goes behind them to investigate the genesis of the structures and its constitution as well as the process of structuration. As tool of radical critique of the structuring process of structures themselves, post-structuralism opens a vast field of liberation for the marginalized.

Particularly, poststructuralist hermeneutics makes us aware of the gaps and silences, in the text, in history, in tradition, in literature, in cultural expressions.Postmodern and poststructuralist approach to historiography, for example, contests constructs of historical narratives as if they were seamless, and shows the manner in which the voices of the silenced and marginalized are stifled. Though colonial and nationalist historiographies may appear antithetical to each other, they in fact, share something in common on one count. They both have marginalized the voices and narratives of the subalterns.

The subaltern approach has helped to revise mainline historiographies and to come out with a critical subaltern historiography.

Further, if structuralism, especially structural linguistics, shows that the very identity of the various constituents of the language stand in interdependent relationship to each other and to the whole, thus bringing out the radical relativity in the meaning making process, post-structuralism and postmodernism help us realize the infinity of the semantic potential of texts through an unending process of interpretations. Both of them play a liberative role for the subalterns in as much as they release texts and symbols from the tyranny of canons and censures, and create new spaces for the display of the subjecthood and agency of the subalterns.

The Pragmatics of Hermeneutics – East and West

It is possible to identify streaks of this pragmatic and liberational orientation in the Bible and Marxist-inspired liberational hermeneutics, as well as in certain aspects of Buddhist hermeneutical tradition. Well-known is the silence of Buddha on ultimate questions, as is also his critique of unproductive speculation and intellectualism. Moved by the existential question of suffering and ways to overcome it, Buddhism naturally cannot be expected to focus its attention on theoretical issues for their own sake. The Biblical, Marxist and Buddhist traditions focus on hermeneutics as a service to the goal of liberation. This is what I would call the pragmatics of hermeneutics. It is inspired by practical and pedagogical concerns. Against these concerns, we can understand the challenge Buddhism represents to the exaggerated importance given to hermeneutics in the study of ultimate reality as is done in theology and in religious studies.

Postulating that enlightenment as the path to liberation is open to all, Buddhism took forward its pragmatic orientation. Vedas and their intellectual interpretation do not serve this goal. They were in fact rejected. *Buddha*, *dharma*, and *sangha* are practical goals and ideals, which can be striven after without the crutches of texts, interpretation, and knowledge. Moreover, sensing the danger of objectification of the ultimate realty, if the process of conceptualization is deployed, Buddhism became very weary of it. This is not to deny the intellectually rich and vigorous hermeneutical tradition in Buddhist history, which has other orientation and goals than of interpreting the Vedas to bring out their meaning. In short, Buddhism represents a caveat to all interpretations that is divorced from *anubhava*, *anubhuti* and *satori*. Things should be interpreted differently to different people as the Shakyamuni did depending on the needs and capacities of the people. That is what any physician would do – prescribe different remedies for different people and for different maladies.

Pragmatic and pedagogical (*upaya*) concerns have shaped Buddhist hermeneutics. It could be illustrated with the parable of the burning house from the *Lotus Sutra*:[13] A fire broke out in the house of a wealthy man whose many children were playing inside the very house; lost in their games they were unaware of the fast consuming fire. When all appeals of the father to the children to come out went unheeded, he resorted to a practical way for luring them out of the burning house and to safety. He promised them loudly those very toys which they always wanted, and which he knew they would not resist: bullock carts, goat carts, deer carts, each to their liking. The children rushed out of the blazing house, to find their father outside not with the different carts that he had promised, but with just one bullock cart. However, this bullock cart was not a cheap toy cart, but was of great magnificence, draped with precious clothes, adorned with jewels, and drawn by many white bullocks. The children all receive several such bullock-carts, but they were all of the same appearance and of the same kind. The parable shows the inadequacy of reasoning, in this case on the danger of fire, which would not have brought their liberation. What led them to liberation was the *upaya-kaushalya* (skillful or clever means). The issue here is not whether the man resorted to trickery to get his children out of the burning house, whether he was guilty of falsehood for promising them three different kinds of cart, whether he kept his promise or not. The real issue was to save the children from the fire.

Conclusion

In conclusion, let me point out a few areas, which would require further explorations. In our global world, one of the crucial questions is *alterity*. How does one deal with differences and identities? How are these constructed? Classical and modern hermeneutics have many insights to contribute to the issue of *alterity* – cultural, ethnic, linguistic, geographic, etc. They create a world where pluralism can be at home by allowing myriad interpretations. The sea of interpretations is open for everyone to swim and move about. Inter-cultural or cross-cultural hermeneutics saves this pluralism from being a disoriented freedom and autonomy. Cross-cultural hermeneutics brings the interpretation in conversation with each other, and for mutual transformation. It helps us to enter into the world of the other and create room for the other in one's own world. How do we approach cross-cultural hermeneutics when the other is not simply a neutral entity, but a marginalized, a discriminated and a victim? Subaltern hermeneutics needs to explore how it could give a liberational perspective to cross-cultural hermeneutics.

Further, subaltern approach would call for a communitarian hermeneutics for which concepts like pre-understanding (*Vorverständnis*) and hermeneutical circle need to be retooled to the questions and concerns of *community*. There are still strong traces of what I would call liberal and individualistic hermeneutics both in the East and in the West, and which is now challenged by a subaltern approach to the issue.

Another area which I have not dealt with, but which I realize is extremely important is the field of *tradition and hermeneutics*. It is indeed a vast and critical area. Let me just allude to a beautiful metaphor given us by Abhinavagupta in his commentary on Bharata's *Natyasastra.* Abhinavagupta is comparing the past and present to the lower and higher rungs of a ladder. There is continuity with the past, but the past is not oppressive since one climbs up (which is not possible without the lower rungs of the ladder). Standing on the higher rung, one has a better vision of reality, which was not possible in the past. Positioned on the higher rung, we are able also to understand the past better. Hermeneutics cannot be stuck as an interpretation of tradition, its heritage, and its symbols. As it should serve the cause of liberation, so it needs to be oriented towards the future, even when it interprets the past. The lower rung could also be served as a trampoline for a better future, instead of allowing it to be an obstacle to progress and to a higher tomorrow.

Notes

1 Cf. Richard E. Palmer, *Hermeneutics: Interpretation Theory in Schleiermacher, Dilthey, Heidegger, and Gadamer* (Evanston: Northwestern University Press, 1969); George Wright "On a General Theory of Interpretation: The Betti-Gadamer Dispute in Legal Hermeneutics," *American Journal of Jurisprudence* 32, no. 1 (January 1987), http://scholarship.law.nd.edu/ajj/vol32/iss1/8.

2 In an earlier contribution, I had developed certain perspectives on subaltern hermeneutics and showed how it helps overcome the five different polarities in interpreting religious traditions. See Felix Wilfred, "Towards a Subaltern Hermeneutics," in *Asian Dreams and Christian Hope*, 2nd edition (New Delhi: ISPCK, 2003), 245-266.

3 Cf. Anand Amaladoss, *Indian Exegesis: Hindu-Buddhist Hermeneutics* (Chennai: Satya Nilayam Publications, 2003), 102; M. Leelavathy, "Evolution of Indian Theories of Hermeneutics," in *Indian Theories of Hermeneutics,* ed. P. C. Muraleemadhavan (Delhi: New Bharatiya Book Corporation, 2002), 129-144; T. Vasudevan, "Hermeneutics and the Dhvani Theory of Interpretation," in *Indian Theories of Hermeneutics,* ed. P. C. Muraleemadhavan (Delhi: New Bharatiya Book Corporation, 2002), 343-348.

4 As cited in Anand Amaladoss, *Indian Exegesis*, 103.

5 I am reminded of the well-known work of Roger Haight, *Jesus the Symbol of God.* More appropriate, from the perspective of dhavani, would have been a title like, *Jesus the Metaphor of God* which has much greater evocative power than the word "symbol."

6 Paul Ricœur, *Interpretation Theory: Discourse and the Surplus of Meaning* (Fort Worth: Texas Christian University Press, 1976), 87.

7 Gispert-Sauch, "Orthodoxy and Heterodoxy in Hinduism and Buddhism," in *Christian Orthodoxy, Concilium* 2014/2, ed. Felix Wilfred and Daniel Pilario (London: SCM Press, 2014), 114.

8 Werner Jeanrond, *Theological Hermeneutics* (New York: Crossroad, 1991), 67.

9 See Joachim Jeremias, *The Parables of Jesus* (London: SCM Press, 2003).

10 See Edward Said, *Orientalism* (New York: Pantheon Books, 1978).

11 See Daya Krishna, Indian Philosophy: A Counter Perspective (Delhi: Oxford University Press, 1991).

12 See K. Kunjunni Raja, *Indian Theories of Meaning* (Chennai: Adyar Library and Research Centre, 2000).

13 See *Lotus Sutra* chapter 3.

Chapter 2

Celebrating Difference
Doing Philosophy Otherwise

Nishant Alphonse Irudayadason
Professor, Jnana-Deepa Vidyapeeth, Pune

Misunderstanding or being misunderstood in ordinary everyday communication and event is a common human experience. The challenge to have a correct understanding of an event or an experience that makes a profound impact on our lives is even greater. Such experience would include religious and meta-religious experience or a cordial friendship. We are brought to realize at once that meaning making is not univocal. We do not share a homogenous space in the process of understanding and meaning making. Derrida once raised an interesting question: "Are we Jews? Are we Greeks? We reside in the difference Jew and Greek, which perhaps the unity of what we call history."[1]

This search for who we are seems to offer a fertile ground for our probe into the question of the equivocal aspect of meaning making. It follows that a comparative study is a better and more appropriate approach to address this question. However, we should take care not to make a superficial comparison between philosophers or poets or mystics or different traditions to end up in syncretism. we need to rather engage in a serious dialogue with people or traditions, precisely to note the different space or non-space they occupy and then attempt to see if they are comparable from any semantic axis that can hinge this difference without however not subsuming this difference and reducing it to some kind of uniformity. In addition, the choice of comparison we have made here is not between two philosophers or philosophical traditions, but between two mystics and mystical traditions – Tirumular and Luria (Tamil Śaiva mystical tradition and Jewish Kabbalah mystical tradition. We will also relate them to the Greek philosophical tradition by referring to some philosophers including Plato and Derrida.

The Ineffable Mystical Experience

The mysticism of Tirumular is expressed in poetic form suggesting an intrinsic link between mysticism and poetry.[2] Toynbee says that the truth apprehended in the mystical experience is naturally expressed in poetry. Ordinary language is unable to communicate this experience. In other words, mystical experience is ineffable and resists conceptualization. It cannot be described, but appreciated as a work of art. That is why Tirumular speaks of it as "a nameless experience" (*nāmam a̱ra ni̱ṟral*). Bryant ranks poetry into two categories: *saguṇa* (with attributes) and *nirguṇa* (without attributes). The former is based on historical events, presenting a narrative in poetic form, and the latter is based solely on a personal experience of an intuitive poet and it reflects an intimate personal experience. The poetry in *Thirumandiram* is *nirguṇa*, that is, without attribute as Tirumular speaks intensely of openness to the transcendence from his personal experience. In his *Jñāna-sūtram*, Bōganāthar said that the mystical experience is incomprehensible in propositions, but comprehended in the moment of sharing.[3] While trying to communicate what is ineffable in itself, a mystic uses a paradoxical and nebulous language.[4]

The nebulous language contains simplicity of deception (*ēmā̱ṟrum eḷimai*). Tirumular uses ordinary language in his poems to address both the initiated and uninitiated to mysticism. His poems have therefore two levels of meaning: linguistic and symbolic veiling the deeper meaning to the uninitiated by the use of symbols, but borrowed from everyday life. The nebulous language envelopes and hides the sacred in the ordinary, the transcendent in the worldly, and wisdom in the paradox. This language is cryptic and can be understood by the insiders. Tirumular calls it *śūnya-sambhāṣṇai* whose equivalent in Sanskrit is *sandhyā- bhāṣa*.

Tirumular uses several terms to talk about his mystical experience. He designates it as *yoga- samādhi*, evoking the idea of infinite space. This space is neither outside nor inside, but in between the two. It evokes the meaning of a veiled depth, and inexpressible consciousness; a transcendental consciousness of non-duality.

Penetration of oneself by oneself (*korugi-k-kiḍakkum tu̱rai*) is a mystical state in which the human person attains liberation. The term he uses for liberation "*vīdu*," which literally means home and thus liberation is home coming. Paradoxical as it may seem, it is a homecoming, a coming back to oneself but after having transcended the narrow confines of self-identity. Tirumular suggests that even Vedas have not talked about this experience: "Tranquility begins where Vedas end" (*Thirumandiram*, 128/126).[5] In *Tiru-viḷaiyāḍal-purāṇam*, a Śaiva literature is also found a similar idea, "*vēdam kiḍandu taḍumāṟum vañca veḷi*," "the veiled pure space that Vedas find difficult to explain." This idea highlights both the limits of the Vedas and the ineffable nature of the mystical experience.

Siddhas use the term *veḷi*, which literally means space and *para-kayam*, eternal space to refer to the final liberation. Tirumular calls the state of liberation "*tōyāda tu-veḷi*," pure spotless space (*Thirumandiram*, 1768/1751). The Siddhas also employ the *veṭṭaveḷi* to designate the infinite and transcendental consciousness, different from the consciousness of the "I" conditioned by temporality. Outside of historical time, *veṭṭaveḷi* continues the movement of the past towards the future through the present. It is a "space" where there exists neither day nor night (*Thirumandiram*, 80/62, 1856/1835). A true *yogin* is *kāla-atīta*, who will go beyond time; he lives in *akāla*, non-historical or primordial time. *Akāla*, which has neither before nor after, is eternity, eschatology, that which is always to come in Derrida's parlance.

Tirumular uses another word *kaḍuveḷi*, indeterminate vacuum, which the Siddhas replaced by a well-known term in Indian philosophy, *śūnya*. *Kaḍuveḷi* or *śūnya* should not be understood as emptiness in the ordinary sense, but should be understood as non-substantiality; it is openness itself, indescribable by concepts, beyond the matrix of space and time, the abandoning of duality and every discursive thought. *Kaḍuveḷi* is nothingness, but also fullness; it is consciousness without content. It is not a negation of what is, but a negation of all determination. It is an undifferentiated state, an "empty space," deprived of a fixed centre. This is not a theory, but the end of all theories about reality. It refers to the absence of both subjectivity and objectivity, thus destroying every conceptual opposition. For this very reason, it is the state of bliss and tranquility, which Tirumular calls *yoga-nirvāṇa* (*Thirumandiram*, 1466/1451). For Tirumular, *nirvāṇa* is neither existence nor non-existence, lest it is limited. There is a loss of the concept of the "I" in the cosmic consciousness without limit, which Tirumular calls "*pērinpaṭṭu-aruḷ-veḷi*," supreme bliss (*Thirumandiram*, 123/121).

In other words, the term *nirvāṇa* can evoke the idea of absence. Speaking of the mystical experience of joy, Eckhart said, "A teacher says that pure knowledge, even here, in this body, containing so much joy than the joy of all creatures is really just nothing compared to the joy that pure knowledge conceals in it." The concept of nirvana is paradoxical; for Stace, it is "empty-full paradox."[6]

Tirumular compares mystical experience to the experience of joy in loving union, "*anuboga-k-kāmam*" (*Thirumandiram*, 2943/2831). It is so intimate that it can neither be expressed in words nor be depicted even in art. We can only experience this joy and pass on to mystical silence, *summā*. The term *summā*, in the literature of the Siddhas, refers to the mystical silence, although we can use no word to designate this silence without doing violence to it. This mystical silence is the silent language of the heart. It is the state where transcendence and immanence are brought together at once, the state in which the self becomes a witness in the quiet. For Tirumular, this silence is not merely the absence of words, but also the tranquility of the consciousness (*Thirumandiram*, 1896/1876) *Summā* or *mauna* is the inexplicable bliss, peace of mind, that Siddhas refer to as *aṟi-tuyil*, sleep without sleep or again *yoga-nittirai*, vigilant sleep. It is a state where clouds of obscurity disappear. Tirumular names this state *tūṅgi-k-kaṇḍār*, perception while asleep (*Thirumandiram*, 129/127).

Appālaikku appāl, beyond the beyond is another term used by Tirumular to speak of mystical experience (*Thirumandiram*, 1768/1751). In all mystical literature, there is a tension between the impossibility of expressing the experience and the desire of the mystics to verbalize, hence the paradoxical expression "beyond the beyond." Tirumular recognizes that expressing in words what is inexpressible is a paradox (2468/2585). This experience is inexpressible precisely because it does not follow certain logic of language. It is a state when one cansay, "I am you." Tirumular says that the copula "am" is not of the logical order, but of the mystical order. Thus, he invites us to understand the teaching of the Upaniṣads: *tat tvam asi*, which means "you are that."

Différance and Trace

While attempting to permeate into the heart of Derrida's philosophy, we might wonder if his philosophy does not fall in line with some kind of mysticism. It is with this objective that we shall now discuss Derrida's elaboration on his thinking of différance and trace, but by relating it to the Jewish mystical tradition Kabbalah. It is unlikely that Derrida has drawn inspiration directly from Kabbalah but his acquaintance with the philosophy of Walter Benjamin who has also contributed to the sharpening of Derrida's thinking; it is more than likely that Derrida knew some aspects of the mysticism of Kabbalah.

In order to facilitate our attempt to bring together Derrida'a philosophy and the mysticism of Kabbalah, let us briefly dwell on the two important philosophical notions of Derrida, différance and trace. He employs the term différance to suggest a new way of understanding the relationship between the pairs of binary opposition and its foundation. Derrida's deconstruction of the binary opposition is not a simple reversal of the privilege accorded to one binomial over the other, but the unveiling of the dynamic between the binominals of a pair: both are already and always mutually "contaminated," each inscribing within in what Derrida called the trace of the other.

Speaking of différance and trace, Derrida does not follow the rules of philosophical and logical discourse, though these rules themselves are included in différance, but adopts another logic adventurous search. "If there is a certain wandering in the tracing of différance, it no more follows the lines of philosophy of its symmetrical and integral inverse, empirical-logical discourse. The concept of play keeps itself beyond this opposition, announcing, on the eve of philosophy and beyond it, the unity of chance and necessity in calculations without end."[7]

For mystics, some form of discourse is beyond the rules of logic, and even precedes those rules. In his book *Mysticism and Philosophy*, Stace argues that mystics generally regard their experience as ineffable precisely because they try to express an experience whose logic is relational and which precedes all empirical experiences of multiplicity and differentiation. As we have noted earlier, the language Tirumular employs to express his mystical experience is nebulous, off-logic and even paradoxical. It is therefore not surprising that Derrida immediately after recalling the idea of "off-logic" *(hors-logique)* in discourse evokes mysticism while interrogating its preeminence.

The reason for interrogating the preeminence of mysticism, according to Derrida is that it carries with it the idea of the absolute, the principle of unity, God and can make present it to the subject in a singular act of conscience. In an interview with Rötzer broadcasted in the German radio, then published in German titled *Französische Philosophen im Gespräch* in 1987, later translated and published in English in 1995, he said the following:

> At any rate, unfortunately or fortunately, as you like it, I am not mystical and there is nothing mystical in my work. In fact my work is a deconstruction of values which found mysticism, i.e. of presence, revelation, of absence of a mark, of the unspeakable. If I say I am no mystic, particularly not a Jewish one as Habermas claims at one point, then I say that not to protect myself, but simply to state a fact. Not just that personally I am not mystical, but that I doubt whether anything I write has the least trace of mysticism.[8]

However, an attentive reading of Derrida's article titled "Difference" help us observe striking similarities between some of his major themes and those of Kabbalah. In order to bring out the similarity between the two, we shall discuss certain concepts of Lurianic Kabbalah such as *Tsimtsum*[9] and *Ein-Sof.*[10] We shall then compare them with Derrida's understanding of différance and with his criticism of the metaphysics of presence and logocentrism by making use of Platonic *khora* (χώρα). In doing so, we will seize the opportunity to show the similarity between Derrida's différance and the mysticism of Kabbalah as well as that of Tiumular. Our objective is not to make Derrida a mystic, but to show that his philosophy has some affinity with mysticism. This comparison should not be considered a definitive interpretation as this would then become essentialist and would ruin the very spirit both of Derrida's deconstruction and of mysticism.

Derrida holds that the identity of everything is dependent on its difference from all other things. This means that every entity contains within itself the system of differences, which constitutes that entity which is not unique, single, and self-sufficient. Its identity is shared between itself and the system of differences that allows it to be defined. This idea seems conflicting with the mystical experience of singularity, of the absolute and the foundation of unity. However, this unity is simple, that is before any experience of multiplicity. The experience of the oneness of the mystic, indistinguishable from any ontic reality, leads to the belief that, at the deepest level of experience, everything is found in everything else. "All are one" is a proposition close to the thought of Derrida insofar as every being contains a trace of the entire system of differences, which gives it its full meaning. We can subscribe to the idea that the mystical experience of unity comes before the act, whatever name we may give to it: différance, *Tsimtsum*, creation, etc., whereby multiplicity comes to exist. The Kabbalists hold that once multiplicity has occurred through *Tsimtsum* then reinforced by the *Sheviratha-kelim*[11] (breaking of the vessels), division, alienation, and exile are spread throughout the world.

This idea is similar to that of Tirumular. To better substantiate our claim, let us have a quick glance at the idea of Tirumular on the divine and on *māya*. The divine, for Tirumular, as in Kabbalah is transcendent; he is even transcendentally transcendent (*parāparam*). No attribute is sufficient to speak of his real nature (*svarūpalakṣaṇa*) except through negation such as "neither... nor" or "neti... neti" in the Indian tradition.

Tat-Param is a name given to the divine, but he cannot be limited to this name alone, which evokes only a few attributes. *Sadasivam* is another name for the divine. He is *aru-v-uru*, which means he is with and without form. Hence, we cannot designate him only as *aru*, without form or *uru*, with form. In our imagination, we can conceive of him in all three possibilities: formless, with form, both formless and with form, but it is a wonder as inexplicable as the joy of the loving union. The divine is beyond speech and thought. Designating him by one of these attributes is limiting him. This is the mystical paradox: God is so transcendent that we cannot give any attribute, and yet so immanent that he remains united to us. Tirumular expressed this paradox through several words *antarayāmin*, internal ruler of the self (*Thirumandiram*, 27/26), *viśvarūpa*, or the universal form (*Thirumandiram*, 10/9), etc. In the Kabbalist language, in himself, the divine is *Ein-Sof* but he contracts in during the process of creation.

According to Lurianic Kabbalah, the fragmentation of the world is due to the *sefirot*,[12] originally each of them distinct in itself and not linked with others. This idea is untenable for a unique and well-defined self-identity is contradictory in itself. As Derrida notes, a well-defined self-identity may eventually give way to a vision of an integral world wherein a thing can be itself only when it contains in itself all the rest, what the Kabbalists call *Tikkun ha-Olam*.[13] The *shevirah* is the result of a way of thinking and being, always looking for an ultimate difference and distinctiveness. However, the foundation of all thought, the difference paradoxically starts failing itself. According to Derrida, the trace of otherness remaining in the heart of the same crosses the boundaries of all beings. By a striking coincidence, Kabbalists use the same terminology "trace," *reshinu* located in the vacuum created in the course of the divine *Tsimtsum*. As Derrida's trace ensures that the difference never complete, the *reshinu* ensures that *Tsimtsum* is never in its totality.

Concealment of Self-Presence

Moltmann in his book *God in Creation*[14] traces the origin of this concept of divine withdrawal to the ancient Jewish doctrine of *Shekinah*, according to which the infinite God can so contract His presence that He dwells in the temple. In the seventeenth century, Isaac Luria applied this notion to creation such that the existence of the world outside God is made possible by an inversion of God. Lurianic kabbalah claims that the first act of *Ein-Sof* was not one of revelation and emanation, but, on the contrary, was one of concealment and limitation. The starting point of this theory is the idea that the very essence of *Ein-Sof* leaves no space whatsoever for creation, for it is impossible to imagine an area that is not already God, since this would constitute a limitation of His infinity. . . . Consequently, an act of creation is possible only through 'the entry of God into Himself,' that is, through an act of *Tsimtsum* whereby He contracts Himself and so makes it possible for something which is not *Ein-Sof* to exist.

Scholem explains the paradox that the *Ein-Sof*, the infinite God, is *Ayin*, nothingness: "In the self-limitation of the divine Being which, instead of acting outwardly in its initial act, turns inward towards itself, Nothingness emerges. Here we have an act in which Nothingness is called forth."[15] In a certain sense, *Tsimtsum* and *Ein-Sof* are equally paramount, because if in the latter, are distinguished individual beings, it is the former that allows for this differentiation.

According to Schneur Zalman letters are the vehicles of *Tsimtsum*, since they are the first elements with which the finite world is created and thus differentiated from *Ein-Sof*. In them, *Tsimtsum* takes flesh and the space it opens up between letters allows for the unity of sound, and the space between words, allows for signification. The Lurianic Kabbalists stress the character of differentiation of *Tsimtsum* by identifying it with *Din* (judgment) power, which is the source of moral, spiritual, and material distinction in the world. *Tsimtsum* veils the fullness of *Ein-Sof* to himself, insofar as it is the origin of space and time and the vehicle of unveiling, thus deferring the presence of *Ein-Sof*. Individual beings can exist separately from the divine fullness, because their union with *Ein-Sof* is constantly deferred in space and in time. If *Ein-Sof* were present fully, space and time would disappear and the "differential matrix" allowing for the distinction of individual beings would be blurred. Derrida seems to have appropriated the concept of *Tsimtsum*. In his book, *Memoirs of the Blind*, he refers to the conditioned vision resulting from the withdrawal [*retrait*] of traits, which form the portrait.[16] These traits are similar to Venetian blinds that structure the light passing through them, allow for a particular kind of vision. Derrida goes even further to compare the removal of traits and other structural elements of art to the withdrawal of God and emphasizes the idea metaphorically that if we see God without "blinds," we would be blinded by the intensity of his light.

> Is it by chance that in order to speak of the trait we are falling back upon the language of negative theology or of those discourses concerned with naming the withdrawal [retrait] of the invisible or hidden god? The withdrawal of the One whom one must not look in the face, or represent, or adore, that is, idolize under the traits or guise of the icon? The One whom it is even dangerous to name by one or the other of his proper names? The end of iconography. The memory of the drawings-of-the-blind [déssins-d'aveugles] it has been only too clear for quite some time now opens up like a God-memory [memoire-Dieu].[17]

Lurianic Kabbalists believe that space and time, as well as individual beings, are constituted by *Tsimtsum* and therefore by absence. In Lurianic Kabbalah, the very essence of the finite being is the absence, that is, the concealment and contraction of *Ein-Sof*. *Tsimtsum* creates absence of the heart being, giving it a place, "spacing" that allows for the differentiation of finite entities, and characterization of their property. Is individual identity is defined by a relative absence, that is to say, by the concealment of the divine light. *Tsimtsum* leads to the assertion that every finite presence is constituted by absence. For the Kabbalists, the very nature of finite and temporal existence is to be impregnated with absence. They identify this absence with the divine trait (Din) that brings judgment and distinctions into the finite world. For Derrida, the present moment has no meaning in itself because we cannot experience it outside the past and the future. Therefore, the present is never present completely, but is only as a trace contaminated by the absence of the past and the future. Located beyond the logic of non-contradiction, trace marks the place where the binary opposites such as identity/difference and presence/absence continuously intersect.

For Lurianic Kabbalists, time is both the vehicle and the result of *Tsimtsum*. Full presence is possible only for a timeless God. Since human person is a created being in time, it is inevitable that his/her presence is always constitutive of absence. What he/she is at a given time, for example in the present moment, is constituted by what he/she is not: what he/she was in the past and what he/she will be in the future. His/her very identity is constituted by a past that is no more and by a future that has not yet arrived. It is from this perspective that we can understand Lurianic thought, namely that *Tsimtsum* the *Shevirah* and *Tikkun* are present at all times.

Tsimtsum, insofar as it generates finitude and limit, conditions death and ignorance. Indeed, the very subsistence of finite entities is some form of death and ignorance. Consciousness is inscribed in the very heart of finitude.

Coincidentia Oppositorum

The binary opposition, which underpins the History of Western philosophy appears when each binominal of the pair takes part in the difference of its opposite, for example, "the intelligible as differing-deferring the sensible, as the sensible different and deferred."[18] Derrida uses this idea of *coincidentia oppositorum* as a means to overcome the privilege of a one binomial in a pair of conventional binary oppositions of Western thought, thus deconstructing the fundamental idea of the Western metaphysics.

To this idea of Derrida, corresponds the Kabbalistic view according to which, the opposites are contractions and mutual concealments. One of the binary opposition, deconstructed by philosophers referred to as postmodern is the binary truth/lie. For example, Jabes in his book *The Book of Questions* says, "Reb Jacob, who was my first teacher, believed in the virtue of the lie because, so he said, there is no writing without lie. And writing is the way of God."[19]

The Kabbalists, in their conception of creation as *Tsimtsum* (concealment), deconstruct, in their way, the opposition between truth and lie. *Ein-Sof* creates the world by an act of concealment. This concealment was made through the Hebrew alphabets and through language in general. Letters take flesh in the Torah, which becomes the prototype of creation itself resulting from a linguistic process. Scripture, the divine revelation for creation is also a concealment of the divine truth; this revelation/concealment inaugurates "lie." Creation, from a certain perspective, is manifestation, realization, and perfection of divine truth, but from another perspective, it is alienation, denial, delusion, and deception. Schneur Zalman claims that "even though it appears to us that the worlds exist, this is a total lie"[20] Lie, as hiding the truth and as a permanent possibility of linguistic deception is indispensable if there is creation and revelation. Lie, for Kabbalists, exists in *coincidentia oppositorum* with the truth.

Tirumular speaks of the divine that illuminates the non-liberated soul (*paśu*) by his grace, but he also obscures the soul by the three malas or impurities. This divine power to obscure the individual soul is called *tirodhāna-śakti* and its obscuration is so intense that it deprives the individual soul from knowing his/her own self and the divine (2259/2233). This is part of the divine play: he simultaneously conceals himself from the individual non-liberated soul and grants him/her the grace for knowledge. Tirumular underscores the importance of *coincdentia oppositorum* in the divine play of revealing and concealing.

The Kabbalists use the terms *achdut hashwaah* to express the idea that *Ein-Sof*, the infinite God is a "unity of opposites." According to Azriel, *Ein-Sof* unifies within itself being and nothingness "for Being is in Nothingness after the manner of Nothingness and Nothingness is in Being after the manner [according to the modality] of the Being... This teaches us that Nothingness is Being and Being is nothingness"[21] *Ein-Sof* is "absolutely undifferentiated in a complete and changeless unity…He is the essence of all that is concealed and revealed."[22] For Azriel, *Ein-Sof* is also "the principle in which everything hidden and visible meet, and as such it is the common root of both faith and unbelief."[23]

A thorough analysis of the Lurianic Kabbalah can help us discover a set of symbols applicable to God, world and humanity, which overcomes the binary oppositions of traditional metaphysics. Each symbol expresses *coincidentia oppositorum* between supposedly contradictory ideas in thought and speech. Luria affirms the following:1) the divine principle of the world is both *Ein-Sof* (infinite) and *Ayin* (absolute nothingness). 2) Creation is both *hitpashut* (emanation) and *Tsimtsum* (contraction). 3) *Ein-Sof* is creator of the world, but also constantly "created" through spiritual and ethical acts of human persons. 4) *Sefirot*, original elements of the world, can be fully realized only in a fragmented and differentiated world.

For Tirumular *coincidentia oppositorum* is the inevitable to think of the divine, whatever name we give him. He is both transcendent and immanent; the Tamil word *kaḍavul* to denote the divine involves both, "*kaḍa*" which means transcendence and "*ul*" which means immanence. He is *aru-v-uru*, both formless and with form. He is Śiva and Rudra, both caring and scary. As Otto says, all religious experience is ambivalent. We always find a double dimension: fascinating and despicable. *Coincidentia oppositorum* is already found in the *Taittirīya Saṃhīta Veda* dated around the eighth century BCE. This Veda contains a litany of hundred names of the divine. Later in the epic *Mahābhārata*, dated between third century BCE and the third century CE, there is a litany of a thousand names of the divine. Strangely, these litanies attribute many negative qualities to the divine such as rogue. The only way to explain this phenomenon is accept Otto's thesis that these litanies are examples of *coincidentia oppositorum*.

A careful study of two key elements of Kabbalah, *Tsimtsum* and *shevirat ha-kelim* can shed some light on the Kabbalistic understanding of *coincidentia oppositorum*. In *Tsimtsum*, there happens a meeting of opposites between positive acts of creation and revelation, and the negative acts of concealment, contraction, and withdrawal. According to Luria, God did not create the world from a new and finite substance, but by contraction and concealment of a single infinite substance, which before contraction, is both "nothing" and "everything." *Ein-Sof* reveals the structure of the finite world through a selective concealment of his own infinite. By concealing his absolute unity, he gives rise to a finite and differentiated world. Therefore, *coincidentia oppositorum* exists in *Tsimtsum* between creation and negation, and between revelation and concealment.

For Luria, the realization of *Ein-Sof* is still linked to a second *coincidentia oppositorum* between creation and destruction, symbolized by *shevirat ha-kelim*. *Ein-Sof* is fully itself only when the *sefirot* are broken before being restored by humankind (*Tikkun ha-Olam*). Source and creator of all, *Ein-sof* however, becomes himself only through a rupture with the result of an alienated world in need of restoration (*Tikkun*). Thus, just as the human person depends on *Ein-Sof* for his/her existence, *Ein-Sof* depends on humanity to be what he is. *Ein-Sof*, *Shevirah* and *Tikkun* point to *coincidentia oppositorum* among views in opposition, according to which human person depends on God and God depends on human person.

God depends on us, because he dwells in us who are his "temple." This idea of Tirumular is not only an indictment of the binary opposition between mind and body, the first pair binominal privileged over the second, but also a reminder that it is through human person that God engages in extraordinary task of recreating the world. Schneur Zalman held that the truth of opposites is necessary for God and the world to be united in their essence. He argues that the true meaning of the world is in a dialectical movement from non-being to being, with return to nothingness. He says, "The purpose of the creation of the worlds from nothingness to being was that there should be *Yesh* (Creation), and that the *Yesh* should be *Ayin* (Nothing)."[24]

Khora

In one of his dialogues titled *Timaeus*, Plato uses the term *khora* to refer to a place where in the demiurge engraves images of forms. It is well known that Plato narrates the creation of the world by the demiurge. According to Plato, there are two kinds of realities: the intelligible, invisible forms and the visible, tangible things modeled after the forms. However, Plato also introduces a third kind, which is *khora*. The Platonic *khora* is a place from which all things grow to the extent that *khora* receives the seeds of forms, which are like the "father." Having received the impressions of forms, *khora* generates sensible things, which are, so to speak, "children." Plato compares *khora*, the receptacle to a "mother" or "nurse." More importantly, he also says that "it is by the same name that it [that is khora] has to be called, because of its own virtue at all it withdraws, receives indeed constantly all things, and similar to any of those who enter it, it never appropriates any form in any respect, in any way." *Khora* remains formless and yet must have a name.

Sometimes Plato uses many positive images to speak of *khora* such as receptacle, space, matrix, and mother, as if it were the author of Aristotle's *hyle* and Descartes' *extensio*. At other times, he speaks of *khora* in negative terms: neither logos nor mythos, neither being nor non-being, neither sensible nor intelligible, neither present nor absent, neither active nor passive. In this trope, it has neither meaning nor identity; even the "receptacle" appears in its interiority. It gets everything, but becomes nothing. It is, for Derrida, the unspeakable and impossible other. Yet it is beyond the metaphysical one and good. It is nothing insofar as it is without character. We can only say it is the possibility for something to occur.

For Derrida, from the mysterious aspect of the receptacle a follows discourse equally mysterious about it in Plato's thought, as well as in the history of interpretations of Plato's *Timaeus*. Like *khora*, the discourse concerning it "oscillates between two types of oscillation: the double exclusion (neither/nor) and the participation (both this and that)."[25] The oscillation of the discourse is explained by the fact that *khora*, as Derrida says, is an "anachronism."[26] Every time it is called by its name, it cannot be what it is, because, as a third kind, it always comes before the intelligible forms and sensible things modeled after forms. *Khora*, as Derrida points out, is both older and more recent than things it produces. This "anachronism" means that it is the receptacle of all things, and yet it receives without receiving, it contains all things but is not part of anything. Nevertheless, it must be named. Only to the intelligible forms or the sensible things, we can give names such as "mother" or "nurse." In order to name *khora*, we are forced to make use of its contents whether they are intelligible forms or sensible things. If we find a name within the receptacle to name the same receptacle, then the condition of this name, to paraphrase Derrida, becomes undecidable.

As Derrida gives the precision, use of the name "mother," for example, is not a metaphor, since the concept of metaphor is founded on the opposition between the sensible and the intelligible, the very opposition contained in *khora*, but excluded from lack of form that defines it. We can see this paradox in another way. Whenever we try to make a closure to the receptacle of all, it is necessary that we go beyond the limit of everything to occupy a position outside of it. Whenever one occupies such a position, it is not a receptacle of all, since there is a position outside of it. Thus, that the position of *khora*, the receptacle is occupied neither in its interiority nor its exteriority. The difference between the inside and the outside is no longer certain and no longer determined. That is why Derrida calls *khora* "non- place."

Khora is therefore related to Derrida's différance.[27] "*Différance* is the nameless of this open-minded, uncontainable, generalizable play of traces. And khôra is its sur-name."[28] For the Kabbalists, *Ein-Sof* is both the transcendent being and the nothingness, since he empties himself and contracts himself to open up a space (*tehiru*) in which the world is born. *Khora*, for Derrida, in as much as it is différance and desert giving place to all, comes before religion. *Khora*, like the desert, is a pre-original "place," an impossible "origin": a place that is organized neither by religions, nor known by philosophical theologies, but it is "the most anarchic and anarchivable place possible, not the island nor the Promised Land, but a certain desert that which makes possible, opens, hollows or infinitizes the other."[29] *Khora* is a placeless place, but makes place for singularity; like Derrida's différance, it is the very possibility of gift opening itself to those who, precisely because of their difference, are "aliens" in all categories such as social, economical and political. It is a play opportunities conditioned by différance in favor of those who are different and therefore marginalized. This favor does not arise from a semantic logic, but from a deconstructive logic, namely that the marginalized can have a chance when possibilities are wide open.

Conclusion

By way of conclusion, we need to ask if the hermeneutical appropriation of mystical approach to philosophy has relevance for socio-political issues of our times. Certainly, it gives an alternative to the metaphysical approach to reality. Traditional metaphysics posits unity between the self and the other to the point of absorbing the other into the self or posits a total separation between the self and the other to the point of self constantly opposing the other, thus giving way to an inevitable conflict and violence. We might also say that at the very basis of colonialism, understood in the broad sense of the term, there lies a certain metaphysical thinking. Otherness from this perspective is a negligible intrusion and, therefore, can either be assimilated or eliminated in an effort to reconstruct the whole in its pure and natural state. However, a certain mystical approach to philosophy would help us realize that the relationship between the self and the other is undeniably irreducible. That there is inter-dependence within the play of difference between the self and the other is not only a moral imperative, but also an ontological condition. This perspective continually structures life in terms of relationship – not a relationship in which the other is subsumed into the self, but one in which the otherness in its difference is always retained.

To be able to relate to the other while retaining his/her otherness, dialogue becomes imperative. If we want to enter into a genuine dialogue with the other, we need a philosophy shaped by mystical experience; we need to go beyond the excessive preoccupation with rationality and move towards a reason of heart as was suggested by Pascal. This is possible through the phenomenology of empathy, notes Edith Stein. Scheler and Stein have already shown us the way to address the question of phenomenology of mysticism, though there are still many new avenues possible for further research.[30]

In one of his books titled *Phenomenology and Mysticism*, Steinbock discusses the relationship between phenomenology and hermeneutics in mysticism.[31] He rightly names his approach to mysticism hermeneutical phenomenology. The two philosophical currents seem opposed to each other, because phenomenology proceeds by bracketing all our previous knowledge, including what was handed over to us by our tradition, while hermeneutics affirms the important role of prejudice we have inherited from our tradition, in Gadamer's sense of these terms. By adopting an approach to mysticism through these two currents, Steinbock ensures that we can still question some practices of our tradition, transgress them when necessary and yet can be safeguarded against anarchism. Otherwise, there would no possibility of discerning openness and closure except through a continuous dialogue between phenomenology and hermeneutics, especially when mystical experience calls for social commitment. In other words, we must constantly get out of ideologies through the spiral of hermeneutical phenomenology: while hermeneutically appropriating from our own tradition what leads us to openness to difference and otherness, we need to fall back on the phenomenology of our personal mystical experience. We can create a meaningful node of mystical philosophy and socio-political commitment, without bringing to a closure neither mystical experience, nor social commitment.

Notes

1 Jacques Derrida, "Violence and Metaphysics: An Essay on the Thought of Emmanuel Levinas," in *Writing and Dfference*, trans. Alan Bass (London: Routledge, 2001), 191.

2 For more information see T. N. Ganapathy, "The Mysticism of the Tirumantiram", in T. N. Ganapathy and K. R. Arumugam (eds.), *The Yoga of Siddha Tirumular: Essays on the Tirumantiram* (Quebec: Babaji's Kriya Yoga and Publications, 2006), 231-278.

3 T. N. Ganapathy, *The Yoga of Siddha Bōganāthar*, vol. 1 (Quebec: Babaji's Kriya Yoga and Publications, 2003), 81-82.

4 For a detailed study on nebulous language see Roderick S. Bucknell and Martin Stuart Fox, *The Twilight Language: Explorations in Buddhist Meditation and Symbolism* (London, Curzon Press, 1986); T. N. Ganapathy, "The Twilight Language of the Tirumantiram," in T. N. Ganapathy and K. R. Arumugam (eds.), *The Yoga of Siddha Tirumular: Essays on the Tirumantiram* (Quebec: Babaji's Kriya Yoga and Publications, 2006), 279-322.

5 All translated citations are *Thirumandiram* are taken from Siddhar Thirumoolar, *Thirumandiram: A Classic of Yoga and Tantra* (3 vols.), trans. B. Natarajan, ed. M. Govindan (Quebec: Babaji's Kriya Yoga and Publications, 1993). The fist number is from the English translation and the second number is from the Tamil text in 3 volumes.

6 For a detailed discussion on this idea, see Walter Stace, *Mysticism and Philosophy* (London: Macmillan, 1980).

7 Jacques Derrida, "Différance," trans. Alan Bass, in *Margins of Philosophy* (Chicago: University of Chicago Press, 1982), 6.

8 Florian Rötzer, *Conversations with French Philosophers* (Atlantic Highlands: Humanities Press International, 1995), 74.

9 The Hebrew word *Tsimtsum* literally means "shrinking," "withdrawal" or "contraction." Isaac Luria, a Kabbalist Rabbi employed this term to suggest that God vacated a region within himself in order to create the world. According to the tradition of Kabbalah mysticism, God brought into being a vacuum in which to create something other than Him. He could then fill this vacuum or empty space by the simultaneous process of self-revelation and creation.

10 *Ein-Sof*, "without end" refers to the transcendental dimension of God. See Brian L. Lancaster, *The Essence of Kabbalah* (London: Arcturus, 2005), 228. In Kabbalah, *Ein-Sof* is understood as God prior to his self-manifestation in the production of any spiritual realm.

11 *Shevirat ha-kelim* or breaking of the vessels is the first disaster of *Tsimtsum* because it requires a contraction force of light, which gives rise to evil and judgment. Excess of judgment is derivative of the primordial *Tsimtsum*, which is the cause of the inability of the vessels to bear the light. According to Luria, the ten vessels that were originally meant to contain the emanation of God's light were unable to contain that light and were hence either displaced or shattered. See Lancaster, *The Essence of Kabbalah*, 99.

12 A *sefirah* (pl. *sefirot*) is a channel of divine energy or life-force. This most fundamental concept of Kabbalah is that in the process of creation an intermediate stage was emanated from God's infinite light to create what we experience as finite reality. *Sefirot* also refers to the emanations of God, the essential symbols of Kabbalah, indicating immanence of God and defining the mutual relations between God and human person.

13 Kabbalistic practice is embodied in the notion of *Tikkun ha-Olam*, literally the "repair" or "restoration" of the world.

14 See Jürgen Moltmann, *God in Creation* (New York: Harper and Row, 1985), 86-87.

15 Cited in Moltmann, *God in Creation*, 87.

16 For a detailed discussion on this see John D. Caputo, *The Prayers and Tears of Jacques Derrida* (Bloomington: Indiana University Press, 1997). 320.

17 Jacques Derrida, *Memoirs of the Blind: The Self-Portrait and Other Ruins*, trans. Pascale Anne-Brault and Michael Baas (Chicago: University of Chicago Press, 1993), 54.

18 Derrida, "Différance," 14.

19 This quote of Jabes is taken from Marc C. Taylor, *Erring: A Postmodern A/Theology* (Chicago: University of Chicago Press, 1987), 97.

20 Cited by Rachel Elior, "Chabad: The Contemplative Ascent to God," in *Jewish Spirituality: From the Sixteenth Century Revival to the Present*, ed. Arthur Green (New York: Crosswords, 1987), 157-205.

21 Cited by Gerschom Scholem, *Origins of the Kabbalah*, trans. A. Arkush (Philadelphia: Jewish Publication Society, Princeton University Press, 1990), 423.

22 Azriel, "The Explanation of the Ten Sefirot," in Joseph Dan, *The Early Kabbalah*, trans. Ronald C. Kieber (New York: Paulist Press, 1966).

23 Scholem, *Origins of The Kabbalah*, 441-2.

24 Schneur Zalman, Likkutei Torah, Leviticus, p. 83, cited by Rachel Elior, *The Paradoxal Ascent to God: The Kabbalistic Theology of Habad Hasidism*, trans. J.M. Green (New York: New York University Press, 1993), 137.

25 Jacques Derrida, "Khōra," in *On the Name*, trans. David Wood, John P. Leavey and Ian McLeod, ed. Thomas Wood (Stanford: Stanford University Press, 1995), 91.

26 Ibid., 94.

27 See Caputo, *The Prayers and Tears of Jacques Derrida*, 40.

28 John D. Caputo, *Deconstruction in a Nutshell* (New York: Fordham University Press, 1997), 105 (emphasis in original).

29 Jacques Derrida, "Faith and Knowledge: The Two Sources of 'Religion' at the Limits of Reason Alone," in *Acts of Religion*, ed. Gil Anidjar (New York: Routledge, 2002), 55.

30 Cf. Max Scheler, *On Feeling, Knowing and Valuing: Selected Writings*, ed. Harold Bershady (Chicago: University of Chicago Press, 1993); Edith Stein, *On the Problem of Empathy*, trans. Waltraut Stein, 3rd edition (Washington: ICS Publications, 1989).

31 See Anthony J. Steinbock, *Phenomenology and Mysticism: The Verticality of Religious Experience* (Bloomington: Indiana University Press, 2007).

Chapter 3

Trifocal Hermeneutics
Mimesis, Krisis, Poiesis

Keith D'Souza
Saint Pius College, Mumbai

Hermeneutical activity is largely governed by three distinct focal points: *mimesis*, *krisis* and *poiesis*.[1] *Mimesis* has to do with past-based or retrospective creative representation, *krisis* with present-based analysis and resolution of dysfunctional phenomena and *poiesis* with futuristic creative projection.

Responsible hermeneutics takes cognizance of these three unique dimensions of communicative activity, even though a specific exercise of interpretation may largely focus on only one of the three types of interpretive foci. It is understandable that any given hermeneutical activity will tend to focus largely on a specific focal point –*mimesis* or *krisis* or *poiesis* –, butfor such an activity to be productive and not dysfunctional in terms of the generation of meaning and purpose, it will need to factor in the real or virtual significance and influence of other hermeneutical foci.

The necessity of a responsible and comprehensive trifocal hermeneutics is also evident in terms of culture-based interpretive action. While each community or culture may operate from a dominant hermeneutical focal point at a particular time in its history, this focal point needs to be complemented by other focal points and in some cases, corrected by these alternative focal points either from outside or from within the cultures concerned. The complementary nature of the three hermeneutical foci in theory and in cultural practice will be dwelt upon in the second part of the essay.

The Trifocal Nature of Hermeneutical Activity

There are mainly three types of interpretive action, each of them respectively governed by three distinct – but not separate – dispositions. The first has to do with *receptivity*, i.e., cultivating a respectful, grateful, and indebted disposition towards mimetic social phenomena that are a cumulative effect of the past. The second involves *engagement*, i.e., cultivating a critical yet proactive and productive approach towards elements of social crises, including those that emerge because of the inherited past. The third entails *creative projection*, i.e., cultivating a desire to compose and construct new interpretive processes and products, in relation with, or independent of the influences of *mimesis* and *krisis*.

Each of these types of interpretive action may itself be divided into various subtypes. Three of the most important such subtypes have been highlighted within each hermeneutical focus. Some of the more famous hermeneutical theorists may be easily seen to have worked out systematic positions that represent a particular type and subtype of interpretive focus. The need, however, is to acknowledge the limitations of operating from only one focus at all times and in all situations. Even if it may be difficult for an individual interpreter or community of interpreters to develop a position from, or operate from different hermeneutical foci simultaneously, it is at least necessary to recognize the validity and the significance of these other interpretive foci. From a long-term perspective, it is important that any interpretive action consciously factor in these other foci, in order to circumvent the possibility of being insular and chauvinistic.

Mimetic Hermeneutics

The most basic form of hermeneutical activity is that of creatively imitating or representing past interpretive and communicative activity. This *mimesis* of the past is based on a sense of fidelity to the cumulative deposit of socially interpreted life patterns and cultural products. It may also be based on a spontaneous, premeditative use of interpretive means inherited from the past. There are at least three types of hermeneutical theorizing, which recognize or affirm the significance of *mimesis*. Each of them is based on a particular locus of interest, namely, personal or existential experience, tradition-based communitarian experience and the experience of encounter between different cultural communities.[2]

An example of the first type of theorizing is that engaged in by the 'early Heidegger,' for whom human beings find themselves already in the midst of a 'ready-at-hand' interpretive framework.[3] This framework is taken for granted, and constitutes an ideational and affective 'home' – an existential opening – from which and through which humans encounter the world of experience.

In such a world, there can be no subjective or objective world existing independently of each other, because every act of interpretation presupposes a relational existence between subject and object. The conditions for perfect objectivity, understood as the possibility of engaging in neutral and value-free observation and judgment, cannot easily be met, for there is always an interpretive standpoint from which one judges.

An example of the second type of mimetic-based hermeneutical theorizing may be found in the works of Gadamer, who took this ontological interpretive understanding to its logical social conclusion. Gadamer validated the *mimesis* of the past in terms of a legitimate fidelity to the *habitus* and cultural *situs* of tradition.[4] In opposition to both the instrumental and objective methodology of the Enlightenment and the divinatory, affective, and subjective methodology of Romanticism, Gadamer proposed a mediatory interpretive process. This entailed recognition of the cumulative existential prejudices from the past, which constituted the necessary or unavoidable conditions for the possibility of knowledge and interpretation in the present.

While most hermeneutical theorizing focused on interpretation within a particular tradition, it was mainly in the latter half of the twentieth century that 'post-modern' attention began to be paid to alternative or 'other' traditions. An example of a theorist who systematically developed the contours of a 'diatopical' or crosscultural hermeneutics is Raimundo Panikkar. One of the main points emphasized in his literary corpus was the need to recognize the mimetic richness found in other traditions and to engage in an activity of dialogue which would hopefully result in a 'mutual fecundity'[5] between these different mimetic trajectories.

In a globalized world, it has become impossible to ignore other collective mimetic interpretations. This awareness by itself is not sufficient to elicit respect for the 'other.' In fact, a dominant contemporary cultural development seems to be that of affirming one's mimetic heritage in the face of other mimetic traditions. In this regard, the interpretive strategies advocated by Panikkar, Levinas and the later Ricœur[6] seem to be qualitatively superior to those practiced especially by Heidegger, in terms of creating a global community of interlocutors engaging in an ongoing polylogue, instead of the phenomenon of a multitude of insular and possibly hegemonic soliloquies.

Mimesis in our age thus needs to take on an intercultural, intercommunitarian and interdependent tenor or texture. The monochromatic nature of modernity needs to make way for a possible and workable solidarity within postmodernity – a solidarity that transcends the insular reiteration of mimetic activity limited to specific traditions, and instead seeks to find a common chord with and among others who may sing a different mimetic tune. Besides this, when mimetic interpretation goes awry in communitarian discourse that is either *ad intra* or *ad extra*, there is a need to have recourse to a *krisis*-governed consciousness and methodology to realign the contours and development of mimetic expressions both within and between communities.

Critical Hermeneutics

Mimetic interpretation contributes towards the creation of identity of persons and communities. This development of identity includes a sense of personal and communitarian meaning and purpose. However, in any given community, whenever there is an internal desire for change, or an exposure to alternative meaning systems and ways of life, the stability and fixity of these identities and inherited systems of meaning and purpose are likely to be called into question.

Krisis comes to the fore when *mimesis* becomes traumatic, in some form or the other, when the status quo is perceived to be dysfunctional. However, the insistence of the upholding of mimetic interpretations and actions in a situation of social flux may quite likely lead to a dysfunctional and conflict-ridden situation. The need for social redressal, and ultimately for some form of *therapeia* or healing is called for.

This moment of *krisis* – a turning point or decision for change – may be initiated either by those more socially sensitive or enlightened, or those more affected and marginalized by the force of past interpretations which do not seem to match the evolution of current social relationships. This attempt at a revision of the past may be perceived to be a threat to some agents within any given society, especially to those who have a stake in the conservation of tradition and the sustenance of identity.

Among the many possible forms of *krisis*, I will highlight just three. The first is primarily personal and subjective, though it could also feature as a collective exercise; the second is operative at the interpersonal and the social level and the third may be more radical, leading towards systemic or structural change.

The first form of *krisis* has to do with the use of reason in a reflective capacity. In this case, *mimesis* is no more considered hermeneutically self-sufficient, but is also subject to an external source of validation. This recourse to reason as an independent resource for knowledge is at least as old as philosophy itself, when rational processes were recognized as being different from, and even superior to mimetic processes sustained by powerful cultural and religious myths. However, in recent history, it is mainly from the seventeenth century onwards that the recognition of the autonomy of this faculty gained widespread social credence, albeit largely in the intellectual world. That this capacity and desire of human beings to use ostensibly pure rational processes to adjudicate between competing truth claims was to later be christened the '*Enlightenment*' speaks volumes about the perceived merits of *krisis* as opposed to *mimesis*.

Another manifestation of *krisis* has to do with the external expression of reflection governed by universal criteria of appropriate communication. It is not only the human capacity to reflect at the personal level that brings about change, but also our capacity to develop an interpersonal and communitarian discursive platform subject to universal rules of communicative action. Here the four-dimensional criteria worked out by Karl-Otto Apel and Jürgen Habermasare significant. Ideal communicative action needs to be semantically *meaningful*, morally *truthful*, epistemologically or objectively *true* and socially *right* or appropriate.[7] Each of these criteria subjects *mimesis* to increasingly objective and transcendental standards of validation. An example of such standards and processes may be found in the "discourse ethics" worked out by Apel and Habermas.[8]

A third form of *krisis* is one that arises from within an ideological or theological position in response to a phenomenon of *mimesis* that has gone awry. Both ideology and theology have the potentiality to be counter cultural, and to this extent, counter mimetic. Part of this counter cultural propheticism comes from their temporal orientation towards the realization of future ideals, rather than the slavish repetition of past practices. The idealistic values embedded in a particular ideological or theological frame of reference may stem from a form of *mimesis* by themselves. However, while most mimetic communication is housed within particular narrative frameworks, ideological and theological *mimeses* spring from generally more robust metanarratives. Thus, in comparison to, and in conflict with other *mimeses*, they represent a critical counter.

Krisis wraps itself around two axial imperatives: the 'is' and the 'ought,' as opposed to the 'has been' of *mimesis* and the 'maybe' of *poiesis*. The 'is' has to do with objective, scientific *explanation*, whether it entails historical-critical methods in the literary or human sciences, or empirical-experimental methods in the natural sciences. The 'ought' has to do with reflective or discursive *critique* as well as strategies of deconstruction, addressed to manifestations of the mimetic which are perceived to be dysfunctional.

If *mimesis* has been found wanting when one takes recourse to *krisis*, then a realistic alternative has also to be proposed. The 'ought' of *krisis* needs to at least contain within itself the kernel of an alternative vision, if not a well worked out utopian substitute. For this to take place there is need for interpretive *poiesis*, so that necessary and wholesome reinterpretations may give new life to persons and communities subjected to debilitating social forces and practices.

Poetic Hermeneutics

Most interpretive productivity has to do with past and present communicative action. However, human beings are notoriously unpredictable and highly creative animals, as compared to other beings who share their animal status. Most of the social habits, dispositions and ways of thinking that we take for granted are a product of numerous cumulative changes over millennia. Many of these products of civilization, when they first appeared, were seen to be discontinuous with the prevalent mimetic hermeneutic. Either by way of discovery (revelation) or invention (co-creation), novel hermeneutical communication belonged at first to the realm of the poetic, before familiarization made them part of the inherited mimetic matrix of society.

There has been no age in the human past in which the call of *poiesis* has met with such a ready and willing response as in our generation. The forces of modernity and postmodernity have ushered in democratization not only of *krisis*, but also of *poiesis*. While *mimesis* privileges the elders or those who value the 'old' and give more weight to habits borne of the past, *krisis* and *poiesis* seem to best match the disposition of those who are young in mentality, or those who are more open to, and desirous of change and novelty. It is not surprising that the world of *scientia* and especially *techne* has had by far the most poetic activity over the past few centuries, because of the expansion of knowledge based on a new inductive logic. In comparison and in contrast, the academic disciplines of religious studies, theology and philosophy – and the humanities in general – still feature a whole host of continually resourceful and relevant mimetic material.[9]

There are many forms of *poiesis* and each of them differ in their relationship with the mimetic or critical background from which *poiesis* emerges, but I will highlight just three. The first form of *poiesis* is an attempt to communicate what is old and familiar in terms of something relatively novel. Poetics in the ancient Sanskrit tradition "is that intellectual power which enables the poet to present familiar things in a striking and novel way."[10] This poetic ability may assume various forms, such as the "creative fidelity" proposed by Gabriel Marcel, in which fidelity to *mimesis* is not endangered but instead qualitatively heightened by the creativity of *poiesis*.[11] It could also take the more technical and systematic form of completing the hermeneutical circle, beginning with an unreflective form of *mimesis*, passing through a moment of *krisis* and culminating in a more refined and acceptable form of *mimesis*. This movement is especially highlighted in the conciliatory hermeneutical literature of Paul Ricœur, in which all three hermeneutical foci are given their due: the 'first *naiveté*' of *mimesis*, the moment of *krisis* along the hermeneutical circle and the poetic realization of a more salubrious 'second *naiveté*,' which completes the circle.[12]

Another form of *poiesis* is of a more revolutionary nature, in which there is a distinct and direct reaction against, and rejection of a particular framework of *mimesis*, which is perceived to be inherently dysfunctional and violent. Here the relationship between the new and the old is of a contradictory or at least a contrary nature. This may take place at the theoretical level, such as the contrast between idealistic and realistic presuppositions, or rationalist and empiricist ones. This may also have its social equivalents, e.g., in classical Marxism, by way of the postulated uprising of the labor class as part of the historical and dialectical movement towards a state of perfect communism. In these cases, there is a conscious intent to contrast one's poetic projections with the prevailing mimetic situation, bringing about a social rupture.

A third form of *poiesis* is more strictly and appropriately poetic in nature, as it neither seeks to bring meaning to old forms of *mimeses*, nor to counter, oppose or reject earlier *mimeses*. Instead, this form of *poiesis* seeks to break entirely new ground, which may or may not be related to that which has gone before. Here what is entailed is crossing new thresholds of meaning and creating new paradigms of thought. This type of *poiesis* may result from hard work in a new avenue of research, or it may take the form of a purely serendipitous discovery.[13] This form of *poiesis* is also the least functionally or instrumentally directed – at least at the overt, conscious level – as compared to many of the other forms of *mimesis*, *krisis* and *poiesis*. It depends largely on inspiration and revelation rather than purely systematic and resolute human effort.

Trifocal Hermeneutics: Cultural Applications

The metaphor of a triple focus has been purposefully used in this essay. For one who has healthy eyes, no artificial lens – single, bifocal, or progressive – is needed to view the world around and afar. There is a seamless movement from one focal length to another. However, over time it happens quite often that the inflexibility of the eye's natural lens accustoms one to a particular range of focal lengths. It is then that recourse to artificial lenses for other focal lengths are required. This metaphor may be applied to the field of interpretive communication as well. Different hermeneutical theorists may choose to develop largely one focal point of interest, for various reasons. However, it is necessary that they also factor in – either implicitly or explicitly – the existence, function, and complementary contribution of the other interpretive focal points.

The Complementary Nature of the Three Hermeneutical Foci

An enlightened process of interpretation, while perhaps operating within the influence of one of the three hermeneutical foci, will concomitantly recognize the nature, purpose, and significance of the other foci. If this does not happen, then it is quite likely that one's interpretive vision will become myopic or even dysfunctional in the long run, if not the short.

What is true of individual hermeneutical theorists may also be true of entire cultural communities. At any given moment in the historical development of a community, a particular focal point may be more developed, through which reality is viewed. There may be resistance to entertain other interpretive foci. However, healthy interpretive dynamics demand at least recognition, if not an actual employment of these other foci. This is necessary not only for the wellbeing of a particular community, but also for the quality of its relations with other communities.

Mimesis without attention to *krisis* and *poiesis* will tend to be reactionary and anachronistic, or worse, tend towards isolationism,exclusivity, and fundamentalism – often entailing the presupposition of belonging to a superior culture. Such an interpretive position is generally closed to innovation, and would likely result in a generation gap between those who live in a mimetic world and others – those more cognitively and affectively open – who are ready and willing to enter into a critical and poetic mode of interpretation.

The democratization of education and the vast reaches of mass and social media brought about by information and communication technology has made it not only possible but also necessary to learn more about, rather than vilify the 'Other.' In this context, if one does not give due consideration to *krisis* and *poiesis*, this would constitute a case of culpable ignorance at best, or xenophobia at worst, with respect to other cultural or national communities, as well as other ideologically inspired interpretive communities.

Krisis without attention to *mimesis* and *poiesis* could lead to the development of an irreverent or disrespectful attitude towards the past and a nonchalant or careless attitude towards the future. It could also result in a case of "analysis paralysis," in which too much critique leads to a soft or hard case of nihilism with regard to ultimate or even proximate meaning, value, and purpose. Collateral damage created by those operating from *krisis* – especially those who show disrespect towards tradition – could include the creation of a defensive and reactionary movement on the part of those who are in most need of a perspective change. Moreover, engagement in critical activity without projecting an alternative and more wholesome scenario would amount to irresponsible interpretation, which may cause more problems in some cases than it attempts to resolve. Proponents of critique and deconstruction need to propose simultaneously alternatives to that which is being critiqued or deconstructed. These solutions need to be realistic, and not simply reproduce the ailments of the past in new forms such as reverse discrimination, in which the victims of the past now become the agents of retaliatory forms of interpretive violence.[14]

Poiesis without attention to *mimesis* and *krisis* would be like a wild cannonball, i.e., rootless, without tradition, and rudderless, without rational and critical principles for discerning guidance. It is fanciful to imagine that one can be purely imaginative and creative without taking recourse to anything of value from the past. No projective activity begins entirely from scratch. It is also foolhardy to venture into creative activity without giving some thought to reasonable and critical principles that need to guide such activity.

Even though it is necessary that one recognizes the value of the triple-foci, in practice it is very rare to find all these three components actually worked out by any one theorist, or even employed in any particular hermeneutical activity. The mimetic myopia of a multitude of ancient civilizations is inversely mirrored in the critical and poetic – and similarly narrow – temperaments of our contemporary age. The ideal, thus, is that every interpretive act based on a particular focus also needs to consider the contribution of the other two foci. While one may initially operate from a particular hermeneutical focal length, growth along the trajectory of hermeneutical maturity would necessitate the recognition of, and the actual employment of the other focal lenses.

Hermeneutics as a Cultural Activity

Different cultures tend to focus on different hermeneutical focal points, based on the prevailing issues and values within such cultures at different points in their history. While globalization is slowly resulting in the sharing of best practices at the pragmatic and economic levels of human existence, regional and cultural differences continue to manifest themselves, sometimes vigorously and even violently. In this context, there is an urgent need to develop a sense of *phronesis* or practical wisdom with regard to which hermeneutical focus to employ in which particular situation and in what manner, if one is to generate salubrious personal and social living conditions.

Communities living in the Northern hemisphere and the 'Westernized' parts of the globe have had their share of mimetic hermeneutics in past millennia, but since the Enlightenment have come to increasingly recognize *krisis* as a productive hermeneutical strategy, within the theoretical, practical and social spheres of life. The cultivation of this critical consciousness has precipitated many social reform movements – in the Western world and in Western-influenced colonies – that have led to significant paradigm shifts in the way race, gender, class, caste and nationality have come to be understood and redefined. The social dispositions assumed by many of us who live in the second decade of the twenty-first century have taken years of bloody struggle for many of our prescient ancestors to establish and many of our activist peers to sustain.

While *krisis* in the Western world has consequently given rise to an abundance of *poiesis* especially in the scientific and technological sphere, the neglect of *mimesis* has resulted in a limiting of the horizon of human existence to the proximate and secular realm.[15] A collective inability to tap into the power of *mimesis* has resulted in a growing metaphysical and religious nihilism. Even though *mimesis* has inadvertently found its way into the substructure of Western consciousness – in terms of prevailing social values and habits[16] –

there is a postmodern tendency to harbor "incredulity toward metanarratives" at the conscious level, which limits the personal and social influence of religious imagination.[17] Besides this function of *mimesis*, the recovery of this past-based inspiration could also help to reinforce efforts at the critical and poetic levels to create a more just and inclusive social order at the larger global level, given the power that materially and economically developed nations possess to ameliorate dismal living conditions and wounded human relations across the globe.[18]

Those communities that live in the Southern and Eastern hemispheres of the globe have inherited *mimesis*. They also continue to invest a lot of energy in *mimesis*. Even those nations in these regions exposed to rigorous forces of colonization continue to retain a core cultural residue that characterizes their original identity. Contemporary globalization has not served to obliterate this residue, and in some cases, has elicited just the opposite response, featuring powerful affective reactions to what is perceived as a new form of alienation and marginalization. Just as the West seems to have a resistance to entertain *mimesis*, for various reasons, the South and East seem to resist *krisis*. In such situations, even a seemingly innocuous concept such as "human rights" may be considered or alleged to be an alien cultural imposition rather than a universally agreed upon measure or standard for integral human development, based on common human values.[19]

Apart from collective phobia, perhaps one of the reasons for resistance among more traditional (mimetic) societies is the perceived lack of consistency among those who engage in strategies associated with *krisis*. Critique is then looked upon as merely instrumental and part of a power game, unable to challenge its agents to similarly and consistently engage in self-reflection and self-critique. This may happen when a cause is taken up on a narrow interest-based and instrumental manner – whether it be race, caste, class or gender-based. In such cases, the cause itself may be perceived as partisan and insensitive to larger interests, prompting *krisis* to be rejected as a warped or cryptic form of *mimesis*. Thus, consistency and comprehensiveness is needed in *krisis*, else one ends up fighting only insular and collectively narcissistic battles, insensitive to, and unconcerned about the needs of other affected communities. This becomes even more patent when the struggles associated with *krisis* merely give rise to reverse forms of discrimination, instead of new, wholesome relationships between erstwhile victors and victims.

This inconsistent and instrumental resort to *krisis* may take place even at the methodological level, e.g., when the texture of postmodern writing seems to bear a resemblance to that of the modern mentality it opposes. Not only is there a similarity in terms of the polemical texture and the noetic certitude in both orientations, but the binary opposition that has resulted between these ways of processing reality – as 'postmodern' may well be considered as a euphemism for 'anti-modern' – is precisely what is intended to be critically eschewed. In a similar vein, alterity or 'otherness' needs to be transcended as a distinct category today, as mass migration and displacement at a global level are steadily blurring the lines between community-based identities and human beings are becoming more and more socially hybrid entities.[20] The fabrication of 'otherness' by postmodernists may be thus perceived to be of the same cloth as that of 'sameness' by the modernists. Discursive *phronesis* entails the adoption of strategies that bypass both of these binary positional oppositions and instead finds better ground in the adoption of a humble listening to the narratives from different worlds and the values they bear, without preemptively dismissing sameness or otherness.[21]

When it comes to *poiesis*, the division is chronological than geographical. This is understandable, as the young are generally in the chronologically best position to address crises, and possess the necessary time and drive to explore alternative paradigms that will help them and future generations to live life to the full. While poetic activity is most obvious in the discipline of the natural sciences and in the technological and communicative fields, there have also been significant shifts of understanding and practice at the social level. Startlingly new modes of social relationships and identity issues have emerged on the global mindscape – some of which were unthinkable and unmentionable just a few decades ago, even in progressive Western societies. Concepts such as the 'post-human' and 'trans-human' may soon become common currency.[22] Given the somewhat disquieting and rapid nature of these developments, the need for *poiesis* to be governed by *phronesis* is even more necessary. Much more than in the worlds of *scientia* and *techne*, the world of social relations – ubiquitously dominated by various forms of violence – is in urgent need of new governing dispositions and prevailing habits. The need for *phronesis* to guide *poiesis* is even more evident in this area. This is because understanding the human world with wisdom and compassion is perhaps far more demanding and difficult than dispassionately understanding the more objective and stable natural world.

Conclusion

The function of such intercultural seminars – for which this essay has been composed – is precisely to invite participants to an expansion of consciousness,[23] so that they may at least acknowledge, if not actually employ these three distinct types of hermeneutical foci. Similarly, it may be unrealistic to expect any given community to pay equal and consistent attention to all three foci, but it is imperative for integral personal and social wellbeing within any culture that interpretive agents take cognizance of the trifocal nature of hermeneutics, if not explicitly, at least implicitly. Beyond the welfare of any particular community, the wellbeing of the entire human family depends on such interpretive sensitivity, wisdom, and breadth of vision.

Notes

1 *Mimesis* is a Greek word for imitative representation, "from Greek *mimos* imitator or actor," according to the *Chambers Dictionary of Etymology*, ed. Robert Barnhart (New York: Chambers, 1988), 662-63. *Krisis* is a Greek word, meaning "a separating, discrimination, decision, from *krinein* to separate, decide, judge" (*Chambers Dictionary of Etymology*, 235). *Poiesis* is yet another Greek word, meaning "composition, poetry, from *poiein* to make or compose" (*Chambers Dictionary of Etymology*, 810).

2 For examples of the first two types of mimetic employment, see William Schweiker, *Mimetic Reflections: A Study in Hermeneutics, Theology and Ethics* (New York: Fordham University Press, 1990). On p. 134, Schweiker asserts that, "by reading Gadamer, Ricœur, and . . . Kierkegaard, I am reconstructing mimesis as a way to speak of the fundamental acts of understanding, narrativity and selfhood."

3 The 'early Heidegger' is largely associated with the ontological hermeneutics presented in *Being and Time*, trans. John Macquarrie and Edward Robinson (New York: Harper and Row, 1962), especially Division One, "Preparatory Fundamental Analysis of Dasein."

4 See Hans-Georg Gadamer, *Truth and Method*, 2nd rev. ed., trans. Joel Weinsheimer and Donald G. Marshall (New York: Continuum, 2000), especially the sub-section titled, "Prejudices as Conditions of Understanding," with a further sub-division dealing with "The Rehabilitation of Authority and Tradition," 277ff.

5 See Raimundo Panikkar, *Myth, Faith and Hermeneutics: Cross-Cultural Studies* (New York: Paulist Press, 1979), 244.

6 See Richard Kearney, "Paul Ricœur and the Hermeneutics of Translation," in *Research in Phenomenology* 37 (2007): 147-159, where Kearney demonstrates how the process of translation may be used as a model for dialogical hermeneutics. Following Ricœur, he argues that, "All translation involves some aspect of dialogue between self and stranger" (152), and, "Linguistic hospitality calls us to forgo the lure of omnipotence: the illusion of a total translation that would provide a perfect replica of the original" (151).

7 See Karl-Otto Apel, "Regulative Ideas or Truth-Happening?: An Attempt to Answer the Question of the Conditions of the Possibility of Valid Understanding," in *The Philosophy of Hans-Georg Gadamer*, ed. Lewis Edwin Hahn (Chicago: Open Court, 1997).

8 See Jürgen Habermas, *Moral Consciousness and Communicative Action*, trans. C. Lenhardt and S. Nicholsen (Cambridge: MIT Press, 1990), and Karl-Otto Apel, *The Response of Discourse Ethics to the Moral Challenge of the Human Situation as Such and Especially Today* (Leuven: Peeters, 2001).

9 The remote mimetic materials in the sciences and in technology fit more into a museum-like intellectual space, and are largely of historical, not theoretical interest. As a result, students of science and technology are not concerned about the history of their professional fields, as compared to students of religious studies, theology and philosophy, for whom ancient canons of literature still hold revelatory and inspirational possibilities.

10 Suresh Dhayagude, *Western and Indian Poetics: A Comparative Study* (Pune: Bhandarkar Oriental Research Institute, 1981), 120.

11 See Gabriel Marcel, *Creative Fidelity*, trans. Robert Rosthal (New York: Farrar, Strauss & Co., 1964). The existential and interpersonal overtones of Marcel's argumentation of

such fidelity could easily be extended to include a creative or poetic fidelity towards tradition and community.

12 See Paul Ricœur, *The Symbolism of Evil*, trans. Emerson Buchanan (Boston: Beacon Press, 1967), 350, where the author speaks of a "criticism that is no longer reductive but restorative." In *The Rule of Metaphor*, trans., Robert Czerny, Kathleen McLaughlin and John Costello (Toronto: University of Toronto, 1977), 318, Ricœur distinguishes between a "reductive explanation," equivalent to a form of *krisis*, and "a recollection or a retrieval of the original meaning," equivalent to a form of *poiesis*.

13 Commenting on the history of the concept of imagination in Western poetics, Suresh Dhayagude remarks thus: "No other concept in the history of thought has perhaps gone through such extreme changes in fortune. At one time it was revered as a divine gift, at another a claim to it was suspected as imposture; it was valued at one time as the source of divine wisdom; it was condemned at another, as shear madness" (Dhayagude, 109). In comparison, the notion of *pratibha*, the Sanskrit word for imagination or creative genius, is understood more consistently, salubriously and productively in the Indian tradition. According to Dhayagude, "the distinction between fancy and imagination. . . has no parallel in Indian poetics" (Dhayagude, 120). This is perhaps because *pratibha* is understood and accepted to be, "a kind of intellect, but it is not the analytical and discursive intellect. It will be more correct to characterize it as a kind of vision or intuition into the significance of things" (Dhayagude, 115). In general, cultural and religious imagination and expression in India has been better received socially, as compared to their reception in post-Enlightenment Western societies, subject to the rational and critical scrutiny of modernity.

14 See my article titled "Interpretation and Violence: Reasons and Resolutions," in *Violence and its Victims*, ed. Ivo Coelho (Bangalore: ATC, 2010), 70-93 for different forms of violence which result from interpretive activity.

15 In his encyclical *Fides et Ratio* (Mumbai: Pauline Publications, 1998), §7, Pope John Paul II laments that philosophical reflection in the West has forgotten its primary vocation: "Abandoning the investigation of being, modern philosophical research has concentrated instead upon human knowing."

16 See George Soares-Prabhu, "The Kingdom of God: Jesus' Vision of a New Society," in *The Indian Church in the Struggle for a New Society*, ed. D. S. Amalorpavadass (Bangalore: NBCLC, 1981), 579-608. The author emphasizes three important values in Jesus' vision of a new social order: "freedom, fellowship and justice are... the parameters of the Kingdom's thrust towards the total liberation of man" (601). While Western – especially European – society may be considered to be far less mimetic than other contemporary societies, these three parameters may be considered as spiritual precursors of the more secularly accepted values of the French revolution, viz., "liberty, fraternity and equality," respectively. These values are considered to be socially fundamental in most Western nations.

17 See Richard Kearney, *Poetics of Imagining: Modern to Post-Modern* (New York: Fordham University Press, 1998), where he discusses numerous postmodern theorists who struggle to formulate "an ethics of alterity by re-inscribing ways of imagining which elude both the prison-house of mirrors and the cheerless conformity of Grand Theory" (218). The "prison-house of mirrors" would be the equivalent of nihilism, and the "cheerless conformity of Grant Theory" would be the equivalent of a mimetic disposition, which in the Eastern world is not so cheerless, but in fact still a vibrant manifestation of meaning and purpose.

18 This call to economic reform is featured in Pope Benedict XVI's encyclical, *Caritas in Veritate* (Vatican City: Vatican Press, 2009), and in Pope Francis' incessant appeals to world leaders to help ameliorate the present economic systems and political relations which have led to severe social inequalities.

19 Even though, this concept may have had its origins in the critical consciousness of Western 'Enlightenment,' the nature and application of such a concept need not be perennially associated with only one culture.

20 See Homi Bhabha, *The Location of Culture* (New York: Routledge, 1994), where the author discusses concepts such as hybridity, liminality, interstitiality, border-crossing, etc.; all intended to convey the blurring of cultural indices which normally fix personal and communitarian identities.

21 Perhaps a wiser approach is that presented by Paul Ricœur in *Oneself as Another*, trans. Kathleen Blamey (Chicago: University of Chicago Press, 1992), in which sameness and selfhood are arrived at via a detour of the encounter with otherness.

22 According to Gregor Puppinck, "*Post-humanism* is the domination of individual wills over human nature. As a result, it is replacing human rights with 'rights of individuals' . . . Assisted suicide, euthanasia or abortion are post-human rights . . . *Trans-humanism* is about the surpassing and substitution of human nature by biotechnology . . . Eugenics becomes therefore a component of an increased human nature. It is a trans-human right." See http://www.zenit.org/en/articles/how-human-rights-are-becoming-post-and-trans-human-rights, accessed 13 November, 2014.

23 See my "Levels of Existential Development," in *The Dynamics of Development: Negations and Negotiations,* ed. Keith D'Souza (Bangalore: ATC, 2014), 287-309, in which I propose a hierarchy corresponding to this expansion. Lower states of consciousness have to do with furthering personal interests; higher states are concerned about communitarian interests; and the highest states feature a concern with transcendent interests. This state of transcendent consciousness is further divided into an 'altruistic' state, in which one recognizes alterity and sub-alterity, then a higher 'agapeistic' state, in which one engages in compassion and care for the 'other,' and finally a 'mystical' state, in which both subjectivity and objectivity are transcended. Mimetic approaches would typically sustain a communitarian consciousness, whereas critical and poetic approaches, when used with *phronesis* (practical wisdom) would be able to take one to higher levels of personal and social consciousness.

Chapter 4

Religion, Culture and Communication

George Karuvelil
Professor, Jnana-Deepa Vidyapeeth, Pune

Walter Kaufman in his influential book *Critique of Religion and Philosophy* takes Christian stalwarts like St. John the evangelist and St. Paul to task for trying to "assimilate their religion to the fashion of the day."[1] John's crime is that he presented Jesus as logos, a term that was familiar in the Greek culture; Paul is criticized for trying to become "all things to all." Kaufman's contention is that the genuinely a religious person –like a Hebrew prophet – would beconcerned about the message (truth) and not its reception; to focus on reception, as Sts. Paul or John did it is to contaminate the message. Kaufman is not alone in thinking that culture contaminates truth. Consider an episode on stigmata telecast a few years ago on the National Geographic Channel. One of the points discussed in this well made documentary is the location of the stigmatic wounds. Traditionally, stigmatists like St. Francis of Assisi and Padre Pio had the wounds on their palms. But a change was seen in the case of some twentieth century stigmatists. Their wounds were on their wrists, and not palms. It is to be noted that this migration of wounds from palms to the wrists occurred after a French physician Pierre Barbet (1925-95) hypothesized that Christ's crucifixion could not have been on his palms but on his wrists. Commenting on this Joe Nickell of the *Skeptical Inquirer Magzine* poses the question as to why God would change the location of the stigmata after Barbet's book, as if God did not know where Jesus was nailed during crucifixion! The underlying assumption seems to be that stigmata could not be from God;

something that changes so easily with the changing cultural moods cannot be a matter of truth; truth and culture stand in fundamental opposition to one another. Consider a third instance. It is well known that Jews and Muslims who have strict prohibitions on depicting the deity do not ordinarily see religious visions whereas Hindus and Catholics who are more liberal in this matter have visions. This is seen by many critics as evidence against these happenings having anything to do with divine reality; they are to be taken as mere cultural or psychological products. They ask if God wants to communicate something to human beings why he would be so dependent on culture.

I will not counter the skeptic's claim in this paper and show that divine communication is more than a cultural product having truth-value, as it requires a full-fledged discussion of epistemological issues. I hope to show that awareness of even the most rudimentary principles of communication will enable us see that divine communication will necessarily have a cultural component. The first part of the argument places some key insights of hermeneutics (especially of Gadamer and Ricœur) into the context of a Communication theory. I use communication theory so as to bypass a lot of unnecessary baggage that hermeneutics carries from its history.[2] It also helps to avoid diverting our attention to discussions on whether hermeneutics is identical with or a successor discipline to epistemology.[3]

Fundamentals of Communication

The first thing to note about communication is that it is a triadic relationship between the communicator, the message, and the receiver. This relationship also involves two kinds of action.[4] The first is performed by the communicator who encodes a message in signs and sends it across to the receiver hoping for a particular response from that person. The second kind of action is done by the receiver who decodes the message by selectively attending to the available stimuli, interprets it, and responds to it in the manner he or she seems fit. It is important to note that the acts done by the communicator and the receiver are independent of each other. Or else, communication would be misunderstood as the communicator (A) transferring his or her thoughts and ideas (message) directly to a passive receiver (B), known as the Bullet Theory of communication.[5]

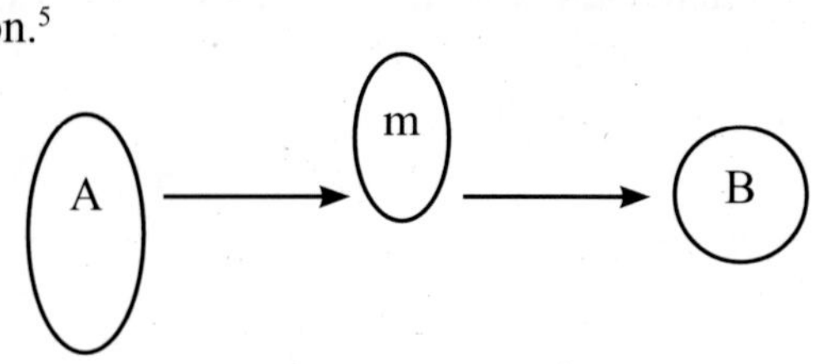

Figure 1 (from Schramm, 1971, 22)

Good communicators have known that Bullet Theory is a wrong way of understanding communication; successful communication depends not only on the communicator but also on the recipient, the addressee. This prompted Socrates (*Phaedrus,* 276) to compare the one who writes down his thoughts to a farmer who scatters seeds without any consideration of the kind of soil on which it would land. When the independence of the actors and their acts is taken into account, the relevant diagram would look like this:

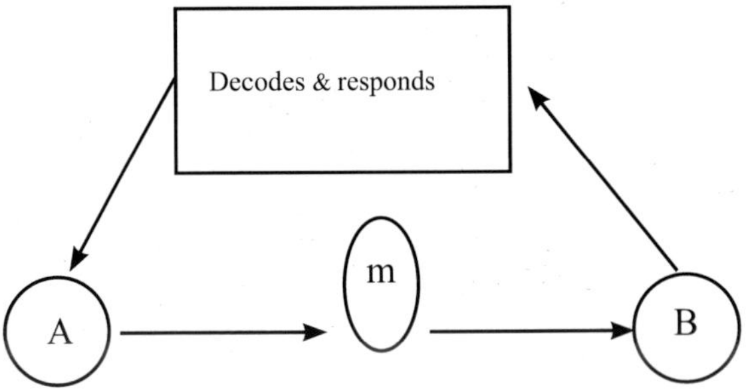

Figure 2 Communication as relational (adapted from Schramm, 1971, 23)

The independence of these two actions arises from the fact that the relationship between the communicator and the receiver is not merely a form of inter-stimulation.[6] Rather, both are persons with their own egos and subjectivity where each lives within an encompassing horizon that is different from that of the other. Each person's lived horizon is made up of a different set of accumulated experience, values, and prejudices, exposure to ideas and education, and cultural heritage.

The fact of having such existential enclosure influences all the three elements as well as the two acts of communication. The message that A wants to communicate to B has not suddenly dropped from the sky; it arose as a particular episode in the inner life of A, within that horizon. That horizon of accumulated experiences not only provides the communicator with a social, cultural, and linguistic context for the message but also the codes to encode the message. The addressee, in turn, understands the coded message in terms of her own horizon of accumulated experiences. Schramm illustrates the last point with the example of a tribesman who has never seen or heard of an airplane. Such a person "can only decode the sight of a plane in terms of whatever experience he has had. The plane may seem to him to be a bird, and the aviator a god borne on wings."[7] All human communication, whether a discourse (written, oral), or a piece of art, then, becomes a doubly mediated process. Figure 2 therefore, needs to be modified by placing the communicator and the addressee within their respective horizons.

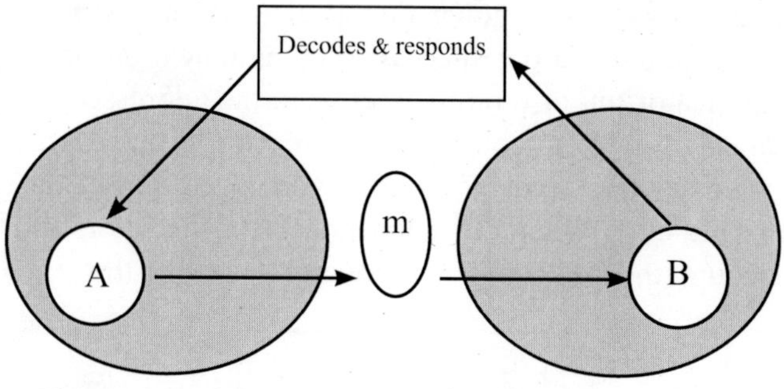

Figure 3 A and B are situated within their horizons

The fact that the action done by the communicator is independent of the action of the recipient, there is always the possibility that a communication might fail. Given the possibility of such failure, the task of communication is to bridge the gap between the source and the destination by aligning the one with the other. Different communication theorists use different terms for this alignment. Schramm uses the imagery of "tuning" the source and destination to each other, in the manner of a radio transmitter and receiver.[8] Barnett Pearce talks about "Coordinated Management of Meaning" (CMM) where the "term *coordination* is used to call attention to the fact that whatever we do does not stand alone,"[9] but we need "to align our actions with those of others."[10] No matter what terminology is used, the alignment of the source and destination is essential to successful communication. An act of reporting would be successful when it is understood as report; the act of persuading is successful when the addressee is persuaded. The task of communication, therefore, is the overcoming of the distance between the source and the destination.[11] The essence of communication, therefore, consists in aligning the source and the destination of the message.

The Forces at Work in Communication

The autonomy of the addressee from the source enables us to see the twin forces at work in communication, which could be called the driving force and the engaging force. The driving force has to do with motivation, that which prods a person to communicate with another. Different theorists have suggested different theories of motivation, Abraham Maslow's theory of a hierarchy of needs being one of the most prominent, though it has its own limitations.[12] His theory of needs, coming at the height of modern thinking, is centred on the individual where the community dimension of fellow feeling and empathy takes a back seat. The manner in which even little children spontaneously reach out to one another show that bonding and fellow feeling are not extra add-ons to individual needs. Such fellow feeling and empathy are especially important in the context of communication. Whatever the source of the communicator's motivation, when motivation is present, it brings with it a sense of "ought" or "must" (e.g., "I ought to write that letter this week"). The logic of "ought" is known as deontic logic as opposed to the logic of "is-ness" (e.g., "I wrote that letter this week). According to Pearce, the logic of communication is deontic.[13] Motivation, with its deontic logic, is the driving force of all communication; where motivation is lacking there can be chatter but no message, and where there is no message there is no communication. Where a message and the urge to communicate are present, the driving force of communication is in place and the communicator is ready to transmit the message.

This internally generated tension makes the communicator, like a drawn bow, ready to shoot. However, the realization that the addressee is an autonomous "other" does not permit the communicator to do such shooting; one's communication has to be controlled, guided, and channelized to engage the addressee. Engaging the addressee involves a restraint on the part of the communicator such that it leads to "a tension between holding one's own position and listening while being profoundly open to the other."[14] It is a matter of having a message to communicate and yet acknowledging that the recipient of communication is different from the communicator. William Gudykunst sees it in terms of a tension between empathy with the other and respect for the otherness of the other.[15] Empathy without respect can lead to condescension and respect without empathy can lead to distancing. In the process of respectfully engaging the other, there takes place a shift in the "ought" dimension of communication with which the communicator began: "the force of the deontic logic (the sense of what I "ought" to do) shifts from intrapersonal to interpersonal."[16] It is a shift from being completely driven from within one's own horizon to submitting to the restraining force of another horizon.

There is a similar tension operative in the recipient. On the one hand, the message that enters the recipient's consciousness has an external source (communicator's subjectivity), possessing a meaning that is independent of what the recipient reads into the message. On the other hand, the recipient can receive the message only through his or her subjectivity, accumulated experience, and tradition. Inasmuch as the message has an external source, the recipient needs to reach out beyond one's own subjectivity and enter into the other horizon, as it were. To paraphrase Paul Ricœur, it is the struggle between the otherness that experiences all spatial and temporal distance as estrangement and the ownness by which all understanding aims at the extension of self-understanding.[17] Thus, just as the communicator attempts to engage the addressee by being sensitive to the horizon of the other, the addressee goes beyond the meaning that is projected from within one's horizon to listen genuinely to the other by entering into the other horizon.

This entry into the horizon of the other, however, does not mean attempting the impossible task of leaving one's own horizon behind. This seemingly impossible task of entering into another horizon without leaving one's own becomes possible because while their respective funds of accumulated experiences remain different, there are also commonalities. This area common to the two holds the key to successful communication. This is the point of access whereby one can enter into the horizon of another. As Schramm recognized, "If the circles have a large area in common, then communication is easy. If the circles do not meet –if there has been no common experience– then communication is impossible. If the circles have only a small area in common – that is if the experience of source and destination have been strikingly unlike – then it is going to be very difficult to get an intended meaning across from one to the other."[18] Figure 3 is then modified in the following manner by situating A and B in their respective existential horizons, with some sharedarea:

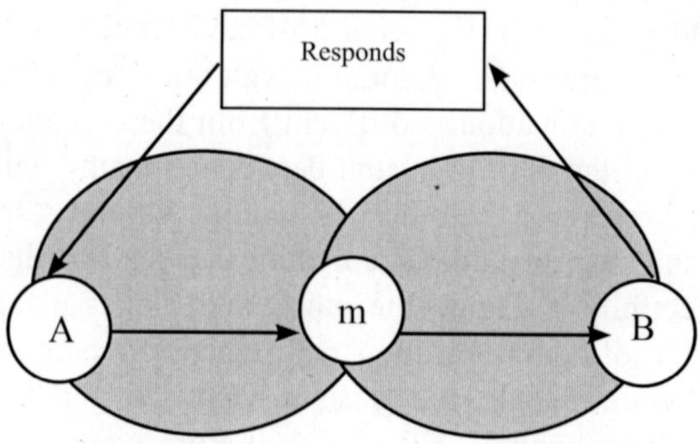

Figure 4 Overlap of two horizons

Dynamics of Communication: Hermeneutic Circle

Managing the tension between the source and the destination of communication is a dynamic process that is captured in the idea of the hermeneutic circle. Hermeneutic circle tells us that all understanding by the recipient of a message begins with the projection or anticipation of some meaning into the encoded message. This projection is done in terms of one's own horizon of accumulated experiences. Recall Schramm's example of person who has neither seen nor heard of an airplane decoding a sighted plane. Such projected meaning, however, is provisional. This provisional meaning is either confirmed or corrected eventually by one's actual encounter with the otherness of the message. Gadamer puts it this way: when a person is trying to understand a text, some initial meaning "emerges only because he is reading the text with particular expectations in regard to certain meaning. The working out of this fore-project, which is constantly revised in terms of what emerges as he penetrates into the meaning, is understanding what is there [in the text]."[19] The initially projected meaning, then, is only a starting point. This may be revised as the communication proceeds. All communication, therefore, involves to-and-fro process.[20] Every turn in this to-and-fro movement is a crucial link to the next, eliciting the next move just as the present one was elicited by the last.[21]

The result of the to-and-fro movement is that the initial commonness (Figure 4) either grows or shrinks. The idea of commonness is so crucial to communication that Schramm considers it almost its defining feature. Tracing the word 'communication' to the Latin *coummunis* (common), he says that communication is an attempt to establish commonness with someone. The common ground is something that is found and achieved at the same time. It begins with an antecedent commonness that the communicator discerns in the addressee, and is modified in the process of the exchange. If the process goes well, the common area shared by A and B grows, and there occurs a "fusion of horizons" where the strangeness of the other is replaced with familiarity.[22]

Implications for Religion

This brief outline of communication theory has profound implications for understanding religious communication, both in terms of inter-human communication as well as divine-human communication.

Human Communication of Religious Message

Let us consider the motivating factor in religious communication. According to Aquinas, the purpose of all religious communication (preaching, catechesis, and theology) was to communicateone's acquaintance with God.[23] More generally one could say that the motivation for religious communication comes from a religious experience or revelation or a sense of having seen or heard or experienced something that is extra-ordinary, not ordinarily seen or heard by others, but something that is beneficial to all. "Woe to me, if I do not preach the gospel" (I Cor. 9:16), said St. Paul. An enlightened Siddhartha (Buddha) had no choice but to preach.

Now we can return to the problem raised by the cultural element in communication with which we began. We noted that the signals coming from the communicator is decoded by the receiver in terms of the resources available to her within her horizon. Gudykunst is explicit that the rules for interpreting signals come from culture.[24] The history of Christian missions is replete with examples where the cultural ignorance of the missionary has led to disasters in communication. Robert Schreiter gives some good examples.[25] One is uproar caused when an image of St. George killing the dragon was sought to be installed in a Catholic cathedral in Koyo to in the 1950s. The puzzled missionaries found that dragon had a completely different significance for the Japanese. For them, not only was it not a symbol of evil as it was for the Westerners, but was the symbol of the emperor. Therefore mounting the image of St. George slaying the dragon amounted to Christianity destroying Japaneseness!

If the rules for interpreting communication signals are culture-bound in this manner, it holds important lessons for all forms of religious communication whether human or divine. When Kaufmann criticizes the Hellenizing tendency of Paul and John as attempts to "assimilate their religion to the fashion of the day," he forgets that message needs to be communicated in a manner that is intelligible to the recipient. As Robert Audi puts it pithily, "Belief requires understanding. Where of one cannot understand, there of one cannot believe."[26] If Christian missionaries are to be criticized, it is not for Hellenizing their message by Paul and John, but for keeping it that way, even when it spread to other cultures like those of India, China, and Africa. (Matteo Ricci and followers in China and Robert De Nobili and others in India are notable exceptions to this tendency.)

Another benefit of understanding communication theory is in terms of interreligious dialogue. A felt need for dialogue with people of other religious persuasions has been the main driving force of writers like John Hick and Paul Knitter who called themselves "pluralists." They saw that if dialogue is to take place there should be a "level playing field" where no religion is considered superior or inferior.[27] Their quest for the level playing field led them to move away from their existential horizons to conceptual abstractions (from eclesio-centrism to Christo-centrism to theo-centrism to Reality-centredness) in search of some position that is supposedly neutral between the interlocutors. A communication perspective on religions makes us aware that no communication takes place on neutral grounds. The level playing field required for inter-religious dialogue is not any neutral ground away from the lived horizons of the communicators, but the common territory shared by those engaged in dialogue. It further implies that this level playing field need not be the same for all different inter-religious dialogues. Dialogue between two Christian denominations, for example, will obviously have more common ground than say, dialogue between Christians and Muslims; the latter will surely have more commonly shared religious ground than between Christians and atheists. Thus, there is not one but many level playing fields available for inter-religious dialogue, depending on the religions and non-religious horizons that seek dialogue. This helps us appreciate better the works comparative theologians who have moved away from global theories of the kind proposed by Hick and Knitter towards exploring the concrete commonality that exists between two or more religions that are being compared.

There is the question as to whether it is possible or feasible to fuse all horizons. Wittgenstein's idea of 'forms of life' has something to say to this question. For Wittgenstein meaning of linguistic expressions is neither arbitrary nor dictated by some "reality" outside of language. Rather, our language is part of a broader context of human life and activity. Its implication is that the fusion of horizons cannot go far unless the concerned horizons also share in a way of life. Immediately after talking about human agreement on the language they use, Wittgenstein goes on to qualify it: "That is not agreement in opinions but in form of life" (*PI* 241).[28] Answering the question as to whether all horizons can be fused, then, will depend on the empirical question as to whether there are also certain shared forms of life among the concerned horizons. In the absence of shared forms of life, the back and forth movement of communication is likely to lead to a breakdown of communication than to fusion of horizons. Wittgensteinian philosopher of religion D.Z. Phillips has observed that "in certain circumstances religious believers will want to stress the differences between their practices and those of other people."[29] It is also important to note even when fusion of horizons takes place, such fusion would seldom, if ever, amount to unification.[30]

The most amazing result of recognizing the intimate link between communication and culture is that it helps to understand some forms of religious diversity. Consider the often-posited opposition between religions of grace and effort. Buddha's instruction to his disciples to "work out their own salvation" and "walk lonely as a rhinoceros" is often taken to mean that Buddhism is a religion of personal effort whereas Christianity is a religion of grace, as if the two were exclusive.[31]

There are two specific problems with this manner of conceiving the matter. First, it neglects the role of effort found in a grace-based religion like Christianity just as it forgets the insufficiency of effort in Buddhism. The same Christian Scriptures, that emphasize salvation through grace (Eph 2:9, for example), also talk of working out one's salvation with fear and trembling (Phil 2:12). Forgetting their bipolarity and seeing them as exclusive of each other has led to prolonged controversies over the role of grace and works. Such bipolarity of grace and effort is not merely doctrinal but also practical inasmuch as Christian spirituality has always emphasized the need to cooperate actively with divine grace for one's salvation. St. Augustine put it in these words: "God, who created you without you, will not save you without you" (Sermon 169, 13). Similarly, when properly understood, the idea of grace is not absent even in traditional Buddhism (in addition to Mahayana Buddhism where it is explicitly acknowledged).[32] Therefore, it seems unwarranted to oppose grace and effort.

Second, if they were exclusive, it becomes hard to understand the emergence of grace in later Buddhism. Shinran, for example, taught that we cannot attain enlightenment by our efforts, but must rely on the grace of Amida Buddha. If the religion of the Buddha was solely a matter of effort, how could such explicit reference to grace emerge later? It can only be a contamination of the Buddhist teaching. However, when the emphasis on grace and/or effort is seen as communication of a message to suit the prevailing cultural conditions of the day, one would expect to find such changes. Look a little closer at the cultural context of the Buddha and Shinran. Historically, Buddhism arises at the same time as the Āranykās, the Upanishads and Jainism. All of these can be seen as revolts against the religious practices where the role of the individual's effort was next to nothing. The emphasis was on maintaining the cosmic order through the correct performance of rituals. The efficacy of the ritual resulted neither from the favor of gods nor from the inner disposition of the one who performed the ritual, but was entirely dependent on the precision with which the ritual was performed and the accuracy with which the mantras were uttered.[33] These, obviously, needed an expert (priest). The one on whose behalf the sacrifice was done (called *yajamāna*) hardly had any role. Seen in this background, Buddha's emphasis on personal effort is a corrective to that cultural situation; the message is the same as that of Augustine: God cannot save you without your consent; there can be no spiritual wellbeing without one's active involvement. The matter is even more obvious in the case of Shinran who, on his own account, was frustrated at not getting Enlightenment even after twenty years of diligent practice. Prompted by a vision he goes and becomes a disciple of Honen and eventually comes to advocate salvation through grace.[34]

Thus, it seems clear that some of religious differences, at least, may be matters of communication. This does not mean that all religious differences are of this kind. What it does imply is that unless we have very strong reasons to consider otherwise, we should not take the differences between religions to be "mutually exclusive" of each other as many writers on religious diversity tend to do.[35] This, of course, does not mean that religions are all the same. There may be important differences, but differences need not amount to contradictions and exclusions. Inability to differentiate the cultural dimension from the religious message inevitably leads to replacing the religious vision with versions of nationalism or culture specific religions. Modern Hinduism that has incorporated even Buddhism, Jainism, and Sikhism into its fold, excluding only Islam and Christianity, is one example where religion is identified with the culture of the Indian subcontinent.[36] The lethal mix of Christianity and national aspirations that functioned as the backdrop to the protracted religious wars in Europe provides another example. The protest of Asian Christian theologians that Christianity is often mistaken for its Western garb is also an indication that the distinction between religion and culture is yet to be sufficiently recognized in Christianity. Buddhism offers, perhaps, has the best track record in distinguishing its religious message from the cultural settings as it has successfully adapted itself to a variety of host cultures.

Divine-Human Communication

We have seen that all human communication –written, oral, or a piece of art – a doubly mediated process – mediated through the horizons of the communicator and the recipient. Inasmuch as horizons are made up of the distinct funds of experience accumulated by human beings in the course of living their lives in the world of space and time, horizons are also the necessary limits arising from our bodily character. Now if a message were to come from a source beyond space and time then it would be communicated directly without the mediation of a horizon. This explains why mystics tend to describe their experience as direct. The immediacy of the divine is what prompted the psalmist to say, "Even before a word is on my tongue, O Lord, You know it altogether" (Ps.139: 4)

On the other hand, divine communication to human beings is direct only in a comparative sense. Compared to the two horizons involved in human communication, divine communication has only one horizon. The source of communication may be undistorted and direct but the human receiver remains within a specific horizon. Unlike human communication that involve a double filtering through two different horizons, so to say, divine communication has only a single filtering at the receiver's end. This makes the message veiled, as it were, by the receiver's own subjectivity. This character of divine-human communication is captured in the paradoxical expression "mediated immediacy."[37] They are immediate in as much the source of the message lacks a space-time horizon, but mediate in as much as the recipient receives the message in within a lived horizon in space and time.

With this basic understanding of divine-human communication, we can return to the skeptical question about the stigmata: Why would the location of wounds change place after Barbet's book? In order to answer this question we should ask three fundamental questions:

(i) Who receives stigmata?
(ii) What is its message?
(iii) How is the message received?

Conclusion

Concerning the first question, looking at the history of stigmata would reveal that not anyone or everyone receives these wounds. Francis of Assisi, the first stigmatist, was a person who was deeply in love with Jesus Christ. Any lover can testify or anyone who has studied love will know the heartfelt longing of the lover to become one with the beloved. Francis' love for Jesus was of the same kind; he wanted to live the life of Jesus in every possible way, including his bodily wounds, which for him was the ultimate sign of Christ's love. The stigmata he received were the culmination of that longing to be united with the Crucified in love. It is not for nothing that he is known as the most Christ-like person after Jesus Christ. Lives of other stigmatists too would reveal that the one who receive these wounds are those who long to be united with the crucified Lord.

Knowing that these wounds occur only by those who long for union with the crucified dramatically affects what we take its message to be. Receiving Christ's wounds in one's own body now can only mean that God has granted the favor of being united with Christ in his suffering and his saving work attained though the crucifixion.

As for the reception of the message, if the message is about God's favor in granting a share in the saving work of the crucified Lord, how would the stigmatist be able to understand this unless the she can recognize that the received wounds are signs of Jesus own wounds? Obviously, this requires that the wounds appear in the same place where the *stigmatist believes* Jesus was nailed. It has nothing to do with where Jesus was actually nailed; it has everything to do with how the stigmatist can recognize the wounds as the wounds of Jesus. Given the message and the manner of its reception, to focus on where the wounds appeared before and after the book of Barbet and to question whether God did not know where Jesus was actually pierced is to completely miss the message and mistake the signal for the signified. If ever there was a case of mistaking the finger pointing at the moon for the moon itself, this should count as a prime example of it.

Notes

1 Walter Kaufmann, *Critique of Religion and Philosophy* (Princeton, New Jersey: Princeton University Press, 1972), 225-235.

2 Issues such as whether hermeneutics provides a different method for human sciences, as claimed by Dilthey, or whether it leads to a different way of understanding truth (Heidegger) can be considered such baggage.

3 See, for example, Merold Westphal, "Hermeneutics as Epistemology," in *The Blackwell Guide to Epistemology*, ed. John Greco and Ernest Sosa (Malden: Blackwell Publishers, 1999), 415-35. Richard Rorty suggests hermeneutics as a successor to epistemology.

4 Wilbur Schramm, "The Nature of Communication between Humans," in *The Process and Effects of Mass Communication*, ed. Wilbur Schramm and Donald F. Roberts (Chicago: University of Illinois Press, 1971), 15.

5 Ibid., 8. It may be noted that the bullet theory of communication has its counterpart in the speech-act theory of J.L. Austin until Paul Ricœur introduced the "interlocutionary" act into it.

6 Robert E. Park, "Reflections on Communication and Culture," *The American Journal of Sociology* 44, no. 2 (1938): 189.

7 Wilbur Schramm, "How Communication Works," in *Basic Readings in Communication Theory*, ed. C. David Mortensen (New York: Harper and Row Publishers, 1973), 31.

8 Ibid., 31.

9 Barnett Pearce, "The Coordinated Management of Meaning (Cmm)," in *Theorizing About Intercultural Communication*, ed. William B. Gudykunst (London: Sage, 2005), 50.

10 Barnett Pears and Kimberley A. Pears, "Taking a Communication Persepctive on Dialogue," in *Dialogue: Theorizing Difference in Communication Studies*, eds. Rob Anderson, Leslie A. Baxter, and Kenneth N. Cissna (London: Sage Publications, 2004), 51.

11 See Paul Ricœur, *The Conflict of Interpretations: Essays in Hermeneutics*, Northwestern University Studies in Phenomenology & Existential Philosophy (Evanston: Northwestern University Press, 1974), 4. For the sake of simplicity, I have avoided the terminology of "speech acts." In terms of the speech-act theory, the act of reporting would be called "illocutionary act" and understanding it as a report would be considered "perlocutionary act" inasmuch as it is the impact produced on the hearer by the act of reporting.

12 For a brief, simple, comprehensive and critical account see Emory A. Griffin, *A First Look at Communication Theory*, 2nd ed. (New York: McGraw-Hill, 1994), 124-133.

13 Pearce, "The Coordinated Management of Meaning (Cmm)," 40.

14 W. Barnett Pearce and Kimberly A. Pearce, "Combining Passions and Abilities: Toward Dialogic Virtuosity," *Southern Communication Journal* 65, no. 2 (2000): 168.

15 William B. Gudykunst, "An Anxiety/Uncertainty Management (Aum) Theory of Effective Communication: Making the Mesh of the Net Finer," in *Theorizing About Intercultural Communication*, ed. William B. Gudykunst (London: Sage, 2005), 298.

16 Pearce, "The Coordinated Management of Meaning (Cmm)," 43.

17 Paul Ricœur, *Interpretation Theory: Discourse and the Surplus of Meaning* (Fort Worth: Texas Christian University Press, 1976), 43.

18 Schramm, "How Communication Works," 31.

19 Hans-Georg Gadamer, *Truth and Method* (New York: The Crossroad Publishing Company, 1984), 236.

20 Paul Ricœur calls this to-and-fro process "inter-locutionary act."

21 Pearce and Pearce, "Combining Passions and Abilities: Toward Dialogic Virtuosity," 171.

22 Gadamer, *Truth and Method*, 273. Gadamer's explicit concern with the horizon of the past and the present, but it seems equally applicable to the horizons of two contemporaries.

23 This is Nicholas Lash's rendering of ST, Ia, q.2. Nicholas Lash, "Considering the Trinity,"*Modern Theology* 2, no. 3 (1986): 187.

24 Gudykunst, "An Anxiety/Uncertainty Management (Aum) Theory of Effective Communication," 284.

25 Robert J. Schreiter, *The New Catholicity: Theology between the Global and the Local* (Maryknoll: Orbis Books, 1997), 33-34.

26 Mark Timmons, John Greco and Alfred R. Mele (eds.), *Rationality and the Good: Critical Essays on the Ethics and Epistemology of Robert Audi* (New York: Oxford University Press, 2007), 4.

27 Paul Knitter, *Introducing Theologies of Religions* (Maryknoll: Orbis Books, 2002), 110; JohnHick (ed.), *Dialogues in the Philosophy of Religion* (New York: Palgrave, 2001), 185.

28 Thomas Crocker sees Wittgenstein's emphasis on human activity to be closely related to Charles Peirce. See, Thomas P. Crocker, "Wittgenstein's Practices and Peirce's Habits:

Agreement in Human Activity," *History of Philosophy Quarterly* 15, no. 4 (1998): 475-93.

29 D. Z. Phillips, *Faith after Foundationalism: Critiques and Alternatives* (San Fracisco: Westview Press, 1988), xv.

30 Gadamer seems ambiguous on this point. On the one hand he would say that "The hermeneutic task consists in not covering up this tension by attempting a naive assimilation but consciously bringing it out." Gadamer, *Truth and Method*, 273. On the other hand, he would also say that two horizons "together constitute one great horizon...," 271. For the incompatibility of the latter claim, See, Xinli Wang, *Incommensurability and Cross-Language Communication*, Ashgate New Critical Thinking in Philosophy (Aldershot: Ashgate Pub. Ltd., 2007), 311.

31 Conrad Heyers, "Rethinking the Doctrine of Double-Truth: Ambiguity, Relativity and Universality," in *Religious Pluralism and Truth: Essays on Cross-Cultural Philosophy of Religion*, ed. Thomas Dean (Delhi: Sri Satguru Publications, 1995, 1997 Indian edition), 179. Masao Abe draws a similar contrast between Christianity as a religion of faith and Buddhism as a religion of awakening. See Masao Abe, "Response to John Cobb," *Buddhist-Christian Studies* 8 (1988): 65.

32 Marco Pallis, "Is There Room For "Grace" In Buddhism?," *Studies in Comparative Religion* 2, no. 4 (1968); http://www.studiesincomparativereligion.com.

33 Anthony Kennedy Warder, *Indian Buddhism*, 1st ed. (Delhi: Motilal Banarsidass, 1970), 23.

34 http://en.wikipedia.org/wiki/Shinran accessed on 11 March, 2001.

35 Hick uses this to justify his postulation of the Kantian *noumenon*. See, John Hick, *An Interpretation of Religion: Human Responses to the Transcendent* (New Haven: Yale University Press, 1989), 234. Similarly, Heyers sees the mystical and prophetic orientations as "one of the more stubborn divisions in the history of religions." Heyers, "Rethinking the Doctrine of Double-Truth: Ambiguity, Relativity and Universality," 176.

36 Swami Vivekananda considered Buddhism a sect of Hinduism. See, *Complete Works*. Calcutta, 1970-1973 (revised reprints of the Mayavati Memorial Edition), III, 536. cited in Wilhelm Halbfass (ed.), *Tradition and Reflection: Explorations in Indian Thought* (Albany: State University of New York Press, 1991), 52. For more details of the process by which Hinduism was made into a national religion, see, Omar Khalidi, "Hinduising India: Secularism in Practice," *Third World Quarterly* 29, no. 8 (2008): 1545-62.

37 Avery Robert Dulles, *Models of Revelation* (Dublin: Gill and Macmillan Ltd, 1983), 148; Rahner, TI, 4:131.

Chapter 5

Towards a Creative Hermeneutics of Praxis

Kuruvilla Pandikattu

Professor, Jnana-Deepa Vidyapeeth, Pune

"Philosophers have hitherto only interpreted the world in various ways; the point is to change it"[1] Keeping this admonition of Marx in mind, this article reflects on the role of philosophy in life. It asks some of questions like what is the relationship between thinking and action, between philosophy and life? and how does theory help us to live our lives better?

To begin with, we study the challenge posed by the existentialist philosopher Albert Camus on the absurdity of life. Then we focus the hermeneutic dimension of life, which helps us to discover meaning and significance of text (and life) as developed by the French philosopher Paul Ricœur and his German counterpart Hans-George Gadamer. This will convince us philosophy has overt and covert practical dimensions, very different from the technical dimension. Then we move to the religious level, where we follow Pope Francis to understand religious as a field hospital, which has the role of healing urgent and immediate wounds. This indicates beyond doubt, that religious always has a necessary practical (pastoral) side to it. This takes us to the queen of sciences, mathematics, where we see the power of abstract calculations (theories), and their deeper relevance for concrete cases.

Similar to mathematics, we argue that philosophy has to have profound practical neither pragmatic, nor technological) implications. From such philosophical perspective, which does not hesitate to look into the abyss of nothingness,[2] we can discover and experience the depth of life, even in its death.[3] Such a philosophy (or hermeneutics), it is hoped, will be creatively practical, providing us with the wisdom to live our (absurd?) lives with gentleness, genuineness and compassion. If philosophy cannot satisfy this role of profound practical involvement with deep commitment, I am afraid it may end as opium for the masses.

The method we follow in this paper is hermeneutical and phenomenological and so we selectively choose some insights from different philosophers and schools of thought. Our main goal is to explicate the profoundly creative praxis dimension of philosophy, with a view to make life richer and deeper.

Philosophy and Seeking Meaning

In order to show how philosophy contributes to praxis, we limit ourselves to Algerian-born French existential philosopher, Albert Camus. As he shows in his famous novel *The Myth of Sisyphus*, the way out of absurdity and the tendency to commit suicideis to seek meaning.

Camus affirms, "There is but one truly serious *philosophical problem* and that is *suicide*."[4] He situates this claim in our life-experiences. Sometimes we see our daily actions and interactions as dictated primarily by the force of habit. We cease to see ourselves as free agents and come to see ourselves almost as machine-like drones. From this perspective, all our actions, desires, and reasons seem absurd and pointless. The feeling of absurdity is closely linked to the feeling that life is meaningless.[5]

Camus relates the feeling of absurdity with the feeling of exile, a theme that is important not just in this essay but also in much of his fiction. As rational members of human society, we instinctively feel that life has some sort of meaning or purpose. When we act under this assumption, we feel at home. Therefore, people without meaning feel like strangers in a world divested of reason. The feeling of absurdity exiles us from the homelike comforts of a meaningful existence.

The feeling of absurdity is linked to the idea that life is meaningless, and the act of suicide is linked to the idea that life is not worth living. The important question, then, is whether the idea that life is meaningless necessarily implies that life is not worth living. Is suicide solution to the absurd? We should not be fooled, Camus suggests, by the fact that there are only two possible outcomes (life or suicide) that there are only two possible answers to this question. Most of us continue living largely because we have not arrived at a definitive answer to this question. Further, there are plenty of contradictions between people's judgments and their actions. Those who commit suicide might be assured life has meaning, and many who feel that life is not worth living, continue to live.

Confronted with the stark meaninglessness of life, we need to ask what keeps us from suicide. Largely, Camus suggests that our instinct for life is much stronger than our reasons for suicide: "We get into the habit of living before acquiring the habit of thinking." We instinctively avoid facing the full consequences of the meaningless nature of life, through what Camus calls an "act of eluding."[6] This act of eluding most frequently manifests itself as hope. By hoping for another life, or hoping to find some meaning in this life, we put off facing the consequences of the absurd, or the meaninglessness of life.

Through *The Myth of Sisyphus*, Camus hopes to face the consequences of the absurd. Rather than accept fully the idea that life has no meaning, he wants to take it as a starting point to see what logically follows from this idea. Rather than run away from the feeling of absurdity, either through suicide or through hope, he wants to dwell with it and see if one can live with this feeling.

Like Camus, our attempt is also to confront this meaninglessness and the act of eluding, without utterly giving up the possibility of making meaning. I like to indicate in this article that by taking this absurd life seriously, as free agents, we can consciously create praxis-orientedphilosophy that may help us to live with this absurdity. One way for such an approach is hermeneutics with its praxis components.

Hermeneutics and Praxis

In this section, we look into some of the significant contributions of two prominent hermeneutic philosophers – Paul Ricœur and Hans-Georg Gadamer – to indicate the practical nature of the study of hermeneutics in particular, and by extension, of philosophy in general.

Ricœur's Hermeneutics Unfolding to Praxis

From the simple act of interpreting texts, Ricœur takes hermeneutics to a critical or dialogical level. In critical hermeneutics the interpreter constructs the context as another form of text, which itself can then be critically analyzed so that the meaning construction can be understood as an interpretive act. In this way, the hermeneutic interpreter is simply creating another text on a text, and this recursive creation is potentially infinite. Every meaning is constructed. Still we need to reflect on the very constructive act of seeking to deconstruct and on the process whereby that textual interpretation occurs.[7]

Critical hermeneutics emphasizes that social reality is historically constituted. Moreover, one of the key differences between a purely interpretative approach and critical hermeneutics is that the "researcher does not merely accept the self-understanding of participants, but seeks to critically evaluate the totality of understandings in a given situation."[8] The researcher analyses the participants' own understandings historically and in terms of changing social structures. The hermeneutic-dialectic perspective, therefore, as an integrative approach, emphasizes both the subjective meanings for individual actors and the social structures, which condition and enable such meanings and are constituted by them.

Therefore, based on his study of Ricœur, the hermeneutic philosopher Paul Kidder[9] takes up the issue of the investigator's prejudice as being a useful starting point for the enquiry. He quotes from Augustine that one should "identify the clear and obvious meanings first and then use this understanding to make sense of the more obscure and confusing passages."[10] Therefore, Kidderaffirms, "what is clear and obvious to one in reading a text is likely to be a function of one's own cultural orientation and one's own prejudices rather than the function of some given accessibility of the text."[11]

So, where do we begin? If we cannot begin with the obvious, are we to begin with the obscure? The answer is that either option is more or less viable, but the crucial thing is that one avoids allowing the starting point to control the enquiry. False assumptions may be excellent roads to genuine understanding, but only if one is open, in the course of interpreting, to the clues that reveal the inadequacy of those assumptions and point the way to needed revisions. Such a hermeneutics allows meaning and understanding to be unfolded as a process. Kidder elaborates:

> Thus hermeneutic properly manifests a circular or cyclic pattern in its unfolding: the progress of the enquiry returns one to the beginning, and the new beginning sets a new course of progress; the interpretation of parts yields a conception of the whole, but that conception brings new meaning to the parts, whose reinterpretation may again require reconception of the whole, and so on, in a circle that would be merely vicious were it not propelled by concrete and cumulative acts of genuine understanding[12]

Such a critical hermeneutics is often called the hermeneutic-dialectic. 'Dialectic' approach is the art of investigating the truth of opinions, testing of truth by discussion and logical disputation. The accepted usage of this term is taken from the original Socratic dialogues.

In an ideal Socratic dialogue, no one is in it to win the debate, but everyone is engaged together in the search for the very best arguments in support of whatever opinion is being considered, along with the very best objections that can be set against those arguments. If in the context of a Socratic dialectic, one proposes an argument to which no one can respond with a substantial objection, it may fall to the same person to become the objector (and Socrates is often put into this situation, particularly with his younger interlocutors). Thus, the hermeneut may or may not have one's own position, but is always open to other perspectives. In this way, it is dialectical and dialogical. Kidder describes this process as follows:

> If I discover that my objection is more reasonable than my argument then I do a virtuous thing, from the point of view of the dialectic, if I immediately abandon my original opinion and seek a new one. This sort of reasoning process, then, has everything to do with persuasion, but it is not one person persuading another to hold a particular opinion; it is rather a matter of putting persuasion into a larger context of enquiry and discovery, allowing the power of argument to sway oneself along with the others, and in a way that is open and deeply attuned to the reasoning on all sides of an issue.[13]

Such a dialogical, critical, and dialectical hermeneutics takes us beyond the rational to the practical and transformatory level, and has bearings on our lives. Cyril Desbruslais agrees with this analysis. "For this as Paul Ricœur has taught us, philosophy must emancipate itself from an excessively rational bias– which is witnessed to by the penchant for conceptual tools and the hankering for rational arguments or "proofs" as also by questionable presuppositions about the comprehensive (rather than the apprehensive) nature of language. Reason is important human quality. But reason has its limits."[14]

Gadamer's Reciprocal Relation between Theory and Practice

The other significant hermeneutic philosopher, the German born Hans-Georg Gadamer also looks at the practical dimension of hermeneutic philosophy. Unequivocally, he claims that his hermeneutics is philosophy and as philosophy, it is practical:

> The hermeneutics that I characterize as philosophic is not introduced as a new procedure of interpretation or explication. Basically it only describes what always happens wherever an interpretation is convincing and successful. It is not at all a matter of doctrine about a technical skill that would state how understanding ought to be. We have to acknowledge what is, and so we cannot change the fact that unacknowledged presumptions are always at work in our understanding. Probably we should not want to change this at all, even if we could. It always harvests a broadened and deepened self-understanding. But that means hermeneutics is philosophy, and as philosophy it is a practical philosophy."[15]

Gadamer holds that the great tradition of practical philosophy lives on in a hermeneutics that becomes aware of its philosophic implications. In such cases, we have "the same mutual implications between theoretical interest and practical action." Aristotle thought this issue through with complete lucidity in his ethics. For one to dedicate one's life to theoretical interests presupposes the virtue of *phronesis* (practical wisdom). Gadamer adds, "This in no way restricts the primacy of theory or of an interest in the pure desire to know. The idea of theory is and remains the exclusion of every interest in mere utility, whether on the part of the individual, the group, or the society as a whole. On the other hand, the primacy of 'practice' is undeniable."[16] Affirming that Aristotle was insightful enough to acknowledge the reciprocity between theory and practice, Gadamer acknowledges as follows: "Hermeneutics has to do with a theoretical attitude toward the practice of interpretation, the interpretation of texts, but also in relation to the experiences interpreted in them and in our communicatively unfolded orientations in the world. 'This theoretic stance only makes us aware reflectively of what is performatively at play in the practical experience of understanding.'"[17]

From these perspectives, Gadamer sees "Hermeneutics as theoretical and practical task."[18] Indeed, the theme of this essay is that his hermeneutics has not only a theoretical dimension but a practical dimension, also, a practical dimension rooted in the profound practical philosophy as explored by Aristotle. Gadamer hastens to make clear that the usual modern conception of theory and its relation to practice is not what he has in mind. Rather, he goes back to Aristotle not only for rhetoric but also for practical philosophy and attempts to shape a hermeneutics that is "both theoretical in its universal dimensions but also practical in not using the abstract methods of science but a practical philosophy that seeks the Good, in the ancient sense."[19]

This compels Gadamer to take up arms against the modern scientific concept of language as an instrument of man, as a "means of communication." Language, he argues, is perhaps the most non-objectifiable element in our world. It takes shape not through scientific manipulation, but through "the praxis of social life itself, which must always reclaim its practical responsibility for the power that has been placed in the hands of man."[20] Here Gadamer plays on the weakest point in modern scientific thought: its inability from within itself to place limits on its own power. "Here the Greek way of thinking about a world in which we can live well and be at home offers something to modern man who finds himself in an alien world of capital, industry, and technology that is spinning out of control. Our modern concept of language, then, is just another symptom of our scientism and of the need to re-explore the Greek way of thinking about man and his relationship to the word."[21]

Thus, Gadamerian hermeneuticsis both theoretical and practical, making human beings feel at home in the larger cosmos. It takes the practical responsibility for the well-being of human beings and so possesses the "practical wisdom."

Religion as Field Hospital

Such a practical wisdom in the philosophical field takes us to the related field of religion. At the religious level, it is very much perceived in the life and mission of Pope Francis. In this section, we want to focus on religion also having such a reciprocal relationship between theory and practice.

Healing the Wounds

One of gifts of Pope Francis as a sympathetic communicator is a peculiar feel for the memorable image: "Shepherds should smell like their sheep;" and seminarians and priests ought to be willing to "make a mess" come readily to mind. One of most striking analogy in an interview[22] given by Pope Francis is this: "I see the church as a field hospital after battle." No doctor doing triage on a battlefield is going to be fussing about his patients' cholesterol or blood sugar levels. He is going to be treating major wounds and trying desperately to stop the bleeding.[23]

He then elaborated on an approach that has been apparent in his ministry as pope, stating that the most important thing that the Church needs to communicate is salvation through Jesus Christ. This proclamation of Jesus Christ is the Church's central message, and people must not lose sight of it.

It is the message of Jesus, the Holy Father said, that "fascinates and attracts more, what makes the heart burn, as it did for the disciples at Emmaus." After people have responded to this message, after they have begun to draw closer to Christ, the issues of how we must reform our lives must be discussed. "It is from this proposition [of salvation in Christ] that the moral consequences then flow," the Pope said.

Limited and Important Role of Theology/Theory

What we find today, the Pope is implying, are millions of people who are, in the general sense, gravely wounded. We are alienated from God, stuck in the no-man's land of selfishness, adrift with no sense of direction, and tempted by every form of errant desire. We require, therefore, not the fine points of moral doctrine, but basic healing. Perhaps this explains why the collective teachings of the Church on ethics are often met with incomprehension or hostility.[24] We need to remember that the theories of the Church (its doctrine and theology) must be coupled with its practice. Therefore, theology has an important and limited role in the self-understanding and development of the Church.

It may be noted that Pope's interview in *The New York Times* provoked media frenzy. *The New York Times* initially headlined its story, "Pope Bluntly Faults Church's Focus on Gays and Abortion." Later itquietly changed its dramatic headline to a more moderate one: "Pope, Criticizing Narrow Focus, Calls for Church as 'Home for All.'"

The Story of i, pi, zero

In this section we draw some insights from mathematics, the "queen of sciences" to apply to philosophy, "the queen of arts and sciences." Here we study irrational, imaginary, and impossible number to see the intricate relation between theory and praxis.

Irrational Numbers

In mathematics π (pi) is an irrational number, which means that its value cannot be expressed exactly as a fraction (when the numerator and denominator are integers). It has an infinite number of non-repeating digits. It is a transcendental number. This means that no sequence of algebraic operations using integers (powers, roots, sums, etc.) can be equal to its value.

Throughout the history of mathematics, there has been much effort to determine π more accurately and to understand its nature; fascination with the number has even carried over into non-mathematical culture. The current record for the decimal expansion of π, if verified, stands at 5 trillion digits.[25]

It is common knowledge that π is very practical in mathematics. For example, it is used to calculate the circumference of a circle ($2\pi r$) and its area (πr^2). There are more interesting every day applications of this interesting number π.[26]

For instance, π appears in all sorts of calculations for physics, engineering, electrical systems. The double helix is DNA revolves around π. It is in the rainbow, the pupil of the eye, and when a raindrop falls into water π emerges in the spreading rings. It appears in colors and in music. It is also used in probability and statistics.[27]

It also appears when calculating the number of deaths in a population. Interestingly, the ratio between the actual length of a river and its straight-line from source to mouth length tends to approach π (Einstein was the one to show this). The Guinness-recognized record for remembered digits of π is 67,890 digits, held by Lu Chao, a 24-year-old graduate student from China. It took him 24 hours and 4 minutes to recite to the 67,890th decimal place of π without an error.Akira Haraguchi, a retired Japanese engineer, claimed to have recited 100,000 decimal places but this has yet to be verified by Guinness.

As every science student knows, π, an irrational number turns up in many places. To summarize some everyday uses of π are:

(i) electrical engineers used π to solve problems for electrical applications
(ii) statisticians use π to track population dynamics
(iii) medicine benefits from π when studying the structure of the eye
(iv) biochemists see π when trying to understand the structure/function of DNA
(v) physicists looking into the behavior of fluid ripples see π and use it in their calculations
(vi) clock designers use π when designing pendulums for clocks

(vii) aircraft designers use π to calculate areas of the skin of the aircraft

(viii) signal processing and spectrum analysis (finding out what frequencies are in the wave you are using) use π since the fundamental period of a sine wave is 2π.

(ix) Navigation, such as global positioning (GPS) is facilitated by π.[28]

Imaginary Numbers

An Imaginary Number, when squared, gives a negative result.[29] Let us try squaring some numbers to see if we can get a negative result:

$2 \times 2 = 4$

$(-2) \times (-2) = 4$ (becausea negative times a negative gives a positive)

$0 \times 0 = 0$

$0.1 \times 0.1 = 0.01$

It is evident that we cannot multiply a number by itself to get a negative answer. Now mathematicians imagine that there is such a number (call it i for imaginary) that could do this:

$i \times i = -1$

Would it be useful, and what could we do with it? Well, by taking the square root of both sides we get this:

$I = \sqrt{-1}$

This means that 'i' is the answer to the square root of -1. This is actually very useful because by simply accepting that 'i' exists we can solve things that need the square root of a negative number.[30] We can explore further. The square root of -9 may be written as:

$\sqrt{(9 \times -1)} = \sqrt{(9)} \times \sqrt{(-1)} = 3 \times \sqrt{(-1)} = 3i$

The square root of -9 is simply the square root of +9, times i.

In general:

$\sqrt{(-x)} = i\sqrt{x}$

So, long as we keep that little "i" there to remind us that we stillneed to multiply by $\sqrt{-1}$ we are safe to continue with our solution! Using i we can also come up with new solutions:

Example: Solve $x^2 = -1$

Using Real Numbers there is no solution, but now we can solve it using our imaginary number! Take the square root of both sides:

$x = \pm \sqrt{(-1)}$

$x = \pm i$

Answer: $x = -i$ or $+i$

Check:

$(-i)^2 = (-i)(-i) = +i^2 = -1$

$(+i)^2 = (+i)(+i) = +i^2 = -1$

The Unit Imaginary Number, i, has an interesting property. It "cycles" through 4 different values each time we multiply:

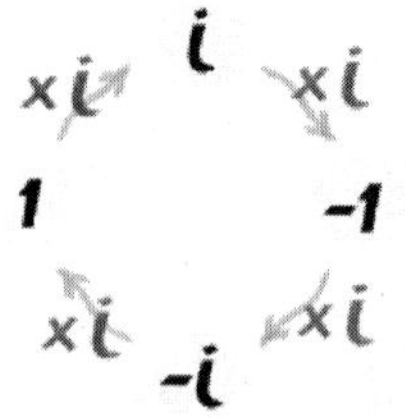

i × i = -1,
then -1 × i = -i,
then -i × i = 1,
then 1 × i = i (back too i again!)

So we have this:

$i = \sqrt{-1}$ $i^2 = -1$ $i^3 = -\sqrt{-1}$ $i^4 = 1$ $i^5 = \sqrt{-1}$ ...etc

Unit Imaginary Number: The "unit" Imaginary Number (the equivalent of 1 for Real Numbers) is $\sqrt{(-1)}$ (the square root of minus one). In mathematics we use i (for imaginary) but in electronics they use j (because "i" already means current, and the next letter after i is j).[31]

Examples of Imaginary Numbers

i: 12.3i; 3i/4; 0.01i; -i/2

Imaginary Numbers are not "imaginary": Imaginary Numbers were once thought to be *impossible*, and so they were called "imaginary" (to make fun of them). Nevertheless, people researched more on them and discovered they were actually useful and important because they filled a gap in mathematics ... but the name "imaginary" has stuck.[32] Imaginary Numbers are Useful: Their practical applications can be found at least in the following four areas of higher science as follows:

Complex Numbers: Imaginary numbers become most useful when combined with real numbers to make complex numbers.

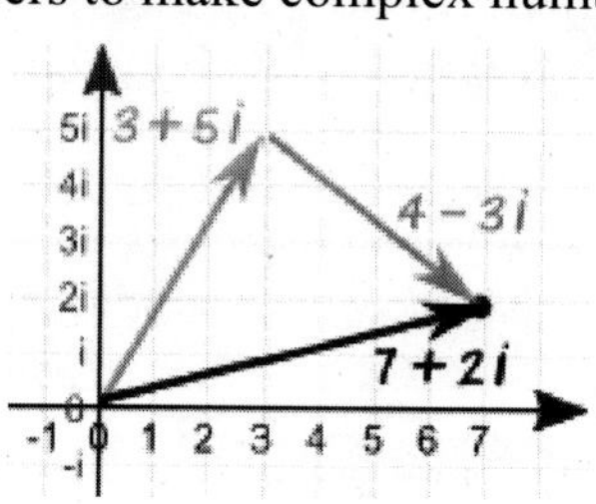

Spectrum Analyzer: Those cool displays you see when music is playing. Complex Numbers are used to calculate them! Using something called "Fourier

Transforms."[33] In fact, many clever things can be done with sound using Complex Numbers, like filtering out sounds, hearing whispers in a crowd and so on. It is dealt with more elaborately in "Signal Processing."

Electric Flow: AC (Alternating Current) Electricity changes between positive and negative in a sine wave. When we combine two AC currents, they may not match properly and it can be very hard to figure out the new current. However, using complex numbers makes it a lot easier to do the calculationsand the result may be "Imaginary" current!

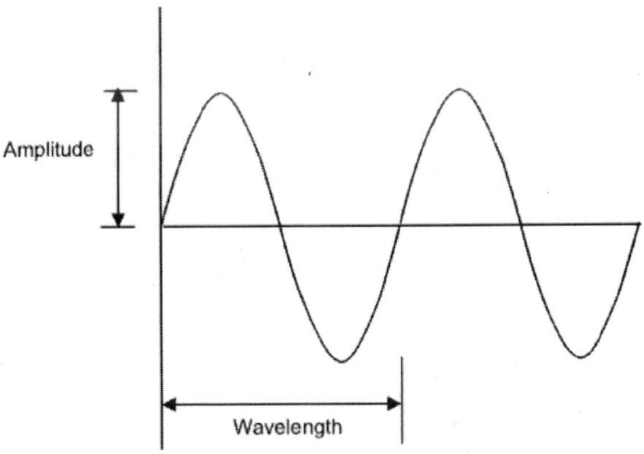

Mandelbrot Set: The beautiful Mandelbrot Setis based on Complex Numbers.

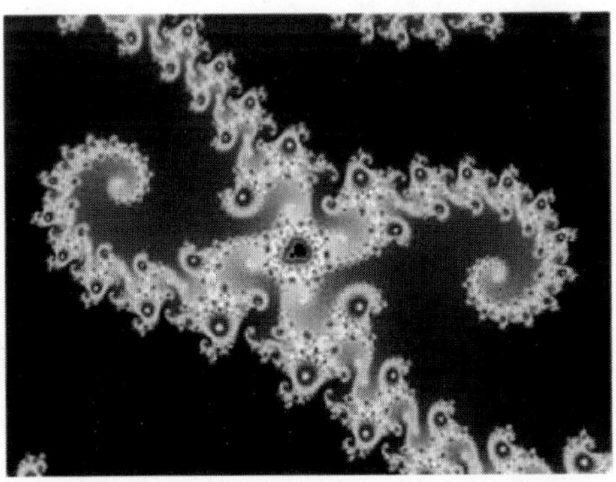

Quadratic Equation: $ax^2+bx+c=0$

The Quadratic Equation, which has many practical applications, can give results that include imaginary numbers Also, in Science, Quantum mechanics and Relativity also use complex numbers.[34] Thus we can assert that Imaginary Numbers are not "imaginary," they really exist, and we use them very frequently in mathematics, physics and other advanced sciences. The general population may need to use them one day.

Impossible Number

Zero is both, a number and a placeholder. Does it really exist? Can we possibly perceive it?[35]

Here are some of the properties of zero.[36]

Addition Property of Zero:

Adding zero to a number does not change it:

For all real numbers x, $x+0=0+x=x$.

Multiplication Property of Zero:

Multiplying a number by zero always gives zero:

For all real numbers x, $x\cdot 0=0\cdot x=0$.

Powers of Zero:

The number zero, raised to any allowable power, equals zero:

For n=1,2,3,…, 0n=0.

In particular, zero to the zero power (00) is not defined.[37]

Zero as a numerator:

Zero, divided by any nonzero number, is zero:

For all real numbers $x\neq 0$, $0/x=0$.

Note: 0/0 is not defined.

Division by zero is not allowed:

Any division problem with zero as the denominator is not defined.

For example, 00, 20, and 5.70 are not defined.

Names for the number one:

Any nonzero number divided by itself equals one:

For all real numbers $x\neq 0$, xx=1.

Names for the number zero:

The numbers 3 and −3 are opposites;

They are the same distance from zero, but on opposite sides of zero.

Any number added to its opposite is zero:

For all real numbers x, $x+(-x)=(-x)+x=0$.

Note: the 'opposite of x' is also called the 'additive inverse of x':

It is the number which, when added to x, gives zero.

So, we can ask ourselves why can we not divide by 0? Why is 0/0 "indeterminate" and 1/0 "undefined"? Why is dividing by zero "illegal" or "illegitimate"?[38] Division by zero is an operation for which you cannot find an answer, so it is disallowed. You can understand if you think about how division and multiplication are related.[39]

12 divided by 6 is 2 because 6 times 2 is 12

12 divided by 0 is x would mean that 0 times x = 12

No value would work for x because 0 times any number is 0. Therefore, division by zero does not work. Let us look at some examples of dividing other numbers.

10/2 = 5. This means that if you had ten blocks, you could separate them into five groups of two.

9/3 = 3. This means that if you had nine blocks, you could separate them into three groups of three.

5/1 = 5. Five blocks could be separated into five groups of one.

5/0=? Into how many groups of zero could you separate five blocks?

It does not matter how many groups of zero you have, because they would never add up to five since 0+0+0+0+0+0 = 0. You could even have one million groups of zero blocks, and they would still add up to zero. So, it doesn't make sense to divide by zero since there is not a good answer.

At the end of our exploration we tend to think that zero as such exists only in the mind (not as an entity in the real world, which makes its existence impossible). That is why zero is different from other numbers and so unique. At the same time zero has tremendous practical implications.[40]

Our analysis of the irrational, imaginary, and impossible numbers helps us to understand the power of conceptual or logical thought. Abstracting from real situation, these concepts can be manipulated in the mind and reapplied to the context of real life. Such reapplication transforms the original situation tremendous. All the developed technologies, for example, space flight, information technology and genetic exploration, use this power of conceptual thought to reinvent and reshapereality for the betterment of humans.

Conclusion: Philosophy, Religion as Leading to Phronesis

T. S. *Eliot* has insightfully observed, "Humankind *cannot bear* very much *reality*."[41] We may add that we also cannot bear very much absurdity. We may not be able to see the stark, naked reality. It may be too glaring. Nor can we live all the time in the illusory absurd world. It may be too maddening. It is precisely here that we can relate the theoretical to the practical, the ideal to the real, the universal to the concrete.

For this purpose, Aristotle will help us again. Gadamer find the answer given by Aristotle to the question about the possibility of a moral philosophy holds true as well for our interest in hermeneutics. His answer was that "ethics is only a theoretical enterprise and that anything said by way of a theoretic description of the forms of right living can be at best of little help when it comes to the concrete application to the human experience of life." At the same time, Aristotle maintains, "the universal desire to know does not break off at the point where concrete practical discernment is the decisive issue." The connection between the universal desire to know and concrete practical discernment is a reciprocal one. Therefore, it appears to me, "heightened theoretical awareness is about the experience of understanding, and the practice of understanding, like philosophical hermeneutics and one's own self-understanding, are inseparable"[42]

Thus, philosophy needs to discover practical application. However, its practical nature cannot be reduced to that of science or technology. It should still maintain its theoretical (contemplative) dimension and be open to deeply (not technically) practical consequences. Here phronesis turns out to be related to but notidentical with episteme and techne.[43]

Thus as seekers, we cannot afford to make philosophy primarily a profession or career, but a concrete passion with commitment. We may pursue *sometimes* search for knowledge as a goal in itself. Most of the time, we need to search for value not for its own sake, but for a larger cause. Thus, we can legitimately theorize and make abstract manipulations if we apply it to life at a deeper level. Our ability to reason, abstract, and manipulate are assets to be used for gaining practical wisdom.

As seekers, we are invited to search for meaning and significance – in spite of the apparent and real absurdity. We are called to cultivate wonder and amazement and not get used to life. This reminds us Ricœur's call for a "second naiveté." After having experienced the bitterness and betrayal of life the "second naiveté" enables us embrace life in its beauty and frailty.

Thus, philosophy has to be always public philosophy, not meant for an elite club, but open to the ordinary people, making their lives more profound and genuine. It is true that an "unexamined life is not worth living," but a life examined and found meaningless is worse. A life examined, purified, and deepened – including its meaninglessness – is worth. Such an examined life enables us to encounter each other and live our lives deeply and passionately with one another taking earnestly our superficial dislikes and genuine differences. Otherwise, the danger remains that along with religion, science and philosophy may become the opium of the people.[44] That is Karl Marx's challenge for contemporary society! Only thus, can we encounter the challenge raised by Camus and live genuinely and honestly, fostering life in its frailty.

Notes

1 *The Theses on Feuerbach* contain one of Marx's most memorable remarks: "the philosophers have only interpreted the world; the point is to change it" (thesis 11). The original German version is: "Die Philosophen haben die Welt nur verschieden interpretiert, es kommt darauf an sie zu verandern." It may be translated better as: the philosophers have only interpreted the world in different ways; the important thing is to change it. See Karl Marx and Friedrich Engels, *The German Ideology: Including Theses on Feuerbach and Introduction to the Critique of Political Economy* (Amherst: Prometheus Books, 1998).

2 Friedrich Nietzsche's quote is relevant here. "Beware that, when fighting monsters, you yourself do not become a monster... for when you gaze long into the abyss. The abyss gazes also into you." Friedrich Wilhelm Nietzscheand Walter Arnold Kaufmann, *Beyond Good and Evil: Prelude to a Philosophy of the Future* (New York: Vintage Books, 1989), 146.

3 See Kuruvilla Pandikattu, *The Depth of Death: Scientific Insights, Religious Openness* (New Delhi: Serials Publications, 2010).

4 Albert Camus, *The Myth of Sisyphus, and Other Essays*, 1st American ed. (New York: Knopf, 1955), 3.

5 For this section I am indebted to the good summary of the novel provided by Spark Notes online;http://www.sparknotes.com/philosophy/sisyphus/section1.rhtml (accessed on 22 December 2015).

6 Ibid.

7 Paul Ricoeur, *The Conflict of Interpretations: Essays in Hermeneutics* (Evanston: Northwestern University Press, 1974); http://press.anu.edu.au/info_systems/mobile_devices/ch06s03.html (acccessed on December 22, 2015).

8 Paul Kidder, 1997, "The Hermeneutic and Dialectic of Community in Development," *International Journal of Social Economics* 24, no. 11 (1997): 1194.

9 Ibid.

10 Augustine and D.W. Robertson, *On Christian Doctrine* (New York: Liberal Arts Press, 1958).

11 Kidder, "The Hermeneutic and Dialectic of Community in Development," 1194.

12 Ibid., 1194-1195.

13 Ibid., 1197.

14 In his forthcoming work titled *Philosophy of Liberation*, Cyril Desbruslais recalls Blaise Pascal, "The heart has its reasons which the reason does not know."

15 Hans-Georg Gadamer and Richard E. Palmer, *The Gadamer Reader: A Bouquet of the Later Writings, Topics in Historical Philosophy* (Evanston: Northwestern University Press, 2007), 244-245.

16 Ibid., 245.

17 Ibid.

18 Ibid., 246ff.

19 Ibid.

20 "Greek Philosophy and Modern Thinking,"*Ibid.* 267 (editor's introduction).

21 Ibid. See also Hans-Georg Gadamer, *Reason in the Age of Science* trans. Frederick G. Lawrence (Cambridge, MA: The MIT Press, 1993).

22 At the center of the media maelstrom was a 12,000-word interview with Francis arranged by several Jesuit publications around the world. The publications contributed questions, and these were put to Pope Francis in August by Jesuit Father Antonio Spardo, the editor in chief of the Jesuit publication *La Civiltà Cattolica*. The interview was published in September 2013. This lengthy and wide-ranging interview to the editor of *Civilta Cattolica* was subsequently published in sixteen Jesuit-sponsored journals from different countries.

23 Robert Barron, "The Field Hospital is Open" Word on Fire, http://www.wordonfire.org/resources/article/the-field-hospital-is-open/470/ 2013.

24 Ibid.

25 "How Do You Use Pi in Everyday Life?" *Yahoo Answers*.Accessed December 23, 2015. https://answers.yahoo.com/question/index?qid=20110313121210AAyorhq. For this section, I am heavily indebted to this site.

26 Ibid.

27 Ibid.

28 Ibid.

29 "Imaginary Numbers." *Maths Is Fun*. Accessed December 23, 2015. https://www.mathsisfun.com/numbers/imaginary-numbers.html.

30 Ibid.

31 Ibid.

32 And that is also how the name "Real Numbers " came about (real is not imaginary).

33 Ibid.

34 Ibid.

35 Hossein Arsham, "Zero in Four Dimensions: Cultural, Historical, Mathematical, and Psychological Perspectives;" http://home.ubalt.edu/ntsbarsh/zero/ZERO.HTM (accessed on 23 December 2015).

36 Adapted from Fisher-Burns, Carol JV. "Basic Properties of Zero and One." *One Mathematical Cat*. Accessed December 23, 2015. http://onemathematicalcat.org/algebra_book/online_problems/basic_zero_one.htm.

37 Ibid.

38 Ibid.

39 "Dividing by Zero."*Math Forum @ Drexel: Ask Dr. Math FAQ:* Accessed December 23, 2015. http://mathforum.org/dr.math/faq/faq.divideby0.html.

40 Ibid.

41 T. S. Eliot, "Burnt Norton," from *Four Quartets*, in *Collected Poems*, 1909-1962 (New York: Harcourt, Brace & World, 1970), 176.

42 Gadamer, Hans-Georg, and Richard E. Palmer. *The Gadamer Reader: A Bouquet of the Later Writings*, *Topics in Historical Philosophy* (Evanston, Ill.: Northwestern University Press. 2007), 245.

43 "*Epistêmê* is the Greek word most often translated as knowledge, while *technê* is translated as either craft or art. Some of the contemporary distinction between theory and practice are not found in the relation between *epistêmê* and *technê*. As we move chronologically

from Xenophon to Plotinus, we go from an author who does not distinguish between the two terms, to an author who has little use for *technê* because it is so far from reality. It is in Aristotle that we find the basis for something like the modern opposition between *epistêmê* as pure theory and *technê* as practice. Yet, even Aristotle refers to *technê* or craft as itself also *epistêmê* or knowledge because it is a practice grounded in an 'account' – something involving theoretical understanding. The relation, then, between *epistêmê* and *technê* in ancient philosophy offers an interesting contrast with our own notions about theory (pure knowledge) and (experience-based) practice. There is an intimate positive relationship between *epistêmê* and *technê*, as well as a fundamental contrast." Parry, Richard. See http://plato.stanford.edu/archives/fall2014/entries/episteme-techne/.

44 Karl Marx. "Religion is the sigh of the oppressed creature, the heart of a heartless world, and the soul of soulless conditions. It is the opium of the people."

Chapter 6

Hermeneutical Influences in U.S. Philosophy of Religion and Theology

Brendan Sweetman
Rockhurst University, Kansas City, USA

There is some overlap in contemporary European philosophy between the movements of hermeneutics and postmodernism, and for the purposes of this article, I shall be concerned with their commonalities, rather than their differences. There are a cluster of themes that overlap in both movements that have been influential in the work of the two American thinkers in the continental tradition whose work I shall discuss here, Richard Kearney of Boston College (and of Catholic background), and James Smith of Calvin College (and of Protestant background).Key themes include the rejection of a ready-made world that one can describe by means of ideas and concepts that are expressed in language; the operation of the hermeneutical circle in the interpretation of ideas and texts; the role of tradition in the reading of texts; the influence of history and culture on objective reason, truth claims and worldviews; and the priority of meaning over truth in the search for knowledge.

Richard Kearney on the God who may be

Richard Kearney is a significant thinker who has been very influenced by the phenomenological and hermeneutical traditions, who draws his inspiration from such philosophers as Husserl, Heidegger, Levinas, Derrida, and especially Ricœur. In his book, The God Who May Be: A Hermeneutics of Religion, Kearney uses the methods and techniques of phenomenology and especially hermeneutics to argue for a radical thesis. As he states it: God neither is nor is not but may be….what I mean by this is that God, who is traditionally thought of as act or actuality, might be better rethought of as possibility. To this end, I am proposing a new hermeneutics of religion, which explores and evaluates two rival ways of interpreting the divine – the eschatological and the onto-theological. The former, which I endorse, privileges a God who possibilizes our world from out of the future, from the hoped-for eschaton, which several religious traditions have promised will one day come…[1]

Kearney's use of the concept of onto-theology is a reference to Heidegger's use of the term to describe derogatorily the view of God that is presented in traditional theism; onto-theology describes the tendency to reify God by reducing him to the status of "a being" (even if God is understood to be a special type of being). The traditional view understands God to be anexisting transcendent being, with a number of important attributes, such as omnipotence, omnibenevolence, and omniscience; a perfect eternal being who does not undergo change, and so forth. Kearney invites us to reinterpret what we mean by God, to understand God as a being who may be – to understand God as possibility – and to reject the traditional approach that understood God as actuality, as "pure act," in Aristotle's terminology. Kearney's general approach therefore has echoes of neo-Platonism, and has also been influenced by the recent work of Jean-Luc Marion. Kearney argues that the reifying of God into the categories of Greek metaphysics is a distortion of God, and that we can reinterpret biblical texts and the Christian tradition to arrive at a different understanding of God, an understanding moreover that is more suitable for our present age, an age that may be characterized as one that rejects the traditional view of God and religion.We live, according to Kearney, in a post-metaphysical age.

Kearney invites us to re-understand God in terms of possibility. This means that God can only come to actuality if we – human beings – enable this to happen. How does this work? Kearney offers us detailed and interesting re-readings of central biblical passages and events, such as Moses and the burning bush, the Sulamite woman in the Song of Songs, and the apparitions of Christ to develop a new interpretation based on the idea that God can be understood less in a metaphysical way, and more in an ethical way. This means that God should now be understood as a transforming ethical possibility – "an eschatological summons," as Kearney puts it, a summons to transform human lives to make them more God-like, more divine centered. This eschatological summons enables us to envisage and hopefully to accomplish a re-created world of peace, justice and love. It also exceeds our own capacity, and involves tellingly a relationship with the other, very much in the spirit of Levinas' analysis of this relationship.

Kearney illustrates with a re-reading of Moses and the burning bush narrative in the Book of Exodus.[2] Recall that this is where God identifies himself to Moses as speaking from the bush, and asks Moses to lead the Israelites out of Egypt and into Canaan. God also identifies himself as "I am he who is" or "I am who am." Many important thinkers have commented on these passages in Exodus. For example, St Augustine, as Kearney notes, makes a distinction between God as he appears to us (and to Moses) and God as he is in himself. God as he is in himself is being itself, Augustine says; this safeguards the absolute, inaccessible, and transcendent nature of God, according to Kearney. Augustine and then later Aquinas went on to develop this understanding of God in detail, stressing the immutability or unchangeability of God (one consequence of which is that God does not need man). Aquinas even cites Exodus as confirmation of his proofs in the Summa. This view of God runs all through the scholastics, and the neo-scholastics, and (Kearney points out) it has been well expressed in Etienne Gilson's remark that, "Exodus lays down the principle from which Christian philosophy will be suspended... There is but one God and this God is Being, that is the cornerstone of all Christian philosophy."[3] Without the encounter of Greek metaphysics with biblical religious thought, Kearney believes, philosophers "would have never reached the idea that Being is the proper name of God and that this name designates God's very essence."[4] Thus, onto-theology sought to have its cake and eat it: to equate God with a modality of being while safeguarding His ultimately ineffable and transcendent nature.

Not only does Kearney reject the traditional concept of God as an immutable, self-sufficient pure act of being, existing as an eternal now with no past or future, without movement, desire or possibility,[5] but he also claims that God's relationship to history is now changed. As he puts it: "God will be God at the *eschaton*. That is what is promised...But because God is posse (the possibility of being) rather than *esse* (the actuality of being as a fait accompli), the promise remains powerless until and unless we respond to it.... God depends on us to be."[6] He proposes a new eschatological (instead of an ontological) reading based on new interpretations of this and other biblical passages, and of religious concepts and themes. He claims that the reading he proposes is more attuned to the original biblical context and is one with an emphasis on the ethical, dynamic character of God.

Kearney introduces the views of the great medieval Jewish commentator Rashi (Rabbi Solomon ben Isaac, 1040–1105) who renders the burning bush encounter as follows: "And God said unto Moses, 'I shall be what I shall be.' And he said, 'so shall you say to the children of Israel, I shall be has sent me to you.'"[7] And lest there be any lingering doubt, God adds the binding promise: "This is my name for ever and this is my remembrance from generation to generation." According to Kearney, Rashi can be read as interpreting the "name" (of God) in terms of mandate and mission. According to Rashi, "the vision that you (Moses) have seen at the thorn bush is the sign for you that I have sent you – and that you will succeed in My mission, and that I have the wherewithal to save you. Just as you saw the thorn bush performing My mission without being consumed, so too, you will go on My mission and you will not be harmed."And Rashi adds, tellingly, that this mandate itself prefigures the fact that three months later Moses and his followers would receive the Torah upon the very same mountain. Rashi tells us that the transfiguring God of the burning bush is pledging to remain with those who continue to suffer in future historical moments, and not just in the present moment. Rashi attributes a similar sense to the phrase "This is My Name forever, and My Remembrance from generation to generation" (Exodus 3:15). The transfiguring God is not a once-off deity but one who remembers the promises of the past and remains faithful to them into the eschatological future.

According to Kearney, "One of the best ways to ensure this fidelity is by refusing to yield up the secret of the Name here and now. As Rashi notes, the terms of Remembrance and Name are linked through the common experience of discretion and passing beyond. The word for 'forever' in this verse is spelled in such a way that it takes the form of a word, which normally says to 'hide the Name.' The reference to Remembrance means, accordingly, that God 'taught Moses how the Ineffable Name which is to be concealed is to be pronounced (… other than it is written)."[8] A main point of Moses' encounter is that the future of the covenant is wide open – nothing is predetermined. It is up to us to remain as faithful to God as God promises to remain faithful to us.

Kearney holds that amplifying the meaning of the Hebrew phrase *'ehyeh 'asher 'ehyeh* ("I am who am") in this manner allows for a plurality of interpretations of the verb "to be" used by God in his address to Moses. And what this means is that we should read the formula in terms of function rather than substance, in terms of narrative rather than syllogism, in terms of relation rather than abstraction (this kind of talk is an excellent example of Kearney's philosophical style). One consequence of the infiltration of this transfiguring God into the history of Greek and Latin metaphysics is to inject the latter with a specifically ethical charge. Smoke from the burning bush blurred the clear blue sky of Greco-Roman assurance, according to Kearney. Nobody slept quite so well at night anymore, or breathed quite so easily during the day, and dogmatic definitions of God began to fritter and come undone.[9]

Exodus and similar passages, he goes on to argue, signal a communion between God and humans, a radically new sense – as Levinas points out – of fraternity, responsibility, and commitment to a shared history of "becoming." God may henceforth be recognized as someone who becomes with us, someone as dependent on us as we are on Him. God's relation with mortals is, in other words, less one of conceptuality than of covenant. From which it follows that most philosophical reflections on God are in need of revision. And certainly, the orthodox onto-theological categories of omnipotence, omniscience, and self-causality, originally forged *sub specie aeternitatis*, could do with a radical rethink *sub specie historiae*. Yhwh is now revealed as affected and vulnerable, showing himself henceforth as one who wrestles with himself (Hosea), laments (Jeremiah), regrets (Samuel), seduces and forgives (Psalms). Here we witness a God who persuades rather than coerces, invites rather than imposes, asks rather than impels (what we have, in short, is a quite politically correct God!).We don't have enough space to develop this view further, but Kearney goes on in this vein in detail in a series of clever, interesting re-readings of biblical texts, illuminated by ideas from Husserl, Heidegger, Levinas, Ricœur and Derrida, as he develops this new hermeneutical approach to God for the twenty-first century.

Let us turn now to a few critical reflections on this view. Kearney has employed a hermeneutical approach to produce a radical re-interpretation of traditional theism, and indeed of biblical theism. His view is radical in several respects. He rejects God as *esse*, as an actually existing being, and says that God is rather, posse, possibility.This means that God may exist, but it is up to us to bring him into existence by the way we live. So, it also follows from this that God needs man not just to be fulfilled (as the process theologians argue), but to exist! The first critical point to make about such a radical view is an obvious one. It is one thing to claim that Greek metaphysical categories distort our view of God, and of God's nature (hardly a new thesis), but it is quite another to claim that this distortion also includes the claim that God exists, whereas what we should have been appreciating all along is that God is the possible, not a God who is, as Kearney puts it, but a God who may be. Of course, the claim that Greek metaphysics distorts the nature of God is hotly disputed, and many argue, including Patrick Masterson, that medieval writers, especially St. Thomas Aquinas, actually refined the Greek view using Christian concepts and categories, and developed a sophisticated, nuanced, religiously edifying view of God. As Masterson notes, Christian philosophers of the past constantly argued that God could not be captured in human concepts, that we can have an experience of God, that God is love, and so forth.They also differed from Greek metaphysics generally by saying that God is not a being among beings, and in arguing that God is creator, a notion that greatly enriched the Greek metaphysical view of God.[10] Whatever about Masterson's interesting corrective to a common contemporary misrepresentation of the medieval understanding of God's nature, a key further point is that in order for God's love to have a transforming effect on us – a key theme in Kearney's view – God must first of all exist! I will return to this point in a moment.

It is tempting to describe Kearney's view as what we might call a political view of religion.This phenomenon is common in Western academic circles. It can take several forms, but it usually involves some combination of a rejection of the existence of God, a rejection of traditional metaphysics and theology, a rejection of Christian doctrine, allied with a liberal moral and political agenda. This mindset (a set of "prejudices" in Gadamer's language perhaps), is then brought to bear on the biblical texts and Christian worldview, and used as the basis for the primary categories by which to reinterpret it. Kearney's view might be read as a version of such as approach, one that is even more radical than usual, because he is denying the existence of God (so there appears to be an atheistic motivation as well).We have seen this kind of approach in general in several thinkers in the twentieth century, an attempt to reinterpret a religion in which one no longer believes so that it can be salvaged for an ethical purpose. We see it in Paul Tillich, Don Cupitt, D. Z. Phillips, and it can be traced back at least to Wittgenstein's notion of language-games.[11] The ethical purpose is re-read back into the religious tradition according to the moral and political views of the interpreter.

But such an approach leads to some more difficulties for Kearney's view. For the fact is that Kearney wants to argue for an ethical agenda, and presumably for specific ethical imperatives for how human beings should live, and should become more God-like.There are two problems here, both of them serious. The first is one that has plagued secularist and naturalistic worldviews: how do we justify the moral order independently of the existence of God? And the second is: even if we could do this, how would we know which specific ethical values human beings should follow, especially on the controversial issues of the day? Why should we be guided by Kearney's moral views? Why would his reading be the correct one, and not other readings that are also offered in good faith (including, of course, traditional ones)? In short, what do justice, peace and love mean in Kearney's exposition, when spelled out in detail, and how do we know? This is why one might suspect that a view like Kearney's comes to the table already with an agenda with regard to these matters, and then one reinterprets the Christian tradition as expressing what one already believes (rather than being guided in one's beliefs by what the traditions says).

I think that one of the main problems facing Kearney's view is that he does not believe God exists as a really existing transcendent being. It seems to be that he runs into straightforward logical problems here. First, we can ask logically of Kearney's view what God is like in himself before he comes into relationship with us, irrespective of his relationship to us? What is his nature? Kearney cannot answer this question because God does not exist in himself; we bring him into existence in the way we live. This seems to be understood communally in Kearney rather than individually, though this is not clearly explained. But the second point is a key one: if God is only possible, then this means that he cannot exist. To put it another way: a god who does not yet exist, cannot exist, and therefore is an impossibility not a possibility (as Masterson has astutely put it).[12] This is why we must understand much of what Kearney says about God as metaphor: for example, his claim that God has kept his promise, and so now we must keep ours. If God does not exist, he cannot make or keep a promise! Since there is no metaphysical basis to his view of God, we must read Kearney as a religious skeptic who still wishes to articulate an ethical theory in the absence of God. It is at this point that his view confronts a large problem for hermeneutics in general: the problem of relativism. I will address the views of Smith first before I return to this problem at the end of the article.

James Smith on Biblical Metanarratives

James Smith has written extensively on hermeneutics and postmodernism, particularly in the application of the key ideas to religion. He represents a younger generation of scholars who are favorably impressed with contemporary European philosophy, and who try to apply some of the key ideas from the movements of hermeneutics and postmodernism to the area of religious belief. He has been influenced by Heidegger, Foucault, Derrida, and Lyotard. Smith argues in several of his articles and books (e.g., in his book, *Who's Afraid of Postmodernism?*[13]) that postmodernism and religious belief can have a positive relationship.

Smith is particularly interested in the hermeneutical approach that allows us to read the biblical text from the point of view of our own context, and to bring our own issues and concerns to bear on our interpretations. He is especially interested in a range of attempts today to criticize religious belief from various perspectives (e.g., science, enlightenment rationality, secularist morality, etc.), and he holds that we can use a hermeneutical approach to show the inappropriateness of such criticisms.[14] Smith recognizes that various perspectives can be brought to the biblical text today from different quarters, but he wants to defend the view that a hermeneutical approach is fruitful, and can be used to give some legitimation to religious belief, and the religious way of life.

Smith refers to Jean-François Lyotard's description or even definition of the postmodern age, or what Lyotard calls, "the postmodern condition," as a condition that is characterized by "incredulity toward metanarratives."[15] Now it would seem on the face of it that a movement whose main theme is the critique of metanarratives can have little time for religious belief. For is not religious belief – the religious worldview, understood as a set of metaphysical, doctrinal and moral claims about reality and human life – as clear a case as one can get of a metanarrative? In addition, is it not precisely the sort of metanarrative that hermeneutical thinkers wish to subject to critique? Although, Lyotard does not criticize religious belief directly, we can still ask would his incredulity toward various metanarratives not apply equally well to religious belief? Against this reading of Lyotard, Smith and others, including evangelical scholars J. Richard Middleton and Brian J. Walsh,[16] and the catholic scholar, R.C. Bauerschmidt,[17] have argued that although religious belief, more specifically the biblical worldview, is a metanarrative, it can nevertheless escape the kind of critique that a hermeneutical reading of a metanarrtive would normally invite. This is because it contains an ethical aspect that prevents it from succumbing to the "violence" associated with metanarratives.

Let us briefly recall how a hermeneutical critique of a metanarrative, or a worldview, or a definitive reading of a text or artwork, or a set of ideas that are being proposed as true, as telling us about what is really the case or about what really obtains, is supposed to work. One of the central ideas in hermeneutics is that there is no ready-made world to describe using language, where the language simply describes concepts, and the concepts represent some aspect of reality. This mirror theory of language (sometimes called the "fido/fido" theory) is rejected by continental philosophers, and the key notion becomes "interpretation," where the emphasis is on the context in which a subject encounters the objects of his/her experience, and so meaning and not truth becomes central. Unlike claims to truth, claims about meaning are relative to history, culture, and context, and these influences must be taken into account in our attempts to read great texts, works of art, and ideas of the past.

This means that the hermeneutical approach to ideas, texts, and meanings is saying that no particular worldview or set of ideas can claim to have the truth because the meanings that are constitutive of a worldview cannot be known to be true objectively. This is because there is no objective knowledge. All knowledge is contextual and is influenced by culture, tradition, language, biases, prejudices, background concepts, and so forth, and is, therefore, in some very important sense, relative to these phenomena. Knowledge is relative in the sense that what is true in one culture, e.g. on a moral issue, might not be true in another culture. This is because our culture, traditions, etc. "influence" the development of our moral views. The fundamental point is that the influence of these phenomena on truth or meaning is not trivial or benign; it is such that it inevitably undermines all claims to objectivity or universality that one might assert from the point of view of one's worldview. This stance is a fact about hermeneutics and most of the postmodernist approach, even if sometimes they are not inclined to acknowledge itexplicitly.

James Smith does not agree that religious belief, understood for the purposes of this discussion as the biblical worldview, is subject to the postmodernist critique, and this is in part because he does not agree that the biblical worldview is a metanarrative in Lyotard's sense. Smith argues: i) that scholars who think the postmodern critique must extend to religious belief are mistaken; ii) that those who think the biblical worldview is a metanarrative are also mistaken; and iii) that the biblical approach actually has some similarities to the postmodernist approach, and so can have a more positive relationship with that approach than most philosophers of religion are inclined to grant it.

Smith's view is that what is most problematic about metanarratives is not that they make universal claims, but that they try to back up these claims by appeal to some kind of universal reason, and it is this latter move that is illegitimate. What is at stake, says Smith, is not the scope of these narratives, but the nature of the claims they make.[18] If their proponents hold that the claims of the metanarrative are legitimated by universal reason, then the metanarrative is subject to the postmodern critique. Marxism is one such metanarrative, and what is wrong with it, according to Smith, is that it is actually grounded in narrative knowledge, in myth and faith-commitments, and not universal reason. Therefore, the claim that one's metanarrative can be legitimated by universal reason is simply a sham. So, Smith is optimistic: he thinks we should see this as an opportunity for religion, not as a problem.

The thinking behind this approach is that all metanarratives that appeal to universal reason as a form of legitimation would fail the test of legitimation. It is not, therefore, their subject matter that characterizes them as metanarratives so much as the fact that their proponents claim that this subject matter is universally true or has universal application, and, more specifically, that they try to justify this claim about universal application by appeal to universal Reason. Since any metanarrative that does this inevitably must appeal to a grander narrative (a language-game with its own internal rules) to justify itself (and this grander narrative would not be universally true, just another narrative), then all metanarratives fail the test of legitimation.

Smith believes that the biblical worldview is not a metanarrative. He holds that it escapes the postmodernist critique because "the biblical narrative and Christian faith does not claim to be legitimated by an appeal to a universal, autonomous Reason, but rather by an appeal to faith (or, to translate, 'myth' or 'narrative')."[19] He acknowledges that many would support a program of natural theology to back up the biblical worldview but argues that those who hold that the biblical narrative can be supported by reason are wrong, and that their view would be subject to critique. Smith then suggests that "new space is opened for a Christian appropriation of the postmodern critique of Enlightenment rationality."[20]

Yet, this view inevitably leads to a pervasive epistemological relativism because, as Smith acknowledges, "criteria which determine what constitutes 'evidence' or 'proof' must be game-relative; they will function as rules only for those who share the same paradigm or participate in the same language-game."[21] (The terminology of language-games comes from Wittgenstein, and is also used by Lyotard.) It is precisely in this area, where most philosophers believe postmodernism has its biggest problems, that Smith sees the opportunity for religion. Smith is quite vague on what the opportunity for religion actually consists in but he seems to think that it levels the playing field between the religious language-game and other language-games, those of secularism or naturalism, for example. He seems to be saying that because no language-game can make a claim to universal validity (or perhaps more accurately that any universal claims that are made are not defended by appeal to universal reason), then the religious language-game is just as legitimate as any other language game (although, of course, none of them are really legitimate at all because they are not objectively true). Therefore, this realization enables the religious believer to "open up a space for a radically Christian philosophy."[22]

Smith argues that the Christian faith is not a metanarrative; this is because it claims not to be justified by appeal to universal reason, but by appeal to faith. But Smith's analysis suffers considerable here because he does not tell us just what he means by "faith." For faith is one of those words that has many meanings and it can lead to confusion. It is used both as a verb and as a noun. If a belief is justified by faith this might mean that the evidence is not certain or conclusive (an example would be believing that God exists). Although there is some good evidence for the belief, it might be argued, it is still necessary to commit to the belief, and so we might describe this kind of commitment as believing "on faith." This commitment involves a movement of the will, as well as of the intellect.

The word "faith" might also be used to describe the strength of one's commitment to a view or belief, rather than the fact that the evidence is not fully decisive (as, for example, in the phrase "Mr. Jones is a person of strong faith").[23] Yet another, more pejorative meaning of the term is to describe believing in something without, or without regard to, evidence (this is sometimes how atheists, and some religious believers, describe religious belief); for example, in the statement "faith is not subject to reason." Smith is using the term mainly in this latter sense.When Smith says that the Christian metanarrative is justified by appeal to faith, he seems to be referring to the notion that since we do not justify our beliefs by appeal to reason, we must believe on faith, that is, without evidence. He cannot be referring to the first sense of "faith" mentioned above – that our belief is backed up by evidence, but it is just that we do not have quite enough evidence. This meaning would require him to recognize natural theology, and to accept the objectivity of reason and logic.

However, if this is the sense of faith he is relying upon – believing without regard to evidence – it is very hard to see how he can avoid running into serious problems, problems that religious belief simply could not cope with. The first problem is that the biblical metanarrative does make universal claims; therefore, in this way, the scope of the claims and the legitimation of the claims are inseparable issues. For example, the biblical metanarrative claims that every person is created in the image of God (as Smith acknowledges), that we should love one another, that we have dominion over animals, that wives should obey their husbands on some matters, that we should look after our neighbor, that we should not kill, etc.These are intended as objective moral claims.The biblical metanarrative does not say that these claims are simply part of the biblical tradition, and although they sound objective, and are often expressed in objective language, they are really not intended as objective moral claims but are, in fact, relative to the biblical time and place!

For if one is inclined to reject some of the positions above as not being part of the biblical metanarrative (e.g. that wives should obey their husbands), then, following Smith's approach, on what grounds can one do this? Either one could claim that this is not what the biblical worldview actually says, or intended to say, or taken as a whole, must be interpreted as saying, or one could claim that even if it does say this, it is wrong, or at least that we should not hold the same view now, i.e., that we should change the biblical metanarrative. I do not see how one can take either of these options without straightforwardly making precisely the kind of appeal to universal reason that Smith argues we should not make. How could we defend this view while avoiding cultural relativism? And utilizing the postmodernist approach to rule out possible interpretations of texts is close to a contradiction in terms.

A thinker like Smith must show how his view does not end up in relativism in the sense that it implies that contradictory views on, say, moral, social and political matters, are somehow all legitimate. Kearney's view faces the same problem with regard to which biblical interpretation is correct, and he must defend one as being correct since his primary aim is to promote an interpretation in order to defend a set of ethical imperatives that he is advocating as objectively true. And it is not sufficient to say that one is simply embracing relativism from "within," as it were, or that one is not worried by the charge of relativism, or that, since one is calling logic into question, one is therefore above logical objections. These are question-begging moves, because it is exactly this conclusion about narratives, and about logic and reason, which postmodernists have not established.

In short, it is not possible on fundamental epistemological issues to distinguish profitably between the scope of the claims of the biblical metanarrative (or of any metanarrative for that matter), and the way one attempts to legitimize these claims (through universal reason), Smith's view to the contrary. It is not possible to argue for the legitimacy of alternative interpretations, as Kearney does, without explaining how one avoids relativism in this process.This is because if one makes a universal claim – especially an ethical claim like one ought not to steal, for example – one needs to say why one should not do this. And this involves automatically giving a rational argument for this conclusion – or making an appeal to universal reason, in the language of postmodernism.To attempt to justify this kind of moral imperative by saying that this is just what my metanarrative, my interpretation, my culture, traditions, customs, practices, etc. says, is simply to fall back again into relativism, and to undermine the claim that one should not steal. A universal claim by its very nature is not relative, and so requires appeal to universal reason to back it up. Conversely, this means that we can legitimately reject an ethical imperative if is founded on somebody else's interpretation of a set of ideas, or events, or a text; we can reject it in favor or our own interpretation. Indeed, the zeitgeist of the democratic age is to encourage people to pursue their own interpretations, not follow those of others, an approach postmodernists are usually quick to champion, except when it clashes with (and so undermines) their own moral and political agendas.

The hermeneutical approach, as we noted above, quickly lends itself to a political agenda in the sense that worldviews are almost by definition oppressive since they privilege some meanings, readings and interpretations, and marginalize others; hermeneutics, structuralism, and deconstruction thus become the method for rejecting and debunking worldviews. Conversely, it also allows those views and readings and alternative meanings that have usually belonged to minority groups, and that have often been marginalized, to reclaim their rightful place in the marketplace of ideas (Kearney's re-readings of the Bible, for instance). But the central point raised by the problem of relativism that thinkers influenced by this approach have never come to terms with is that that marginal worldviews do not reclaim their place because they are true (for that would be to acknowledge objective knowledge), but because, since there is no objective knowledge, they have just as much claim to legitimacy as any other view.

Derrida is more radical on this point, but perhaps more honest, in saying that these marginal views will also have to be deconstructed in the end. This is a point many supporters of the a postmodernist approach conveniently overlook; they frequently talk as if the marginal views are somehow true, and the mainstream views somehow false, an attitude clearly exhibited in Kearney's work.[24] Postmodernism itself cannot offer a concession that no worldview should get involved in politics, despite its occasional protestations to the contrary (expressed in the claim that it is subject to its own critique), for the desire to criticize other worldviews, especially traditional ones – and in this case traditional religion – and to bring about ethical and political change, is one of the driving forces behind postmodernism. It is also, I believe, one of its deepest and irresolvable contradictions. For all of these reasons, I think we should approach recent hermeneutical and postmodernist approaches in theology and philosophy of religion with a great deal of caution and suspicion.

Notes

1 Richard Kearney, *The God Who May Be: A Hermeneutics of Religion* (Bloomington: Indiana University Press, 2001), 1-2.

2 See ibid., 20ff.

3 See ibid, 24; see also Etienne Gilson, *The Spirit of Medieval Philosophy* (New York: Scribner's, 1940), 69.

4 Ibid., 24.

5 Ibid, 23.

6 Ibid., 4.

7 Ibid., 25.

8 Ibid., 26.

9 I think it is quite significant that these are moral and political points that Kearney is making with regard to this reading of the biblical passage.

10 See Patrick Masterson, *The Sense of Creation* (London: Ashgate, 2008), 125-127.

11 For more on the approach of D. Z. Phillips, see my "D.Z. Phillips on Christian Belief, Immortality and Resurrection," *Philosophia Christi* 16, no. 1 (Summer 2014): 57-80.

12 See Masterson, *The Sense of Creation*, 136.

13 James K. A. Smith, *Who's Afraid of Postmodernism?: Taking Derrida, Lyotard and Foucault to Church* (Ada: Baker, 2006). I have discussed Smith's approach in detail in my "Lyotard, Postmodernism and Religion," *Philosophia Christi* 7, no. 1 (Spring 2005): 141-153. My discussion over the next few pages is based on this earlier discussion.

14 See James K. A. Smith, "A Little Story about Metanarratives: Lyotard, Religion and Postmodernism Revisited," *Faith and Philosophy* 18, no. 2 (April 2001): 353-368.

15 See Jean-François Lyotard, The Postmodern Condition: A Report on Knowledge, trans. G. Bennington and B. Massumi (Minneapolis: University of Minnesota Press, 1984), xxiv.

16 See J. Richard Middleton and Brian J. Walsh, *Truth is Stranger than it Used to Be: Biblical Faith in a Postmodern Age* (Downers Grove: Intervarsity Press, 1995), esp. chapters 4 and 5.

17 See Frederick C. Bauerschmdt, "Aesthetics: The Theological Sublime," in *Radical Orthodoxy: A New Theology*, ed. John Milbank, Catherine Pickstock, and Graham Ward (New York: Routledge, 1999), 87ff.

18 See Smith, "A Little Story about Metanarratives," 354.

19 Ibid., 360 (emphasis in original).

20 Ibid., 360.

21 Ibid., 360 (emphasis in original).

22 Ibid., 362.

23 We need to note that Jones himself very likely does not use the word in this way, that he makes the distinction between his commitment and the truths to which he is committed. Yet when his faith is described in this way by a third party it is usually the depth of his faith that is being referred to, and also that this depth of faith will be significant in any discussion with him about matters that concern his religious beliefs

24 For a more detailed critique of Derrida and postmodernism, see my "Postmodernism, Derrida and *Différance*: A Critique," *International Philosophical Quarterly* 34, no. 1 (March 1999): 5-18.

Chapter 7

The Hermeneutics of Ethical Research
A Case Study of Aboriginal and Torres Strait Islander Communities

Jānis Ozoliņš
Australian Catholic University, Melbourne, Australia

Official European settlement of Australia dates back only to 1788, the arrival of the First Fleet at Botany Bay on the East Coast of Australia, little more than two and a quarter centuries ago, whereas some estimates put Aboriginal occupation of Australia at around 40,000 years or more.[1] The idea that Australia was "*terra nullius*" is simply false. While we need not see Aboriginal civilization through rose tinted glasses nor argue that Aboriginal culture was vastly superior to European culture (or vice versa for that matter), it is patently obvious that it differed and continues to differ in significant ways from Western European cultures – and indeed Asian cultures as well. That it was a complex, sophisticated hunter-gatherer civilization is now well recognized.[2] People who inhabited a land before it was conquered by colonial societies and who consider themselves distinct from the societies currently governing those territories are called Indigenous Peoples. If we accept this definition then it is evident that Aboriginal and Torres Strait Islanders are indigenous peoples.

Indigenous peoples around the globe, estimated to number between 300 to 500 million,[3] face similar problems in the lands where they have been displaced, despite the existence of various UN Declarations. Aboriginals and Torres Strait Islanders continue to face serious problems for various reasons, sometimes because of Government policies and sometimes the ineffectiveness of policy designed to improve life conditions. Just like Indigenous people in other countries, Aboriginals and Torres Strait Islanders are over-represented in Australia's gaols, have low levels of literacy, high unemployment as well as low life expectancy.[4] It is shameful that many Aboriginals live in Third World conditions in a country as prosperous as Australia. Traditional lands and sacred sites have been taken over and quarried for their mineral wealth with little or no compensation to their Aboriginal owners. Aboriginal cultures have been suppressed, exploited, or trivialized. Sacred drawings, for example, appearing on tea towels are examples of both exploitation of Aboriginal Art and its trivialization. It may also expose a crass ignorance and a complete lack of understanding and appreciation of Aboriginal culture. The arguably well-meaning policy of assimilating Aboriginals into white society under the naïve view that somehow Aboriginality could be bred out after a few generations and all peoples would form one uniform white Australian population was not only a dangerous lunacy that devalued Aboriginal peoples themselves but also attempted to destroy their culture and way of life.[5] It is no wonder that many Aboriginal and Torres Strait Islanders regard Governments of all political shades with suspicion. It is paramount, therefore, that all people, especially researchers, acknowledge previous wrongs through a more sensitive respect for the culture and customs of Indigenous communities. This is particularly important for researchers who wish to invite Aboriginal and Torres Strait islander people to participate in their research.

The United Nations' Draft Declaration on the Rights of Indigenous Peoples (Article 12) affirms the right of Indigenous people to their cultural traditions and customs, and to have their cultural property returned to them, if it was taken without their permission.[6] Article 29 states that indigenous people are entitled to the recognition of full ownership, control and protection of their cultural and intellectual property.[7] They have the right to special measures to control, develop and protect their sciences, technologies and cultural manifestations, including human and other generic resources, seeds, medicines, knowledge of the properties of fauna and flora, oral traditions, literature, designs and visual and performing arts.[8]

Inconsidering the hermeneutics of ethical research with Aboriginal and Torres Strait Islander peoples (ATSI peoples), we need to be aware of the forces shaping not only individual identity, but also community identity and, for people displaced from their traditional ways of life, the struggle to preserve culture, tradition and particular ways of life. A central concern, to some extent taken for granted, in any discussion of research with ATSI peoples, is the preservation of the community and its traditions in the face of its relentless erosion by the surrounding majority Australian culture. There are lessons here also for small nations with a particular ethnic identity that are surrounded by a larger majority culture.[9]

For ATSI peoples, the self is to be understood within the context of a community and so an aboriginal person will refer to himself or herself as belonging to a particular community and to a particular place. Belonging to land and to a community are central to an aboriginal person's sense of identity. This is because all beings are connected: destruction of the land brings destruction of oneself and community to which one belongs. Similarly, acting in a manner that harms the community harms the individual, since the individual does not exist without the community.[10]

The interrelationship between individual, community, and place for an Aboriginal person is understood holistically; both spiritual and physical aspects of the world are integrated, with one affecting the other. Thinking evil thoughts does not remain simply a spiritual matter, but manifests itself in the physical world as misfortune. For survival, an aboriginal person needs to balance both spiritual and physical aspects of the world, and so the importance of the community becomes evident. If we reflect briefly on the influence of a particular community on the process of the formation of the self, what we mean by self can be understood not only within an historical consciousness, but also, for Aboriginal and Torres Strait Islander peoples within a distinct narrative woven from the stories of the Elders of the community. In relation to this, there are two things we might distinguish: 1) How the experience of others of historical events, stories and narratives and the meanings that they give to those events shape the sense of self that we develop; 2) Our personal reflections on our own experience of historical events, stories, and narratives. For Aboriginal and Torres Strait Islander peoples belonging to the land and a particular community act powerfully to influence individuals' sense of who they are. This is because the narratives, experiences, and stories are not about what has happened in the past, but are present here and now, shaping individuals and placing them within a shared communal journey.[11] For Aboriginal and Torres Strait Islanders, their own reflections, which are not the most important, for shaping their identity, but what has been transmitted to them by the Elders of their kinship group.

For Western people, there is a dual hermeneutic here and possibly a third. From 2) we have i) Our own experiences which are mediated and shaped by the historical and narrative consciousness of those who have given meaning to events that have gone before and which now colors our own perceptions and interpretations and ii) our own reflections on our own experiences, mediated and shaped by those events and experiences which are our own. A third element are those others contemporaneously interpreting and giving meaning to the common experiences that we have. It is the interplay of these elements, which give rise to our sense of who we are, of our sense of self. Thus, the historical events that shaped the ideas and values of our parents and grandparents in their turn shape not only our ideas and values, but largely shape our sense of self, for it is these, which determine our attitudes to others and the ways in which we act towards them. Our own experiences, contaminated as they are by the values of those with whom we have been in intimate relationship influence our sense of self and of our place in the world, as will those others, outside our immediate circle, who influence the way in which we think. For ATSI peoples, the intimate interrelationships between those who are family and members of the particular tribal group to which they belong are central in shaping their sense of identity. Thus, even people of aboriginal descent who are urban dwellers will refer to themselves as a man or woman from a particular tribal family from a specific part of the country.[12] Though their own experiences and interpretations of these are also important, it is the sense of belonging to a timeless present in which all experiences are part of their lives that is most influential.

There is a need within us all to belong and so it is through the communities to which we belong that we develop a sense of self and of ourselves as persons. As Ricœur reminds us, there is no self without the Other.[13] Human beings, being gregarious creatures, need others to have a sense of solidarity of working towards common goals. Exile from one's country would not be difficult to bear if it did not mean being torn away from those whom one loves and from the community in which one has one's roots.[14] To reiterate, the community and the land to which they belong are particularly important for Aboriginal and Torres Strait Islander peoples and shape their sense of who they are. Researchers wishing to work with Aboriginal and Torres Strait Islander peoples and their communities need to understand the values and the culture of the particular communities in which they intend to conduct their research. They need to be aware of a different hermeneutics operating amongst ATSI communities in the interpretation of events and experiences of their own. We shall outline some of the important values that researchers need to be aware of and take into account if they want to conduct research in ATSI communities.

The NHMRC document *Values and Ethics*, notes the development of much fruitful collaboration with Aboriginal and Torres Strait Islander communities, particularly in the areas of health care provision.[15] It can be acknowledged that there is a greater involvement of Aboriginal and Torres Strait Islanders themselves as researchers, but it is also true that some suspicions remain. There remains much work to be done to allay suspicions and to mend deep mistrust within communities about what researchers are trying to gain from them.

Negotiated Consent

Central to research with Indigenous peoples is the question of informed or negotiated consent. It is sometimes thought that it is questionable, given the vulnerabilities of indigenous communities in Australia, whether it is possible to achieve negotiated consent. Although we do not have space to explore in detail what is meant by informed consent, briefly we take it to mean that the participants fully understand what they are being asked to do and are able to make a voluntary decision to participate. It is also understood that they are aware of the risks involved in the research and are able to assess, in an informed way, the nature of the harms and benefits that participation might lead to personally. Informed consent is particularly important for Indigenous peoples because it is to be understood somewhat differently to our Western conceptions of it.

If Indigenous people are to be involved in research, it is not just informed consent of the individual that is crucial, but everyone in the group. If knowledge is understood as belonging to the group and not to the individual, then even if he or she is the only one having custody of it, only the group for whom the individual might have custodial responsibility is able to give consent to its sharing. Moreover, as Daes elegantly states: "Heritage can never be alienated, surrendered or sold, except for conditional use. Sharing therefore creates a relationship between the givers and receivers of knowledge. The givers retain the authority to ensure that knowledge is used properly and the receivers continue to recognize and repay the gift."[16]

In Australian Aboriginal and Torres Strait Islander communities, heritage and culture are not owned by any person, but are held in custody: what belongs to a kinship group – stories, language and cultural practices are sacred – since these are part of what identifies them as who they are.

In order for Indigenous people to participate in a research project, researchers have to be willing to acknowledge that the knowledge that the indigenous people are willing to share with them demands a reciprocal willingness on the part of the researchers to share whatever benefits accrue from the research with them. There is a need to understand that for Indigenous people, though they may be considered participants by the researchers, their own view is that they are partners in the research endeavor and hence it is the group that exercises control over the research process in an active way. That is, participants are actively contributing to the research rather than merely responding to the demands of the researchers.[17]

Given that the Indigenous people as participants are sharers in the research process, it follows that such sharing continues throughout the research process. That is, negotiation and consultation need to continue throughout the research undertaken. This means that consent is never finalized, but must be continuously negotiated. Given this understanding of the nature of the research process, it is sometimes better to speak of negotiated consent rather than informed consent, though the consent would be expected to be informed and voluntarily given.

Part of the reciprocal arrangements may involve the researchers in providing some tangible benefits to the community for their participation in research. In many cases, there may not be a great deal of benefit to them and in that eventuality, the community might expect that the researchers provide benefits in some other way. These are not bribes, but a recognition that if some benefit is given to the researchers it is only fair that some benefit also accrue to the community that has shared their knowledge with the researchers. For example, if the researchers are a medical team, they might consider providing the community with some medical services during the time that they are carrying out their research. If they are a team of educators, they might consider providing some extra help with tuition or assist the local teachers in some way.

Australian Institute of Aboriginal and Torres Strait Islander Studies (AIATSIS) Guidelines

The *AIATSIS Guidelines* present fourteen principles, which it is argued need to be taken into account in considering the involvement of Aboriginal and Torres Strait Islanders in research. These principles are:

1. *There must be recognition of the diversity and uniqueness of peoples as well as of individuals.*[18] The diversity of people and depth of different languages, cultures, histories, and values needs to be recognized. The views of one group of a community should not be assumed to represent those of the whole community. Differing ways of seeing things should not be dismissed as having little consequence, for these differences may reveal significant perspectives that may enlighten the researcher with an open mind. What is revealed to the researcher may not necessarily be easily translated into a Western idiom or Western concepts without doing considerable violence to what has been said. This difficulty points to the considerable challenges in undertaking research with indigenous peoples.

2. *The rights of Indigenous peoples to self-determination must be recognized.*[19] This principle acknowledges that research projects with indigenous people must be conducted in accordance with the United Nations (2008) *Declaration of the Rights of Indigenous Peoples*. This means that indigenous peoples have a right to be fully involved in projects that impact on their lives and that they have a right to maintain control over and protect their heritage, culture and traditional knowledge. They need to be free to pursue their own cultural, economic, and social development. This requires that researchers ensure that research conducted in Aboriginal and Torres

Strait Islander communities involves them not only as participants, but also as fellow researchers to the extent that this is possible, recognizing that this will not extend to all areas of research expertise. Principle 10, which states that Indigenous people have the right to full participation appropriate to their skills and experiences in research projects and processes, stresses the importance of full involvement at the appropriate level of indigenous peoples in research.[20]

3. *The rights of Indigenous people to their intangible heritage must be recognized.*

4. *Rights in the traditional knowledge and traditional cultural expressions of Indigenous peoples must be respected, protected, and maintained.*[21] Thisprinciple is built on the previous one by acknowledging the significance of protecting what is intangible about Aboriginal and Torres Strait Islander peoples' heritage and traditional expression of their culture. It also acknowledges that much of Aboriginal and Torres Strait Islander culture is not written down and there are significant issues with imparting what is traditional knowledge to those who do not belong to the group. Certain stories and narratives are sacred to particular kinship groups and cannot be shared, even with other kinship groups. Writing down, audio or video recording of certain stories and narratives can be a serious violation of what is sacred to a particular group. There are also indigenous technologies, ways of using seeds, knowledge of flora and fauna, which are specific to particular communities, as well as visual and performing arts that need to be respected.

5. *Indigenous knowledge, practices, and innovations must be respected, protected, and maintained.*[22] Where there are differences in the way in which knowledge is gained, such differences need to be respected. Since such processes are part of the cultural property of indigenous people, it should be understood that failing to respect different ways of both gaining and assessing whether something counts as knowledge could be understood as disrespecting the value of a culture. This is not to say that there may be genuine reasons for claiming that something asserted to be known is not actually something for which one has indubitable and incorrigible evidence. It may be that it is simply false. This should not be regarded as a principle that asserts the relative nature of knowledge; rather it is a plea for respecting the way in which knowledge is said to be acquired. Winch's (1958) discussion on what is to be accepted as knowledge is salutary. Winch describes a discussion between Achilles and the Tortoise, where they are discussing three propositions, A, B, and Z, which are so related that Z follows logically from A and B. The Tortoise asks Achilles to treat him as if he accepted A and B as true, but did not as yet accept the hypothetical proposition C, "If A and B are true, Z must be true," and to force him to accept, logically, that Z was true. Achilles begins by asking the Tortoise to accept C, which he does. Now the sequence reads, "If A and B are true and C (If A and B are true, Z must be true) is true, then Z." Achilles now says that the

Tortoise must accept this. When the Tortoise asks, why must he, the response is because it follows logically, that is, if A and B and C are true, then Z must be true. The Tortoise says he accepts this new proposition D, but still asks why he must accept Z. The upshot is that an infinite regress is created.[23] Although the moral of the story for Winch is that the process misunderstands the nature of inference, we can also draw from this another lesson, namely, that differences of understanding can lead us to endless discussion from which there is no relief until we recognize why there is such systematic misunderstanding. The way to do this is through dialogue, but it must begin from a respect for the view of the other in the dialogue and a seeking of mutual understanding.

A crucial element in mutual understanding is the recognition that not only are there different paths to knowledge and different interpretations of that knowledge, but also that these different paths to knowledge are part of the intellectual and cultural property rights of Indigenous peoples and so must be respected and preserved. It follows that indigenous cultural and intellectual property, which exists not just in artifacts, but in the cultural practices, resources and knowledge systems of indigenous peoples need to be respected and preserved. Moreover, just as Western culture is not static, it should be recognized that neither are indigenous cultures static.[24] The *AIATSIS Guidelines* argue that it is a principle of research to acknowledge the sources of information and those who have contributed to the research.

Principles 6-9 deal with issues related to informed consent and the process of negotiating agreement with indigenous groups and communities.

6. *Consultation, negotiation, and free, prior and informed consent are the foundations for research with or about Indigenous peoples.*[25] The gaining of voluntary, informed consent from human participants is a cornerstone of ethical research and it has already been proposed that the establishment of informed or negotiated consent is crucial in dealings with indigenous peoples. In particular, a fundamental element in this is the obligation for researchers to give something back to the communities in which they wish to conduct their research. Consultation, say the *AIATSIS Guidelines*, is an important aspect of the process of consent, irrespective of whether the research involves fieldwork or not. This means that the particular community is to be consulted about the aims and objectives of the research, as well as the identification of the appropriate individuals who are to be consulted. There is a very broad requirement that all aspects of the proposed research are fully understood by those who are to be consulted.

7. *The responsibility for consultation and negotiation is ongoing.*[26] Reinforcing the above point, the *AIATSIS Guidelines* stress the importance of continuing consultation and negotiation. This means that consent has to be re-established throughout the research project and cannot be assumed to be given once an initial consent form is signed. Indeed, it may not be

appropriate at all to use a consent form in this process. This would need to be determined in consultation with the relevant community. For the purposes of Human Research Ethics Committees, who are expected to provide final ethical approval of the research project, it would be expected that the process followed in gaining consent would be documented. This is also reiterated by Principle 9. The staging of projects, where this is feasible, is encouraged, since this will facilitate community involvement and ownership of the research.

8. *Consultation and negotiation should achieve mutual understanding about the proposed research.*[27] The importance of mutual understanding is stressed because of the importance of establishing informed consent. Where a group has had little exposure to academic research, understanding what is required can be a difficult process. Voluntary consent, however, involves as much freedom from ignorance about what is required as possible. Arguably, there can be no ignorance present, if people are to give honest, informed, and voluntary consent. In keeping with the mutual nature of research, indigenous participants can also contribute to the design of the research. Of course, in many situations where the research project is relatively simple, or is a wider project of which the data collected from indigenous peoples only forms a small part, there may not be many opportunities for contributions from the indigenous participants. For example, a survey of literacy that works well with a general population when administered to Aboriginal children will not provide reliable results if it does not take into account the different experiences of literacy that they will have. Without adequate consultation, differing views of literacy will not be recognized nor will it allow a different, more culturally appropriate survey to be negotiated with the researcher. A simple Western understanding of literacy will fail to convey the complexity of literacy in general. Negotiation is vital if a narrow focus that is methodologically unsound is to be avoided. Different lived experiences of literacy need to be taken into account, if the efficacy of a new literacy program in a school is to be assessed. Without involvement of the indigenous participants, construction of a satisfactory survey instrument in which the research variables authentically reflect the meaning of literacy understood in the particular context, will not occur. The general principle of honest exchange of information about aims, methods, and potential outcomes, which might ensure better data collection, is crucial.

9. *Negotiation should result in a formal agreement for the conduct of a research project.*[28]

The aim of all good research is to ensure that whatever agreements are made with participants are based on good faith, and free and informed consent. Sometimes this will require formal agreement with the community elders, who may then allow individuals to be approached. Frank disclosure of all available information and that were entered into with an honest view of reaching an agreement. Such a formal agreement needs to be documented, as has already been indicated.

10. *Indigenous people have the right to full participation appropriate to their skills and experiences in research projects and processes.*[29] We have already mentioned this principle above, in relation to the second Principle, but this adds that indigenous people should be involved in research projects as collaborators. In some respects, this proposal may appear somewhat controversial, but this depends on what is meant by collaborating in the research. Clearly, at one level, indigenous people will not be able to take part in the research, as they will not have been trained in the research methods being used by the researchers. That is, it is hardly likely that indigenous peoples will have very much to say to the researcher about how he or she might refine a statistical hypothesis that he or she is using. Nonetheless, where questions directly involve the culture of the people, it is to be expected that they will have a better grasp of its traditions, beliefs, and values. Moreover, if the research lends itself to an indigenous perspective, it should be included in the research.

11. *Indigenous people involved in research, or who may be affected by research, should benefit from, and not be disadvantaged by the research project.*[30] Where there is benefit to be gained by the community though their participation in the research, researchers should ensure that the indigenous community benefits. In some cases, the research will not have any obvious benefit, though it may provide data that might affect future planning as it relates to indigenous people. In some indigenous communities, there is an expectation that a reciprocal benefit should accrue to the participants if the information that has been supplied is of an intimate kind that reveals both personal and community matters. There seems to be some justice in this claim. Indigenous communities have been exploited in many different ways and it is not surprising that they see researchers seeking information from them as stealing their knowledge and exploiting them. For example, a community's intimate knowledge of the flora and fauna in a particular region might be exploited if it comes to the attention of researchers that they use a particular plant to treat certain ailments successfully that Western treatments are unable to help. Such tribal knowledge, passed down through generations belongs to the tribe, not those who would exploit them.

12. *Research outcomes should include specific results that respond to the needs and interests of indigenous people.*[31] Where there are specific results that can be shared, these should be made available in a form that the participants can understand. Moreover, if there are practical outcomes of the research, which might lead to the betterment of the lives of indigenous people, then these should also be indicated in the sharing of the research outcomes. It may also be the case that there will be a few results specific to the needs of the

community. In this case, the researchers need to find some alternative means to ensure that the community benefits from the research. Whatever is offered, however, needs to be proportionate and should not be offered solely as means of coercing participation in the research. Where both researchers and participants are in a position of equality, it is less likely that abuses will occur.[32]

13. *Plans should be agreed for managing use of and access to research results.*[33] The idea that researchers should share their results with those who have participated in their research is not new and has been suggested before. It should be a general principle that wherever possible researchers should make their findings available. In some instances, the findings will have particular relevance to the participants since the aim may be to find out something about the particular population. In other cases, the particular population is only a small part of the research process. In the case of indigenous participants, if certain conditions have been negotiated that include a report of the research findings, this should be adhered to, even if the findings report something adversely.

14. *Research projects should include appropriate mechanisms and procedures for reporting on ethical aspects of the research and complying with these guidelines.*[34] The final Principle proposes that there are appropriate measures taken to ensure that research with indigenous communities and participants complies with the AIATSIS guidelines. These will be similar to the requirements for all research projects, though as already outlined, research with indigenous communities needs to take into account the very specific cultures, values and traditions of those communities. Importantly, compliance should not be seen simply as a legal requirement, but as a way of ethically engaging with indigenous communities.

The *AIATSIS Guidelines* provide a good way of beginning to understand the way in which certain kinds of research should be approached when dealing with an indigenous population. It is, however, evident that it suits studies that involve more than just a single gathering of data by means of interview, questionnaire, or some such combination. There are particular issues that need to be resolved in ethnographic or anthropological studies. Though the advice contained in the *AIATSIS Guidelines* is particularly pertinent for large-scale studies that involve considerable contact with the researchers, this may not be the case for less contact and much smaller intrusions into the lives of the community. The NHMRC document, *Values and Ethics* (2003)[35], arguably provides a more general overview of contact with Aboriginal and Torres Strait Islander communities and so has different emphases than the *AIATSIS Guidelines*.

Values and Ethics

The NHMRC document, *Values and Ethics*, seeks to incorporate much of the *AIATSIS Guidelines* and begins by setting the context of why the document was written. As already emphasized, it cannot be assumed that the culture of Indigenous peoples differs little from that of the dominant Western culture. The *Values and Ethics* document observes that unethical behavior need not involve a deliberate act that causes harm, but may also include a lack of sensitivity to the community that one wishes to ask to be participants in the research. It may involve subtle and sometimes unconscious acts that harm the relationship between researchers and participants. A disregard, for example, of the proper way to approach individuals in a settlement may result in some community members feeling insulted, even though no insult was intended. Asking certain questions of a woman, for example, by a male researcher might be considered inappropriate. Difference-blindness may result in serious misunderstandings, as most Aboriginal and Torres Strait Islander peoples prefer to be called by terms that reflect their cultural origins, such as Nyoongar, Ngaanyatjarra, Koori, or Murri, rather than by a generic term such as Indigenous people.[36] From another point of view, it would be similar to calling Europeans by that generic name rather than by their more particular cultural origins such as English, German, French, or Italian.

Values and Ethics notes that a proper relationship between researchers and Aboriginal and Torres Strait Islander participants does not depend just on following rules, but depends on the development of trust. The same, it could be said, applies to any relationship between researchers and participants. Rules are never adequate because they cannot cover every contingency. Researchers are better off seeking to engage with the communities that they wish to conduct their research in, so that they have a better understanding and sensitivity to the different values and customs within those communities. The need for guidelines arises because of concerns about poor consultation, lack of communication and infringement of deeply held values arising from cross-cultural insensitivity – despite researchers' compliance with the legal requirements of ethical guidelines.

It is possible to reconcile the interests of research and of researchers with the values, expectations, and cultures of Aboriginal and Torres Strait Islanders. This is because there have been several models that have been used successfully to build trust and recognition of cultural values and principles while advancing the objectives of the research enterprise. Some models have placed greater reliance on participatory processes, while others have established innovative institutional arrangements with continuing involvement of communities.[37] Other models have relied on legal arrangements and on giving the Aboriginal and Torres Strait Islander communities control over the research activities.[38]

Six basic values at the heart of Aboriginal and Torres Strait Islander culture and ethics can be identified. These are: 1) Spirit and Integrity, 2) Reciprocity, 3) Respect, 4) Equality, 5) Survival and Protection and 6) Responsibility. These values are important for Aboriginal Identity and for Aboriginal and Torres Strait Islander peoples. Spirit and Integrity bind the other five together over time so that they cannot be separated. The past, the present and the future are absolutely bound up with one another binding the values together so that when issues need to be discussed all the values need to interact together. These six values are outlined as follows.

Spirit and Integrity

This is the most important value that joins all Aboriginal and Torres Strait Islander peoples' values together. The first part, Spirit, is about the on-going connection (continuity) between their past, present and future generations. The second part, Integrity, is about the respectful and honorable behaviors that hold Aboriginal and Torres Strait Islander values and cultures together.[39] Researchers are seen by Aboriginal and Torres Strait Islander communities as owing an obligation to the spirit and integrity of communities, not just to individuals. Aboriginal and Torres Strait Islander communities will examine what is proposed to see that it is consistent with their values, but it falls to the researchers to demonstrate such consistency. An implicit part of spirit and integrity is the basing of community decision-making on shared values.[40]

Reciprocity

The way of shared responsibility and obligation in Aboriginal and Torres Strait Islander peoples' communities is based on diverse kinship networks. This process in their communities keeps their ways of living and family relationships strong. These responsibilities also extend to the care of the land, animals, and country and involve sharing benefits from the air, land and sea, redistribution of income, and sharing food and housing.[41]

Mutual obligations exist among members of Aboriginal and Torres Strait Islander families and communities to achieve an equitable distribution of resources, responsibility, and capacity and to achieve cohesion and survival of the social order. This mutual obligation extends to the land, animals and other natural elements and features. In contemporary settings, the value of reciprocity continues in various forms, and may vary between locations. Examples include the redistribution of income, benefits from the air, land, and sea, and the sharing of other resources such as housing.[42] When applied to the research context, this means that researchers have to be aware that sharing their culture and making themselves available to researchers as participants, creates obligations for the researchers to ensure that the community benefits from the involvement in the research, as we have already discussed.

Respect

Respect for each other's dignity and individual ways of living is the basis of how Aboriginal and Torres Strait Islander peoples live. Within our cultures, respect strengthens dignity, and dignity strengthens respect. A respectful relationship encourages trust and co-operation. Strong culture is built on respect and trust, and a strong culture encourages dignity and recognition, and provides a caring and sharing environment.

Respect for human dignity and worth as a characteristic of relationships between people, and in the way individuals behave, is fundamental to a functioning and moral society. Within Aboriginal and Torres Strait Islander cultures, respect is reinforced by dignity, whichin turn is strengthened. A respectful relationship induces trust and co-operation. Strong culture is a personal and collective framework built on respect and trust that promotes dignity and recognition. Respect for persons is a fundamental moral principle in Western culture also, and arguably, in all cultures. Respect for persons also means that there is respect for differences, as discussed previously, and in the research context, acknowledgement of the contributions that participants make to the research endeavor. This means respecting their opinions and being sensitive to the differences in values and culture.[43]

Equality

Aboriginal and Torres Strait Islander peoples recognize the equal value of all individuals. One of the ways in which this is shown is their commitment to fairness and justice. Equality affirms and recognizes Aboriginal and Torres Strait Islander peoples' right to be different. One of the ways equality is reflected in Aboriginal and Torres Strait Islander peoples and cultures is through a commitment to distributive justice and fairness. Equality means that difference does not matter and allows Aboriginal and Torres Strait Islander people, as well as others to be diverse in their values, beliefs, and cultures.[44]

In the research arena, a failure to recognize fundamental equality led in the past to discrimination and to the devaluation of Aboriginal and Torres Strait Islander culture and to unequal treatment through exploitation. Such treatment has also resulted in the marginalization of Aboriginal and Torres Strait Islanders with the attendant economic and social problems. Whilst researchers cannot be expected to redress decades of injustices, they can at least strive to ensure that the research agreements they reach with Aboriginal and Torres Strait Islander peoples is respectful of them and their cultures.

Survival and protection

Aboriginal and Torres Strait Islander people continue to protect their cultures, languages, and identity. Recognition of their shared cultural identity, which is based on their shared values, is a significant strength.[45] Aboriginal and Torres Strait Islander communities want to preserve and protect their cultures, which are unique. In the past, this has not been recognized. In particular, where researchers have ignored this distinctiveness or sought to undermine it, tensions have arisen. Moreover, repeated marginalization of Aboriginal and Torres Strait Islander values has reinforced these barriers, creating obstacles to research. Researchers will need to work hard to correct this image of researchers as seeking only their own benefit in research and ignoring the needs of the community that they have asked to be involved in their research. Researchers need to demonstrate through ethical negotiation, conduct, and dissemination of research that they are trustworthy and will not repeat the mistakes of the past.[46]

Responsibility

All Aboriginal and Torres Strait Islander communities recognize the same most important (core) responsibilities. These responsibilities involve country, kinship bonds, caring for others, and the maintenance of cultural and spiritual awareness. The main responsibility is to do no harm to any person, or any place. Sometimes these responsibilities may be shared so that others also may be held accountable.[47] The assignment or inheritance of responsibilities within communities ensures the survival of individuals, families, and whole communities. Survival includes maintaining the bonds and relationships among people and between them and their environment. It also includes responsibilities with respect to the spiritual domain. When Aboriginal and Torres Strait Islander peoples are involved in the research enterprise, researchers have additional responsibilities apart from those associated with their research projects. By involving the Aboriginal and Torres Strait Islander communities in their research, both they and the community create responsibilities for one another for which they are accountable. Ethical research occurs when harmony between sets of responsibilities is established, participants are protected, trust is maintained, and accountability is clear.[48]

Conclusion

The most important aspect of research with Aboriginal and Torres Strait Islander communities is to recognize the importance of respect for persons. Researchers need to enter wholeheartedly into negotiation with the community. By realizing that research is essentially a partnership between the researchers and the participants, they will also be able to determine what their obligations are in relation to the community. A key element in this process will be for researchers to seek advice from their own local Indigenous Research Advisory Groups prior to approaching any communities. Having received advice and having obtained ethical approvalthey may approach the community. An essential component of this will be to listen as much as to explain their research to the community. Finally, they need to be prepared to modify their research. Unless they are prepared to do this, no genuine partnership really exists.

Notes

1 Stuart MacIntyre, for example, suggests that Aboriginal settlemént of Australia occurred between 50,000 and 60,000 years ago, but it is difficult tobe precise. Stuart MacIntyre, *A Concise History of Australia*, 3rd ed. (Cambridge: Cambridge University Press, 2009), 4-8.

2 Ibid., 14.

3 United Nations, *State of the World's Indigenous Peoples* (New York: United Nations, Department of Economic and Social Affairs, 2009), 1.

4 Australian Institute of Health and Welfare, *The Health and Welfare of Australia's Aboriginal and Torres Strait Islander People: An Overview*, Cat. No. IHW 142 (Canberra: Australian Institute of Health and Welfare, 2011), vii-viii.

5 See the devastating report written by Peter Read in 1981. Read was the first to coin the phrase, "the stolen generations," which referred to the Aboriginal children removed from their families by a paternalistic government from 1916 until 1970. Peter Read, *The Stolen Generations* (Surry Hills: NSW Department of Aboriginal Affairs, 1981).

6 United Nations, *United Nations' Declaration on the Rights of Indigenous Peoples* (New York: United Nations, 2008), Article 12, 6.

7 Ibid., 11.

8 Ibid., Article 31, 11.

9 Here, we are thinking in particular of the Baltic nations whose cultures are threatened by the majority Russian culture that surrounds them, but is applicable to any cultural minority.

10 N. Pattel, "Aboriginal Families, Cultural Context and Therapy," *Counselling, Psychotherapy, and Health* 3, no. 1, (2007): 1-24.

11 It would be false to call this a shared communal consciousness, since it is not a common consciousness. However, the individual does exist within a continuum that connects him or her with ancestral spirits, his or her kinship group, and the land to which it belongs.

12 An example might be "I am a descendant of Birripi people of Taree." There are complications, however, as there are several other ways in which an Aboriginal or Torres Strait person might identify as such. The definition of Aboriginality used by the Australian Commonwealth Government (and other state instrumentalities) tries to cover the difficulties of identifying who is an Aboriginal or Torres Strait Islander person by using three criteria. This identifies a person as an Aboriginal or Torres Strait Islander if he or she satisfy the following criteria: 1) (s)heIs of Aboriginal or Torres Strait Islander descent; 2) (s)he identifies as an Aboriginal or Torres Strait Islander and 3) (s)he is acceptedas such by the community in which he or she lives. Our main point here is to stress the dual connection between community and land. Seehttp://www.creativespirits.info/aboriginalculture/people/aboriginal-identity-who-is-aboriginal (accessed on 31 December 2013).

13 Paul Ricœur, *Oneself as Another*, trans. Kathleen Blamey (Chicago: University of Chicago Press, 1994).

14 Simone Weil very eloquently explores the importance of cultural roots. Simone Weil, *The Need for Roots: A Prelude to the Declaration of Duties Towards Mankind*, trans. A.F. Wills (London: Routledge and Kegan Paul, 1978).

15 National Health and Medical Research Council, *Values and Ethics: Guidelines for Ethical Conduct in Aboriginal and Torres Strait Islander Health Research* (Canberra: Commonwealth of Australia, 2003), 1.

16 http://www.refworld.org/docid/3b00f4380.html (accessed on 14 June 2014).

17 The Australian Institute of Aboriginal and Torres Strait Islander Studies (AIATSIS) Guidelines for Ethical Research state:"It is essential that Indigenous people are full participants in research projects that concern them, share an understanding of the aims and methods of the research, and share the results of this work. At every stage, research with and about Indigenous peoples must be founded on a process of meaningful engagement and reciprocity between the researcher and Indigenous people. It should also be recognized that there is no sharp distinction between researchers and Indigenous people. Indigenous people are also researchers, and all participants must be regarded as equal participants in a research engagement."Australian Institute of Aboriginal and Torres Strait Islander Studies, *Guidelines for Ethical Research in Australian Indigenous Studies*, (Canberra: Australian Institute of Aboriginal and Torres Strait Islander Studies,2011), 4. [Hereinafter *AIATSIS Guidelines*]

18 *AIATSIS Guidelines*, 5.

19 Ibid., 5.

20 Ibid., 13.

21 Ibid., 6.

22 Ibid., 8.

23 See Peter Winch, *The Idea of a Social Science and Its Relation to Philosophy* (London: Routledge and Kegan Paul, 1958), 55-57.

24 *AIATSIS Guidelines*, 6.

25 Ibid., 7.

26 Ibid., 10.

27 Ibid., 11.

28 Ibid., 12.

29 Ibid., 12.

30 Ibid., 13.

31 Ibid., 14.

32 In support of the claim that practical outcomes can benefit local indigenous communities, the National Health and Medical Research Council (NHMRC) document, *Keeping Research on Track*, claimed the following:"As a result of participating in the research project the community received home repairs, improved sewerage and additional health services; improved on-going health outcomes for the children, that flowedinto other communities through strong cultural links; new knowledge and understanding of the importance of community involvement in research, how to prevent the spread of infectious diseases, and how to achieve improved hygiene, health and living standards." While the above outcomes are claimed only with respect one particular research project, it is evident that if such outcomes as a result of cooperation between researchers and research participants can be repeated, that the benefits to indigenous communities will be considerable. See National Health and Medical Research Council,

Keeping Research on Track: *A Guide for Aboriginal and Torres Strait Islander Peoples About Health and Research Ethics*, (Canberra: Commonwealth of Australia, 2005), 3. [Hereinafter *Keeping Research on Track*]

33 *AIATSIS Guidelines*, 15.

34 Ibid., 16.

35 National Health and Medical Research Council, *Values and Ethics: Guidelines for Ethical Conduct in Aboriginal and Torres Strait Islander Health Research* (Canberra: Commonwealth of Australia, 2003). [Hereinafter *Values and Ethics*]

36 *Values and Ethics*, 2-3.

37 Ibid., 5.

38 A document adopted by the Tangentyere Council in March 1988 attempts to reorient research to better serve the interests of the researched, including widely spread provisions for control of research planning, implementation and use of research results. The Tangentyere Council document (1–2) requires a legally binding contract with researchers that clearly explains: the aims and purposes of the research; the researcher's duty statement; the time framework of the research project; the researcher's wages and conditions of employment; the method whereby the results of the research will be supplied to Tangentyere Council; and an understanding that the researcher will not use the results of the research publicly without the Tangentyere Council's approval (ownership and copyright notwithstanding). A more recent example of the exercise of Indigenous organisation control is found in the contract binding researchers to the objectives of the Pitjantjatjara Council. Among other matters the Pitjantjatjara Council requires the following: the researcher is to respect the confidentiality of any information provided; all materials generated by the research project are to be owned by the Council; a draft of any report is to be presented to the Council and no thesis is to be presented to the university without its approval; copyright in a thesis is to be owned jointly with the Council and the thesis may not be published without the agreement of the Council; the Council, with the researcher's agreement, has the right to publish the research report; and a catch-all – the researcher 'shall comply with any reasonable direction that may from time to time be given by the Executive.' See Australian Institute of Aboriginal and Torres Strait Islander Studies, *Research of Interest to Aboriginal and Torres Strait Islander Peoples, Commissioned Report No. 59* (Canberra: Commonwealth of Australia, 1999), 30-32.

39 *Keeping Research on Track*, 8.

40 *Values and Ethics*, 19.

41 *Keeping Research on Track*, 9.

42 *Values and Ethics*, 10.

43 Ibid., 11-12.

44 *Keeping Research on Track*, 9.

45 Ibid., 9.

46 *Values and Ethics*, 18.

47 *Keeping Research on Track*, 9.

48 Ibid., 16.

Chapter 8

The Analogical Hermeneutics of Latin America Tracing its Relevance to Philosophy and Theology

Corina Yoris-Villasana
Universidad Catolica Andres Bello, Caracas, Venezuela

Even though the word hermeneutics is used commonly today particularly among scholars, it seems necessary to elucidate the term and what we intend to signify by it. We shall hence define this term as an expression or external manifestation of an inner word; as interpretation of a statement that is not, by itself, understood; as a passage from a foreign language to a familiar language.[1] To put it more briefly, it is the "art of understanding." Hermeneutics is a method aimed at a practical command of the manner in which a text is correctly interpreted.[2]

Within the discipline's tradition, we find a diversity of stances relating to the extension of interpretation. This has given rise to two opposing approaches. The first one of them is the so-called "positivistic hermeneutics," which addresses unified meaning or the reduction of polysemy to as few meanings as possible. The second approach is called – though, again, at the risk of oversimplifying – "romantic hermeneutics."

The purpose of this paper is to present a third hermeneutical stream – the one that is called "analogical hermeneutics." It was founded by the Mexican philosopher Mauricio Beuchot. In what follows, I will attempt to stay close to Beuchot's text in order to explain his proposal with utmost clarity. Thereafter, I will review some of the criticism that has been leveled against it.

Brief Biographical Overview and Purpose of the Proposal

Mauricio Hardie Beuchot Puente was born in Coahuila, México, on March 4, 1950. He has authored many books on medieval philosophy, new-hispanic philosophy, analytic philosophy, and mainly, hermeneutics. He created analogical hermeneutics, which nowadays holds an important place in the field of philosophical hermeneutics. This proposal first saw public light at the National Congress on Philosophy taking place in the city of Cuernavaca, in Morelos, México (1993).

In the Introduction to his *Treatise on Analogical Hermeneutics: Towards a New Model of Interpretation*,[3] Beuchot lays bare the aim of his proposal, none other than to be seen "as an alternative between univocism and equivocism."[4]

It is well known that univocism seeks to establish an identity between meaning and its application in order to attain objectivity. This is rather a positivistic notion. In contrast, equivocism focuses on accepting multiple meanings, which is to say, it embraces differences in meaning as well as application. Because it embraces polysemy, it is vulnerable to relativism and subjectivism.

Analogical hermeneutics attempts to forestall extreme positions. It proposes to widen the margin of interpretations. This may be accomplished by establishing a hierarchy that allows the creation of an order, where one interpretation will be "the principal analogate and other interpretations will be secondary analogates."[5]

Beuchot begins his *Treatise* with a review of the different developmental stages of hermeneutics. He emphasizes the importance, when attempting to interpret a text, of setting it in context. One of the questions posed by Beuchot while accounting for the re-contextualization of hermeneutics is whether he goes about it scientifically or artistically. This description turns out to be quite enlightening for introducing the subject of analogy. For Beuchot, hermeneutics is both science and art. He likens it to logic, which straddles both aspects as well. "This is seen in the likeness of logic, which is also both a science and an art: it orderly builds the corpus of its knowledge, and then arranges it as procedural rules, which are applied to concrete reasoning."[6] We cannot disregard the fact that Beuchot has been a medievalist, a cultivator of scholastics, and an accomplished student of that time. Consequently, his analogy of *logica utens* and *logica docens* turns out to be quite appropriate to his intended goal.

When we speak of *hermeneutica docens*, we are to understand a general theory of interpretation, and under *hermeneutica utens* the former's application to a particular case. As Beuchot puts it,

> This is why I would rather speak of a *hermeneutica docens* as a general theory of interpretation; and a *hermeneutica utens*, which is alive; which is applied to the particular case, proportionally adapting

> the rules deduced from its doctrine and practice, in accordance with its prudence or *phronesis*. Accordingly, hermeneutics is a primordially theoretical, derivatively practical discipline, as it being practical stems from its being theoretical. Hence, I have said earlier that is science and art at the same time.[7]

From here, Beuchot moves on to a component analysis of the hermeneutical act, which are its text, author, and reader. In this trilogy, it is where the problem with the extreme approaches – univocism and equivocism – begins. When the author is emphasized, the reading becomes objectivistic; where, by way of contrast, emphasis is placed upon the reader, the reading becomes subjective. Therefore, Beuchot proposes to search for mediation and approaching the author's intention as closely as possible.

Thus we may speak of a "text's intention." However, we must place it at the crossroads of the other two intentionalities mentioned above. On the one hand, there is an obligation to respect the author's intention (seeing the text as still belonging to him/her, at least in part). On the other hand, we must realize that the text no longer says exactly what the author meant; it has exceeded the author's intentionality upon meeting ours. We make the text say something else, that is, what it says to us. Thus, the text's truth encompasses both the author's and the reader's meaning or truth, living on their dialectic. Though we may grant a little more to one or the other (reader or author), we cannot sacrifice either for the other's sake.[8]

As for the text, Beuchot characterizes it with double qualities: "it is connotation and denotation; intension and extension, sense and reference."[9] Once the acting trilogy in the hermeneutical act has been confronted, he proceeds to an analysis of the interpretive process itself. When the reader approaches the text, she asks herself what does this text say and what does it mean? In the process, where one starts by formulating a hypothesis as an answer to initial questions, the hypothesis then turns into a thesis. In other words, we stand before "a hypothetical-deductive argument or reasoning."[10]

This propaedeutic section to his analogical hermeneutics proposal is closed with a discussion about hermeneutical *virtus* – a habit that can be learnt "through study, work, and imitation, so that you may eventually surpass the one who taught you."[11]

Towards a Model of Analogical Hermeneutics

In the chapter where Beuchot develops his proposal, he states his objective with maximum brevity: to provide a middle ground between extreme views in hermeneutics.

Umber to Eco[12] has pointed out to the difficult task of reconciling those who maintain that the true sense of interpretation is to rescue the voluntary meaning supplied by the author – and so interpretation must limit itself to the one and only meaning – with those who hold that the legitimate interpretation is to investigate infinitely many meanings. By recalling this, Beuchot conducts a detailed analysis of the unsolvable conflict between univocism and equivocism.

Hermeneutics becomes necessary mostly in polysemic texts. Consequently, one of the poles of hermeneutics schools intends to grasp an only meaning – the text's "essential" meaning – whereas the other pole attempts the opposite: to break the text down into a maximum number of meanings, which incidentally are fortuitous and uncommunicated.[13]

Beuchot calls the one-meaning-only camp "positivistic hermeneutics," though he makes it clear that it is simply a way of calling it to be better understood by his readers. He then adopts Ricoeur's terminology and names the other camp "romantic hermeneutics" (again, exposing himself to a risk of oversimplifying). It certainly would not be fair to label as "univocist" all who advocate positivistic hermeneutics, just as it would seem unfair to call every romantic hermeneutist an "equivocist." Beuchot wishes to stress the preeminence of a given position; he attempts to signify that those who cultivate positivistic hermeneutics reach for what ideally is a meaning which alone fits all their references. In this way, they hope to attain a better comprehension. At the same time, romantic hermeneutists strive to make way for a manifold set of meanings, so that not just one meaning, but an explosion of expressiveness effectively is saved which suppresses objectivity itself – this ultimately distorts, or at least modifies, "original" meaning.[14]

In a masterful display of logical prowess, Beuchot proves how both positions are self-refuting. Aspiring to univocity runs into such a difficult obstacle as the requirement of empirical verification; but when it refutes non-univocity, it becomes an unverifiable statement. Therefore, it refutes itself.

In response to the Enlightenment, Romanticism, which arose during the 19th century, would turn into that which it opposed, just as its "adversary." In order to explain the self-refuting character of romantic hermeneutics, Beuchot considers a proposal by theologian Friedrich Schleiermacher, in whose view, the task of hermeneutics was "to understand speech just as well as the author, and then even better than him." From where Schleiermacher stands, feeling and intuition are the task of theology. Schleiermacher has come to be regarded as one of the foremost German theologians in the 19th century. He devoted himself to the practice of hermeneutics as a form of biblical exegesis, and on that reading, feeling is the key to finding intellectual harmony with the holy writer.

According to Beuchot, Schleiermacher succumbs to univocism in his writings on hermeneutics. In order to warrant that assertion, he reminds us that Schleiermacher held that "all schools or churches of biblical interpretation are valid and mutually complementary. They are all true, depending on the point of view that each one of them adopts." This comes about because an intellectual harmony with both the biblical text and its author develops. In this manner, Schleiermacher arrives at a univocist tendency, contrary to his equivocistic starting point, given his conjecture "that so deep a submersion can be made into the holy writer and their culture, that not only does a fusion of subjectivities take place, but even the author's subjectivity is surpassed, thus leading to maximum objectivity."[15]

Once the limitations (or contradictions) proper to both extreme schools have been shown, Beuchot presents his proposal. His chosen fulcrum is analogy, in as much as it allows for some semantic versatility – a very important aspect, as it prevents the slide into both univocism and its opposing pole, equivocism.

The account of the different types of analogies (i.e., attribution, proportionality, unevenness) is crucially important, since it underpins the analogical model. Therefore, the analogical-hermeneutical model will enable the interpretation of an extraordinary diversity of texts, be they metaphorical, figurative, or historical, political, psychological, and so on. Analogical hermeneutics admits several interpretations as legitimate. These interpretations possess a truth correlation since the model is based on the proportionality analogy. However, it does not support all interpretations equally because a grading is determined among all those interpretations regarded as legitimate, so the lowest grades may be discarded as wrong.

Likewise, this modality of interpretation, the analogical hermeneutics model breathtakingly harmonizes metonymy with metaphor. There is a clear reference to Jakobson, who masterfully accomplished that rapprochement between both figures of speech. Thus, analogy links both figures because both are analogies. Metaphor has been accepted as an analogy ever since Plato,[16] and is clearly a significant; metonymy, in turn, is also an analogy, even though in a less evident way than metaphor, but it maintains a relationship to meanings.

M. Beuchot explains that, when metaphor and metonymy are combined, resulting in an analogy, we avoid conveying either a purely metonymical meaning "proper to science," or a purely metaphorical one, "proper to poetry."[17] In addition, he holds that when analogy means proportion, analogical hermeneutics has the ability to harmonize syntagmatic with paradigmatic interpretations; the first favors contradictions, whereas the second, being deeply related, pertains to poetic, religious texts.[18] One of the riches of this proposal is precisely this coming together of both axes – syntagmatic and paradigmatic – which enables language to act in all its magnitude in order to generate new meanings.

One of the points Beuchot stresses the most is the dialogical power that analogical hermeneutics possesses. We must not forget that analogy envelops a peculiar relational activity between universality and particularity. That activity strives to grasp the universal as much as possible, without renouncing its subordination to the particular and the preeminence of the latter over the former.[19]

Setting Analogical Interpretation in Motion

How does he implement this analogical interpretation? Making it clear from the beginning that it is not his purpose to teach a method, he states that his search will focus on finding an interpretation that will be situated between the two previously mentioned camps: univocism and equivocism. He must however, lean somewhat more towards equivocity, "for in analogy, though identity and difference are conjoined, difference is predominant." Here he illustrates his proposal by applying it to a post-conquest text from Mexico called "Diálogo de los Doce" (English: *Dialogue of the Twelve*).[20] I shall quote Beuchot's account:

> A univocistic attitude would lead to referentialism and would have us lean towards searching, in full objectivity, for the facts to which it refers, i.e., the reference or references. Contrariwise, an equivocistic attitude would lead us to neglect referentiality so that we may only search for the meaning it could have had for those involved in that action or event. Instead, an analogical attitude leads us to try to involve both things – reference and sense –, and even to rant the latter preeminence. It is true that we have to analyze the objectivity of the text we are being presented with: if it corresponds to an event that took place or whether it is only fictitious; and we have to even take responsibility for the fiction (reconstruction) carried with it regarding facts. Above all, it must compel us to try to understand the meaning that was given there; to try to iconize us, through analogy, into what was happening there on a human, symbological level. To Aztec priests, that dialogue had a meaning; to the Spanish priests, another. And it is not the point to reduce one to the other, but to differentiate the two. We must stay clear of the easy anachronism of revile: overcome the indignation roused by the extermination of the Aztec religion at the hands of Spanish missioners and try to understand their motivations, their presuppositions, et cetera; in short, their context. Of course we may draw the moral or lesson afterwards, so we may sidestep that in the history that concerns us, to bring it before consciousness that can and must be prevented, that it is possible to change it through dialogical persuasion, like some of them did request – for instance, Bartolomé de las Casas,

who, in this sense, went beyond his time and circumstances, his own context.[21]

Mauricio Beuchot enumerates the connections that analogical hermeneutics can establish, and he explains them in detail. He devotes a section to Argumentation and its relationship to Hermeneutics; he unfolds Gadamer's and Vattimo's arguments with respect to the discipline; he discusses its relation to ethics and with religious texts, to name only some of these sections.

Criticism of Analogical Hermeneutics and Response from the Author

In an appendix to his *Treatise*, Beuchot gathers discussions held with distinguished hermeneutists. Using his own proposal, he engages his critics in dialogue. I shall dedicate brief lines to an attempt at gathering criticism and Beuchot's replies.[22]

In an important discussion at the Universidad Nacional Autónoma de México (National Autonomous University of Mexico) with Gianni Vattimo, who, after pointing out positive aspects of the proposal – such as analogical hermeneutics distancing itself from the discursive violence of identity – observed its excessive attachment to objectivity and the search for truth in a post-metaphysical era. His main criticism was that we are in great need of politically committed hermeneutics (not only with theory or with ethics).

Beuchot resorted to Habermas' criticism of hermeneutics' apolitical character, as well as Gadamer's and Ricoeur's replies. He retorted that analogical hermeneutics is forced to "land on a political context since it is based on phronesis, on prudence, which Aristotle thinks as important to ethics as it is to politics." As concerns the observation about "attachment to truth and objectivity," Beuchot clarified it is about a "truth as correspondence, not univocal."

Ambrosio Velasco, also a professor at UNAM, concurred with Vattimo on his (Velasco's) observations when he pointed out that truth, as correspondence should be abandoned in favor of heuristics, the context of discovery. Beuchot replies that the proposal, since it is grounded on analogy, is linked to heuristics, in as much as the latter has a deep connection to abduction (Peirce) and this one possesses an analogous structure.

Years later, in 2007, Beuchot converses (at the same university) with Jean Grondin, a professor at the University of Montreal, who indicated that, in spite of analogy's battle against equivocism, it ultimately asks for an intrusion on the part of equivocity. It is better that the search for identity prevails, for in a considerable number of cases we have reached the true, definitive interpretation of a text.

Grondin's stance ran contrary to that of Vattimo years before. Beuchot, to find harmony between both observations, highlights that the analogical equilibrium must be pursued. He continues to believe that it is not possible to achieve a final interpretation, as Grondin's remark seems to indicate.

Raúl Alcalá comments on a few important things. First, application limits to analogical hermeneutics are not drawn, and so it seems as a method that intends to be the only one; a kind of panacea coming to dethrone all other methods. Beuchot's reply was conclusive: it would contradict analogy itself to fall prey to univocism.

This appendix ends with discussions between Beuchot and Andrés Ortiz-Osés, from the Universidad de Deusto, in the Basque Country. Ortiz-Osés criticizes that analogical hermeneutics lacks dialectical capacity in order to capture mobile, evasive processes. The reply shows vast knowledge of the concept of analogy ever since the time of Aristotle, and reminds us that analogical hermeneutics is distinctive precisely in that it has the potential for reconciling extremes.

He ends by thanking all remarks and reminding that "thus something that has been identified as most intrinsic to hermeneutics has been fulfilled, which is dialogue. And it has been a very considerable dialogue with such valuable interlocutors."

Some Remarks on Beuchot's Model

Even though this presentation on analogical hermeneutics has been expository-descriptive in character, I do not wish to overlook an aspect that directly concerns me, the reason being that it falls within the scope of my specialty. I am referring to the link, established by Beuchot, between his model and Argumentation Theory. It is a bond which I esteem. The "indifference" that has been the hallmark of philosophy towards studies on argumentation is nothing but inexcusable when we take into account that, in order to exercise its own reflection, it needs arguments.

I will try to be succinct, although the topic may be treated as another lecture. Perelman publishes his *New Rhetoric* in the year 1952.[23] By the time Beuchot's *Treatise* was published (1997), several theories different from Perelman's had appeared. To name but a few, let us remember Frans van Eemeren and Rob Grootendorst, who have developed pragma-dialectics, and whose initial goal was to delineate a code of conduct for argumentative discourse.[24]

In *Argumentation. Analysis, Evaluation, Presentation*, F. van Eemeren devotes a section, in the second part of the book, to the study of argumentation based on analogy. In this part of Chapter 6, he addresses arguments by analogy. For this author, analogy-based arguments defend a point of view by showing that something mentioned while expressing that point of view is similar to something quoted in the argumentation, and that it is on the basis of that similarity that the point of view must be accepted.

In general, van Eemeren's outline for an analogy relation is: Y is true of X, because Y is true of Z, and: Z is comparable to X. What then is essential to an analogy relation? Are there differences between Z and X? Such differences, says van Eemeren, may be stated in two ways: by claiming that Z has a certain trait that X lacks, or vice-versa. Both forms of criticism are very serious shortcomings in a critical discussion, because when a set of arguments rests on an analogy relation, X and Z are supposed to share all characteristics related to the argument.[25]

Conclusion

Beuchot's analogical hermeneutics has taken root and born fruit in several countries across America and other continents: Argentina, Brazil, Colombia, Italy, Romania, Spain, Venezuela.

While drafting this lecture, I found the first call to a colloquium on analogical hermeneutics, to be held in Buenos Aires in May of the present year. These various gatherings on Beuchot's proposal amount to a reinforcement of the interest in analogical hermeneutics. These events provide room for discussion and exchange that make it possible for the proposal to be steadily tweaked and perfected.

To close, by paraphrasing Mauricio Beuchot, I would like to remind you that dialogue is the tool that allows philosophy to advance. Dialogue allows us to avoid solipsism "wherein we often hide ourselves away." The richness of philosophy rests precisely upon open dialogues, a tradition that has continued since the beginning of Platonic philosophy.

Notes

1 See A. Domingo Moratalla. *Hermenéutica.* Retrieved from: http://www.mercaba.org/DicPC/H/hermeneutica.htm

2 See E. Coreth, *Cuestiones fundamentales de Hermenéutica* (Barcelona: Edit. Herder, 1972), 31 & ff.

3 M. Beuchot, *Tratado de Hermenéutica Analógica. Hacia un nuevo modelo de interpretación* (México: Unam-Ed. Itaca, 1997).For this paper, we are using the 4th edition (2009).

4 Ibid., 7.

5 Ibid., 48 ff.

6 Ibid., 16.

7 Taken from the Beuchot's own summary of the treatise, and published in "essential profiles of hermeneutics: analogical hermeneutics." Retrieved from http://www.ensayistas.org/critica/teoria/beuchot/Italics are present in the original.

8 Taken from the Beuchot's own summary of the treatise, and published in "essential profiles of hermeneutics: analogical hermeneutics." Retrieved from http://www.ensayistas.org/critica/teoria/beuchot/Italics are present in the original, 5.

9 Ibid.

10 Ibid.

11 Ibid.

12 U. Eco, Los límites de la Interpretación. (Barcelona: Edit. Lumen. Barcelona, 1992).

13 M. Beuchot. "Perfiles esenciales de la hermenéutica: hermenéutica analógica," 6.

14 Ibid. 7.

15 Ibid. 8.

16 See C. Yoris, *La fuerza de los argumentos por analogía* (Caracas: Ucab-Quirón, 2012), 28. Analogy can be understood as a "shared abstraction," as in the case of the Greeks, to whom analogous objects do not necessarily share a relation to each other; what is shared may be an idea, a pattern, regularity, or an attribute. They accepted that comparisons, metaphors, and images might be used as arguments, and they called such cases "analogies." Plato and Aristotle find themselves in this category.

17 See M. Beuchot, G. Vattimo et al., *Hermenéutica Analógica y Hermenéutica Débil* (Mexico City: Unam, 2006), 18 ff.

18 Ibid.

19 Beuchot. "Perfiles esenciales de la hermenéutica: hermenéutica analógica," 20.

20 This text is known as: Colloquios y doctrina christiana con que los doze frayles de San Francisco enbiados por el Papa Adriano Sesto y por el Emperador Carlos quinto convirtieron a los indios de la Nueva España en lengua Mexicana y Española. It was discovered in the Vatican's Secret Archives of Rome in 1922.

21 M. Beuchot, *Tratado de Hermenéutica Analógica. Hacia un nuevo modelo de interpretación,* 52 ff.

22 All references to these discussions have been taken and tightly summarized from Appendix 3: *Recent Discussions on Analogical Hermeneutics*, from the Tratado de Hermenéutica Analógica. Hacia un nuevo modelo de interpretación (English: Treatise on analogical hermeneutics: towards a new model of interpretation), 203-214.

23 C. Perelman & Lucie Olbrechts-Tyteca, *Traité de l'argumentation: La nouvelle rhétorique* (Paris: Presses Universitaires de France, 1958). Translated into Spanish by Julia Sevilla Muñoz (Madrid: Gredos, 1994) in a single volumen sinceits fifth edition (1989), prepared by Michel Meyer, with prologue by Jesús González Bedoya.

24 F. H. Eemeren, & Grootendost, R. *Argumentation, Communication, and Fallacies: A Pragma-dialectical Perspective* (London/Tuscaloosa: The University of Alabama Press, 1992).

25 I have elaborated these reflections on analogy and its argumentative strenght in Analogía y Fuerza Argumentativa (English: Analogy and argumentative strenght). Caracas. Ucab-Quirón. 2012.

Chapter 9

Hermeneutics of the Genius of the Absurd Interpreting the *Dao*道

Alfredo P. Co
Pontifical University of Santo Tomas, Manila, Philippines

Language provides empowerment and control, Alfred North Whitehead had it once said; "I am Master of this College; and what I know not, is not knowledge."(White head 1938, 58-87).[1]

That was well said, and *Lao Zi* could only nod his head and he must have seen how man understands word, how language played a strong role in empowering man and how man uses language to control the other, some 2,500 years earlier.

Nevertheless, *Lao Zi* is a different breed of thinker who uses language with mastery and power. The opus associated with him, the *Dao De Jing* comes in poetry form, and the language comes with an impacting impression never before seen in other thinkers before him, perhaps even well after him. A first time reader of the book is forewarned:

> This is my philosophy, come journey with me, if you can, and even if you can't you will still find in me the seduction of thought, the allusion to reality within and beyond your thought. You will find eloquent signposts which you might start holding on to, but even that will slip your grasp just as life and its power escaping you. Then as you cruise through this mysterious life you will find yourself walking alone in this lonesome journey to the unfathomable. Truth

> will elude you, good and evil will be hard to comprehend, and language will abandon you as it become opaque. But the seduction of your mind will continue to haunt you. Let me warn you as you follow me in this path… I leave no track.
>
> Friends, welcome to his web, welcome to his parlor.

An Invitation to the World of *Lao Zi*

Lao Zi's Dao De Jing, written some two thousand five hundred years ago in some five thousand Chinese characters never failed to catch attention, gaining followings, and merited the greatest number of translations to many languages coming second only to the Bible. But wait, it also merited various translations not just to various languages but also to different realms of human learning; literature, philosophy, the arts, politics, military strategy, physics, medicine, and even business. One could not miss raising the problem of hospitability of language, and the accuracy with which man is able to approximate human understanding through such interpretation.

As a theory, hermeneutics is a philosophy of interpretation covering the realm of aesthetics and theory of understanding of both linguistic and non-linguistic articulation. It turns philosophical as it rises to the conditions of possibilities in the realm of symbolic communication. At the heart of hermeneutics is the problem encountered in reading and making access in the instrument of communication, arising from the urgency of understanding of how one reads and how one communicates. Alas the chagrin caused by language; the depth and spectre created by symbol; the possibility of communication all come into picture when one reads the *Dao De Jing*, making it an exciting text for hermeneutical problems. Resituating the hermeneutical concerns and translation of the *Dao De Jing* come to the basic understanding that the work warns its potential reader, of the innameability and indescribability of what it wants to tell the world, and that is disturbing, to say the least. This happens when attempts to probe more deeply into the universal and common ground of diverse worldviews as they have evolved across age and cultures. No one at this global age can deny the spectre in which we encounter diverse worldviews enveloping religions, cultures, cosmologies, ideologies pinning down human attempt for understanding the *logosspermaticus* of the idea of *Dao* of *Lao Zi*.

How is one to approach reading a work with the opening salvo of this wondrous work? Poem 1 reads:

道可道，非常道。名可名，非常名。無名天地之始；有名萬物之母。故常無欲，以觀其妙；常有欲，以觀其徼。此兩者，同出而異名，同謂之玄。玄之又玄，衆妙之門。

> *The Dao that can be spoken is not the eternal Dao*
> *The name that can be named is not the eternal name*

> *The nameless is the origin of Heaven and Earth*
> *The named is the mother of myriad things*
> *Thus, constantly without desire, one observes its essence*
> *Constantly with desire, one observes its manifestations*
> *These two emerge together but differ in name*
> *The unity is said to be the mystery*
> *Mystery of mysteries, the door to all wonders.*[2]

The poem provides a fertile ground for thinking and working through the text, not for easy understanding than for immense hermeneutical possibilities. Spilling not only into the spectre involved in the thought work of the language but to the working of the language itself.

The antithetical expressions oscillate from one meaning to another and the comprehension that moves from one layer to the other, not to mention the interpretation that ensues without coming to a final sense but at the same time magically magnetize its reader to follow on. One gets to realize that the text does not intend to explain but neither does it endeavor to confuse. It is a philosophy of a different kind; its epistemic goal is multi-dimensional and multi-layered; its ethics is fluid, nay, meta-ethical. However, the spell that it casts is wondrous; the mystics like it, political philosophers are attracted to it, physicists and even strategist are seduced to it.

As a consequence, even early Chinese thinkers each tried to appropriate the concept *Dao* to their thinking, and I noted three major streams of interpretations in ancient China, namely that of *Zhuang Zi*, another of *Han Fei Zi* and that of *Sun Zi*.

Dao in the Book of *Zhuang Zi*

Zhuang Zi takes his reader to a fantasia stimulating his reader through his discourse on the void, the shadow, infinity, life and death. A journey with him is to ascend above the mundane world where one soars into another realm of imagination and dream. He advocated a life of quietism shunning the life of a maddened crowd.

This aspect of *Zhuang Zi's* discourse immediately gives a spectral division of reality that distinguishes the mundane world from the world of imagination. This latter realm is where he throws into light the very oneness of the multiplicity of things and the secondary importance of distinctions. He draws his reader in tow into another dimension of dream and imagination where reality in the realm of conscious world is rendered relative while the contraries within it are but identical. In a passage, we are shattered by his question:

> Suppose you and I argue. If you win and I lose, are you indeed right and I wrong? And if I win and you lose, am I right and you wrong?

> Are we both partly right and partly wrong? Are we both all right or both all wrong?... Then whom shall I ask to be the judge? Shall I ask someone who agrees with you? If he already agrees with you, how can he be a fair judge? Shall I ask someone who already agrees with me? If he already agrees with me, how can he be a fair judge? Shall I ask someone who already agrees with both of us? If he already agrees with both of us, how can he be a fair judge?[3]

This level of discourse requires intellectual centering that brings ones consciousness out of the focus of logic and epistemology or any final validity of human traditional understanding bringing us even to the postmodern attitude. In this real of human cogitation nothing can lead to any finality in the natural world, everything is seen in constant flux and human understanding become intellectual construct of categories of understanding defined anthropocentrically, even very limitedly by a cogitating mind. Instead, *Zhung Zi* summons man to allow his consciousness to look at the higher plane to allow him to see them all as 'one in the *Dao*.' *Zhuang Zi* narrates:

> When there is separation, there is coming together. When there is coming together, there is dissolution. All things may become one, whatever their state of being. Only he who has transcended sees this oneness. He has no use for differences and dwells in the constant. To be constant is to be useful. To be useful is to realize one's true nature. Realization of one's true nature is happiness. When one reaches happiness, one is close to perfection. So, one stops, yet does not know that one stops. This is Dao.[4]

There is nagging urgency that pushes us to soar into conceptual transcendence to see things as one in unity of vision in the *Dao*, which encompasses both the mundane, and the supra-mundane realms of the said and the unsaid. Consequently, argumentation had to cease, and then there, *Zhuang Zi* pushes us to see that a 'great argument' is one that "uses no word"[5] for the actuality of things, the *Dao* is not manifest and "is beyond description."[6]

In this mode of articulating by not articulating, one is led to the metaphysical theme of a universal truth that leads to the *Dao*. The particularities of things thrives only in the mundane existence where we see constant becoming, and it is also there that one sees contradictions of things for it is this ream that we see nothing but multiplicity of things. In such human finality, neither final arbiter nor final truth emerges; all things are relative. To transcend human prejudices one is urged to soar into the realm of dream and imagination and hence to go beyond the contraries and conflicts arising from one's partial understanding.[7] "If one is right while the one is wrong, then the best thing to do is to look beyond right and wrong."[8] Therefore, *Zhuang Zi says,* "Those who dispute do not see."[9]

This view of *Zhuang Zi* presents *Dao* as nature in constant flux and incessant transformation that binds all things into one. One is to move with *Dao* by gliding with life without resistance to the natural transformation. The *Dao* here is interpreted as essentially a plea for the spiritual freedom of man, one that liberates him from the confines of his own mental construct and from the external restraints so that he may be able to liberate himself from his own prejudices, his own partial view of things, his tendency to judge all else in terms of his seeing the world. Because at the very core, all things are infinite. "When there is no more separation between 'this' and 'that,' it is called the still-point of Dao. At the still-point in the center of the circle one can see the infinite in all things. Right is infinite; wrong is also infinite. Therefore it is said, 'Behold the light beyond right and wrong.'"[10]

This perception of the *Dao* as the Truth, the Way, the One and the Encompassing makes *Zhuang Zi's* interpretation of the *Dao De Jing* bordering the mystical. A man of *Dao* therefore is one who comprehends and lives in the underlying unity of the *Dao* who achieved a happiness that goes beyond all changes in the phenomenal world. Even death is viewed by him as no more than a necessary and proper correlation of life the most logical, and indeed natural and desirable, transformation following life in an eternal process of cosmic becoming. "Life arises from death and death from life... There is right because of wrong, and wrong because of right."[11] The "ten thousand things are what they are, yet they form a whole."[12]

To be able to see life and death as forming a dialectical unity is to achieve great understanding. It is to understand the natural flow of *Dao* and to give importance, life, and joy on the here and now. "Be content with the moment, and be willing to follow the flow; then there will be no room for grief or joy."[13] This is called in the old days, "freedom from bondage."[14]

One who reads the Book of *Zhuang Zi* is made to guess as to whether to take his works literally or metaphorically and then when one is finally convinced that a passage or a story is to be taken metaphorically, one is further puzzled locating as to which level of metaphor *Zhuang Zi* is talking to us.

The trajectory of his discourses on the *Dao* is made self-evident by the topics he discussed in his book. A cursory glance at the contents of the *Book of Zhuang Zi* will reveal for itself. Chapter I speaks of *Transcendental Bliss*; Chapter II speaks of *Identity of Contraries*; Chapter III On the *Nourishment of the Soul*; Chapter XI *On Letting Alone*; Chapter XII On the *Universe*; Chapter XVIII; On *Perfect Happiness*; Chapter XIX on the *Secret of Life*, just to name some.This eloquent humorist-philosopher-mystic interpreter of the *Book of Dao* has undoubtedly made his work sound harmless hermit-talks, that it made many readers of Daoism claim that the *Dao De Jing* is a work on mysticism.

Zhung Zi's interpretation of the *Dao* direct his follower into the realm of unity of all things. However, in such Unity one's consciousness expands and blows up all remaining intellectual and human categories of understanding. Suddenly, intellectual categorization becomes inutile for the natural handicaps that always end up in prejudice. Hermeneutics becomes available only in the realms of phenomena but becomes useless in the realm of the absolute. Even perspectivism cannot be harnessed as a point of view, not even relativism nor nihilism. Thought is no longer challenged not because there never was any attempt to do so, but that such effort explodes on its own. One then begins to 'understand' that thought is discriminatory, relative, inutile and could not usher us into the vortex of understanding, absurd or genius? The idea is worth pushing more.

Dao and the Legalist Interpretation of *Han Fei Zi*[15]

However, there was another philosopher of ancient China took to *Dao* with the same excitement, but viewed the idea from another level of inspiration, thus interpretation. *Han Fei Zi,* the only nobleman of the period of Hundred Schools was a political philosopher belonging to a school of thought called *Fa Jia*. As a school of thought, *Fa Jia* was interested in the political problem of consolidation and preservation of power of the sovereign.

His appropriation of the notion of *Dao* in politics was focused mostly on the idea of preservation and strengthening of the state. His work The Book of *Han Fei Zi* urges the ruler to master the art of politics through effective leadership based on a government characterized by lack of mercy, extreme severity, hard-core rigidity, and above all, a politics that is devoid of ethical concerns. However, *Han Fei* was addressing it to the Emperor, and one who is familiar with the ancient Chinese culture should be quick to recall that emperor is looked up to like a living god. Therefore, in a twist of thought, *Han Fei* tried to urge the emperor to rule like a divine sovereign. The emperor is urged to become a perfect model of an enlightened emperor drawing inspiration from *Lao Zi*. We find in Books Six,[16] and the first chapter of Book Seven[17] devoted to the subject on *The Dao of the Sovereign*, and the *Rule by Wu-Wei* 無爲 were important lexicon in the philosophy of *Lao Zi.*

In these chapters, *Han Fei* urged the sovereign to model himself according to the Daoist Sage Ruler. A Daoist Sage Ruler rules by not ruling, governs by not governing, does nothing and, yet nothing is left undone.

Han Fei said: "Just as the sun and moon shine forth, the four seasons progress, the clouds spread, and the wind blows, so does the ruler not encumber his mind with knowledge, or himself bothered with selfishness. He relies for good government or disorder upon Fa, Law and Shu, Statecraft and leaves right and wrong to be dealt with through reward and punishments; and refers lightness and heaviness to the balance of the scale."[18] However, are we not here reminded of the famous quotation from *Zhuang Zi* that says; "The superior must have no activity, so as to employ the world; but the subordinate must have activity, so as thus to be employed by the world?"[19] We further read, "therefore, the ruler of old, although their knowledge spread throughout the whole universe did not himself think! Although their eloquence beautified all things, they did not themselves speak. Although their abilities exhausted all things within the four seas, they did not themselves act."[20]

It is evident that the Daoist concept of the Sage Ruler and Non-action found comfortable use in the political thought of *Fa Jia*. Thus, a ruler, *Han Fei* thought, takes no direct part in the affairs of government, but he simply presides over the land like a semi-divine figurehead, while the elaborate legal machinery of the government functions of its own accord, obviating the necessity for personal decision or personal intervention. We can here give some parallelisms between the *Dao* of *Lao Zi* and the Diving Supreme Ruler of *Han Fei*. Here is the analogy of the sovereign of *Lao Zi* and *Han Fei Zi*.

Daoist Sage Ruler	***Han Fei's* Supreme Ruler**
1. Absolute understanding of *Dao*.	1. Absolute knowledge of the *Dao of Government*.
2. He rises above all conventional distinction of right and wrong, good and evil.	2. He is law unto himself. He rises above the law.
3. Adopts a course of quietude and deliberately refrains from all forces or unnatural activity, a form of "laissez-faire."	3. Head of vast bureaucracy does the same, issuing orders, quietly judging the efficiency of his ministers but refraining from any personal intervention in the actual affairs of administration. He sets up the machinery of government and allows it to run by itself.
4. Withdraws from the World to a mysterious and transcendental realm.	4. Withdraws from the world and deliberately shuns contact with his subordinates, which might breed familiarity. Dwelling deeply in his palace, concealing his true motives and desires, and projects an image of mystery and inscrutability.

Han Fei Zi's ideal ruler resembles the mysterious *Dao* of *Lao Zi* and his motives and inner thoughts are equated with that of the incomprehensible *Wu-Wei*. *Han Fei Zi* himself said,"So, still he seems to dwell nowhere at all, so empty no one can seek him out. The ruler thus reposes in non-action above, and below him ministers tremble with fear."[21] In fine, *Han Fei* wants the ruler to have within his hand the implements and mechanisms set in the government and then to just allow everything to run by itself, thereby employing the Daoist idea of *Wu-Wei*.

The *Dao* of the Ruler in the Political Realm

Han Fei Zi envisioned a ruler that creates the conditions for a good government without directly getting involved in it; leaving the operation in the hands of competent bureaucrats. *Han Fei Zi* contends that in the same way: the ruler, wise as he is, should not but let everything finds its proper place; worthy as he is, should not be self-assumed but observes closely the minister's motivating factors of conduct; and courageous as he is, should not be enraged but let every minister display his ability. Thus, he relieves the ruler of any form of vulnerability, even possible humiliation of any incompetence. He only reigns like a truly divine figure showing total impenetrability, but his thought will seem to have an encompassing grasp to all there is, the elusive figure of the ruler of *Dao*, without even lifting a finger, sets everything working.

The workings of the government hinges and functions not so much on the deliberate exchange of human wills, but from an objective skeletal, as it were, backbone of systematic machinery, sustaining and determining this very deliberate process itself. In other words, *Han Fei* understands the *Dao* as this very system that conjures up the very condition that makes possible human governance and communal relations. For unlike the Westerners, the Chinese immediately presumes the positive reality of a society and a government. Moreover, it is the *Dao* that acts as the mechanism of this government, determining it towards its end.

However, *Han Fei Zi*'s ideal ruler does not require sageliness-within, and kingliness-without model of the Confucian kind. *Fei's* Sovereign is modeled like a divine figure; as an unfathomable abyss that works in mysterious ways, he keep this divine feature even if one would not live up to it. The secret lies not in the ruler but in the supposed impenetrable appearance of the ruler. *Han Fei Zi* himself said, "So, still he [the ruler] seems to dwell nowhere at all, so empty no one can seek him out."[22] Mysterious and unfathomable is the hallmark of a divine Legalist ruler of *Han Fei*. It is thought that divine inscrutability of a man in power assures obedience and completion of the ruler's desired end.

Han Fei's political interpretation of a *Dao* of Ruler is fully anchored on the interplay of psychology and cunning between the sovereign and subject. By simply assuming the position of a powerful ruler despite his incompetence, the ruler generates a specter of an ideal picture of himself through the machinery of the *Dao* that is at work in the government.

The *Dao* in the Art of War of *Sun Zi*[23]

Sun Zi Bing Fa, or *The Art of War* of *Sun Zi* has exercised a potent fascination over China's great minds and of many military strategists of both East and

West. As a text, *Sun Zi Bing Fa* is not only the staple and base of all military men's training but that it also compels the most careful attention yet given by scholars and men of letters. His military sayings are terse yet elegant, simple yet profound, perspicuous and eminently practical.

There are, however, to be found in *Sun Zi's* language and thought elements that recall the mysterious Daoist doctrine. *Sun Zi* claims that the commander of war has to cultivate the *Dao* in him; he has to be subtle and insubstantial, without trace, divinely mysterious and thoroughly inaudible. Through this Daoist sage leader, "the strong appears weak and the weak strong."[24] His army has "no definite shape,"[25] "as water conforms to terrain so the army flows around the enemy," "spills over the ground, changes form with every rock and crevice." The mysterious language describing the great general fascinated the military men and men of letters alike.

Consider the discussion found in many chapters of the military classic. The concept of soft and weak overcoming the hard and the strong in the *Dao De Jing* Poem 36,[26] Poem 43,[27] and Poem 79[28] were borrowed by *Sun Zi* to be interpreted as references to military strategic advice, and in fact has been understood as such as it appears in the first few lines of the *Seven Military Classics*. In Poem 78, we find the first two lines: "Water is the softest and weakest thing in the world, yet it is best able to overcome that which is strong and solid."[29] We may say that at first glance, the sentence may appear to have no military connotation. Actually, in the ancient Chinese Military Classics, water was often taken as an example to illustrate warfare. The great military strategist, *Sun Pin*, says that fighting a war resembles one's coping with water. Just as water flows very naturally adapting to any course or kind of surface, so should the army adapt itself to the circumstances created by the enemy.

In Poem 76 of the *Book of Dao*, we find this line: "Thus, when the troops are inflexible, they love the war...What is stronger and most solid remains low. What is softest and weakest remains high."[30] These words come quite conveniently to the military strategists. As such, the application of *Dao* is no longer just a Metaphysical idea, but it has also become a practical military advice. Again, Poem 57 of the *Book of Dao* gives other striking military statements: "Govern the realm by the right, and battle by strategem" and, "Battles can only be won if rules are broken."[31] This was adopted in *Sun Zi's The Art of War* which reads: "In all fighting, the direct method may be used for joining battle, but indirect methods will be needed in order to secure victory."[32]

Indirect or extraordinary methods and forces are the means to conduct tricky warfare, such as giving the enemy a wrong impression about one's real strength or a strategy involving temporary retreat, thus luring the enemy into a weak position in order to destroy them finally.

As we look closely at Poem 68 of *Dao De Jing*, we read, "The best charioteers do not rush forward,"[33] a practical advice for the warrior to hold back action. Here it may further be interpreted that the leader of an army and his men are admonished to keep a clear mind to fight passionlessly and to refrain from engaging emotionally. *Dao De Jing* Poem 69 reads:

On Military operations, we have:

I do not boldly attack others first
But take action only after being attacked
I do not boldly move forward even an inch
But withdraw in foot.[34]

Thus, only he who adheres to the rule of self-restraint and plays a passive role rather than an active role is likely to win in war.

The final Daoist admonition on war can be found in Poems 30, 31 and 80. For instance, take Poem 30:

He who by Dao purposes to help a ruler of man
Will oppose all conquest by force of arms
For such things are wont to rebound.
Where armies are, thorns and brambles grow
The raising of a great host
Is followed by a year of death.[35]

This valuable passage of the *Dao De Jing* on war leaves no doubt that *Lao Zi* perceives all violent warfare as intrinsically undesirable as they only lead to misery and deprivation, and *Sun Zi* joins him in unison.

Sun Zi is considered by many as an enlightened general who accepts war as a crucial fact too important not to be studied.War is an art that has to be learned. However, his sensitivity to life and penetrating mind made him say, with truth, vision, and conviction, that an enlightened sovereign "does not raise an army because he is enraged, nor does a general fight because he is resentful. For while an angered man may again be happy, and a resentful man may again be pleased, a state that has perished cannot be restored, nor can the dead be brought back to life."[36]

An Option for a New Interpretation

The three schools of thought each provided us ancient Chinese hermeneutic of the nature of *Dao*. However, is there a fresher view of looking of it again? My own readings bring me back to the same first passage of Poem1, but my interpretation goes in this form of summary:

Dao is Dao
The Dao of the Dao is the Dao of the Dao
The only Dao by which man can reach the Dao is by Dao of the Dao

At first glance, it sounded like a play of word, but as one goes over it again with the multi-layered, plurisignificative understanding of the meaning of the word Dao a new understanding emerges.

Dao, for *Lao Zi,* is the Absolute (*Dao*), but it is also the Way (*Dao*) of the Absolute (*Dao*), and the Path (*Dao)* to the Absolute (*Dao*). To state it another way Lao Zi is telling us: There is a Reality that is Non-Reality (a Being that is Non-Being, a Way that is Non-Way), and the Way of this Reality (Absolute) is manifested in the Way (*Dao*) of Nature (*Dao* of the *Dao*). The only Way (*Dao)* in which one can attain the Absolute (*Dao*) is also by following the Path (*Dao*) of Nature (*Dao*).

The first level of *Dao* lies in its solipsist rendition. *Dao* is *Dao* signifies the One, the Absolute, and precisely because it is the One and the simple, it acquires no distinguishing factor. The nature of simplicity resides in its own wholeness and singularity. This singularity could possibly have no name, and can only be referred to as The One, and thus stay unnamable *Wu Ming* 無名[37] and also indescribable. The temptation of the indescribability is the mental movement toward the transcendence leading to metaphysical understanding of the *Dao*.

As a metaphysical term, *Dao* stays constant providing stable reference for all discourses. Thus, people of all lifestyles take refuge even convenience to refer to it with mysterious significance. Everything that is full and mystery is the *Dao*. Thus, *Dao* is *Dao*, the primordial essence or fundamental nature of the universe.

In all its uses, *Dao* takes ineffable qualities that prevent it from being defined or even expressed in words. It can, however be *known* or *experienced*, and its principles (which can be discerned by observing Nature) can be followed or practiced.

*The Dao of the Dao is the Dao of the Dao.*This takes us to the natural level of the term. *Dao* the Absolute and the One creates its manifestation. This articulation is the Way (*Dao*) of Nature (*Dao*). Here the term *Dao* takes two meaning, the *Dao* as the absolute and Dao as the movement of Nature or the natural movement.

In this level of discourse, *Dao De Jing* provides a whole range of explication in various passages of the book. The *Dao* (Way) of Nature (*Dao*) is Natural *Zi Ran* 自然, spontaneous, unaffected, described in *Wu-Wei* 無爲 a "creative action in non action."*Dao* does nothing and yet everything is done, spontaneously and naturally, as sunrise and sunset. It is expected that one who wishes to know the Absolute *Dao* has to observe with natural working of *Dao*. It is effortless, spontaneous, creative, and even perpetual. It is in this level of articulation that many schools of thought making the Book of *Dao* useful for many practical ethical, political, strategic and physical interpretation.

There is, however the third tier: The only *Dao* (Path) by which man can reach the *Dao* (Absolute) is by *Dao* (path) of the *Dao* (nature). The only Way (*Dao)* in which one can attain the Absolute (*Dao*) is also by following the Way (*Dao*) of Nature (*Dao*), we begin to look for the practical application of the nature of *Dao*. It maybe, at this level, that some contemporary thinkers take *Dao* as Meta-ethical.

Conclusion

When one stands back from a cultural or philosophical orientation and proceeds to cross into the global perspective where variant worldviews originate and intersect; disturbing patterns emerge that are not as evidently seen, even perhaps cannot be seen from a more localized narrative forms of life-world. It is often in this spectral global world, diverse cosmologies and grammars of reality that diverse worldviews through the ages have gravitated to some First Principle of Presiding Reality that is the source of its form of life.

I am proposing to refine a traditional account of the character of Daoist thinking that I take that tradition to have mistaken for a meaning change. The refinement does not deny that they may give accounts of the nature of *Dao*. To the degree that we consider such an account metaphysical, Daoists may be said to address the metaphysics of *Dao;* but it seems that it is multi-layered as much as it is plurisignificative.

On one level, *Lao Zi* was telling us of a discourse on the realm of metaphysics and Epistemology but tells us "What is, such that we may or may not know about it? However, quickly in another plain, *Lao Zi* tells us to engage: "What is, such that humans can act in it?"

But in telling us all these, he does not use the familiar concepts of Western sentential philosophy – no propositions, truths (including moral truths), beliefs, practical reasoning, or most of their close and distant conceptual relatives. In Daoist articulation, we find in the language, the creative mind-shift that autofocuses to the experiential or entry side of meaning and understanding – mystical experience, consciousness, evidence, argument, cogitation, discussion, guess, opinion, all epistemological, metaphysical, logical, and practical activities are in multifunctional. All these celebration of human ability and possibility gracefully intermingle with the phenomenal and imaginary world of existence.

We see plurisignificative terms, elevator terms, and other Daoist language emerge one by one; *Dao* 道, *De* 德, *Wu*-Wei 無爲, *Wu Ming* 無名, *Zi Ran* 自然, *Chang* 常, *Xin* 心, *Shi-Fei* 是非, *Tian* 天, urging that man has to become a

Sheng Ren, 聖人 the ideal wise man or exemplar of Daoism. For only a truly wise man of *Dao* can see the true genius of the Daoist message. Only such wise man could have successfully summoned not just his mind but also his heart to be at-one with the *Dao*.

Daoist meta-ethical articulation uses radically distinctive conceptual scheme addressing a different philosophical agenda allowing various domain to gain access but come with little or no final interpretation either.

What makes the *Dao De Jing* inspirational is that it presents an alternative to the philosophy proposed by many and instead urges man to proceed with carefree flight from respectability and the conventional duties of society. Instead of the common Confucian concern for things human and mundane, it holds out a vision of the other transcendental world of the spirit. If Confucius represented the mind of the Chinese scholar-mandarin-gentleman in his office or study, working to become a conscientious bureaucrat, good citizen and a benevolent family man, *Lao Zi* represents the same 'gentleman' in his private chamber or a mountain retreat, seeking surcease from the concerns of official life, perhaps a bit drunk, but more likely intoxicated by the beauty of nature and the world of the spirit.

Dao De Jing reveals that the works is an invitation to a wide range of hermeneutics written in powerful language, philosophy, mysticism, politics, military view and many more domains of human interest written in a graceful poetry

It is perhaps for this reason that ancient and contemporary hermeneutics continue to have difficulty comprehending the message of *Dao* in *Lao Zi*. However, the work contains the distilled essence of Chinese wisdom, infinitely rich in vision, intellectually challenging, spiritually uplifting, aesthetically sublime, and emotionally heartwarming.

Dao's poetic rendition gives wings to the message and allows its reader "to take the flight of a bird soaring high and quitting the terrestrial ground." However, when it became necessary to focus on higher truths, he readily turned to silence and *Lao Zi* very wisely made use of paradox, for unlike the idea of contradiction, which allows two opposing terms to cancel each other; paradoxical ideas simply appear opposing on one level, but they are mutually complimentary with one another. For, just like the ancient Indian wise men would have thought, the higher the truth, the less it can be described or defined. This plurisignificative nature of *Lao Zi*'s language also leaves its readers infinite possibilities for hermeneutics. It can always render each interpretation valid, in the same way that it can allow the same interpretation to be perceived as doubtful or even false.

What makes the world of *Lao Zi* endure time is the brilliance of his style and the depth of his thought. The book of *Dao* is all that is said of it and all that is not said of it. This spirit conveys a deep and fundamental trait of Chinese thinking as a whole, while at the same time it presents the pervasive Chinese attitude towards life, society and the world. *Lao Zi's* work also affords one the only safe and romantic release from the severity and restraint advanced by other philosophies. It is no wonder that the Book of *Lao Zi* continues to attract readers and translators; and it is not surprising that many people continue to agree and disagree with *Dao De Jing*, and agree or disagree they must, for the Book of *Dao* weaves perpetual spell on its readers.

Zhuang Zi perceived that the *Dao* leads one to a plea for the individual's freedom of spirit from the confines of his own mind-world. Thus, his interpretation of *Lao Zi's Dao*, seems a continuity rather than interpretation of the old sage. His articulation of *Dao* leads us to follow him like a happy wanderer of thought taking us into a happy excursion of the mind. Nothing therefore delighted him more than to show the relativity of things, which made him indulge in satire at the expense of conventional society. However, his ultimate interest labored on the mystical union with nature, revealing the infinite possibilities of the *Dao*, affirming that the absolute and the inexhaustible Truth rests in union with Nature.

While most of the classical Chinese philosophers had rich imaginations, none compared with the fantasy of *Zhuang Zi*. No one can understand *Zhuang Zi* without having to journey with him in the realm of the imagination and dreams. For only in imagination and dream will one understand the elusive reality, the relativity of truth, the essence of life, and the infinite possibilities of everything.

Zhuang Zi shared with *Lao Zi* his central conception of the *Dao* as the principle underlying and governing all existence. However, he ignored *Dao* as a guiding principle of life, urging one to rise above the conflicting forces of the *Yin* and *Yang*, above the conflict of truth and falsity, right and wrong, good and evil. A truly realized man is one who comprehends the *Dao* and has achieved a happiness that is beyond all change.

As part of this true guidance for a person to see through life, *Zhuang Zi* claimed that awakening from a dream in which he was a butterfly, he was uncertain what he really was. How often have these dreams and stories been retold through the centuries, even if scholars debated the spuriousness of certain chapters, or argued which of the author's characters were fictitious, which metaphoric, and which actually real. For the literature of *Zhuang Zi* rises above time and space. He was, of course driven constantly into the idioms of the absurd. But one gradually realizes that as one has expanded this realm of consciousness - call it *Nirvana, Samadhi, Satori*, Enlightenment or mastery of the *Dao*, one's thought enters the para-verbal. The absurd becomes the third medium in which communication takes place. Indirection becomes the guidance. Without loss of patience, *Zhuang Zi* tells us repeatedly what he wants to tell us, but always obliquely.

For those who can follow the course indicated by *Zhuang Zi,* disciplining the body has no value in itself. *Zhuang Zi* was neither a *Yogi* nor an Indian ascetic. Either of those approaches to life would have struck him as excessive and unnatural. He was more concerned with an applied philosophy of life projected through an ideal of living simply in harmony with nature and doing no violence to one's own nature.

A modern person, who has his vision focused on the infinite and his ears open to the universe, is conscious of the great continuum spoken of by the Daoist Sage. Perhaps it is caused by the *élan* of the *Dao*. What *Dao* has to convey goes off like a canon in the mind. The ideas come first through a cloud crossing the peak of a towering mountain. However, when the cloud clears, one realizes that Sage not only speaks to our time but also aims at its very heart of eternity.

Chinese investigation to the realm of understanding and interpretation took a rather multi layered, multi textured articulation different from the history of western hermeneutics. It must have been due to the nature of the Chinese language and its mode of expression. In a language that is not based on the grammar and syntax of the Latin based language; it is literally liberated from the notion of temporal grounding of past, present and future tense. Hermeneutics takes a new host, and the discourse has to take a new turn.

It is in *Lao Zi* that we come to admire the impressive and originality of his discourse on *Dao* and subsequently *Zhuang Zi* pushed the idea to its omega point. There *Dao* was raised to a new level of consciousness where every human explication, cogitation, interpretation become superfluous if not senseless. There language is rendered inutile, sterile and must therefore be dropped as one soars away from the terrestrial ground. For those who dwell in human language, true and non-true, good and non-good, being-non-being becomes oxymoronic if not down to earth absurd, but to one who manage to reach that height of consciousness, that is pure genius. It is not hard to say, that *Lao Zi* was indeed Genius of the Absurd.

...*Lun Xun*, the father of contemporary Chinese literature said; "there never was a road, but people kept walking the path, then suddenly the road appeared." All of a sudden, we nod our heads in recognition that *Lao Zi* was a genius….and we are prisoner to his language. "My Language…..Your Prison."

Notes

1 Alfred North Whitehead, "Understanding," *Lecture Three in Modes of Thought* (New York: Macmillan, 1938), 58-87.

2 Lao Zi, *Tao Te Ching (Dao De Jing)*.Cf. the following translations: *Tao: A New Way of Thinking Chang Chung-Yuan* (London: Harper and Row, 1975); *Lao Tsu Tao Te Ching*

(New York: Vintage Books); *The Way of Life Lao Tzu* (New York: The New American Library, 1955), Poem 1. From hereon, it wll be referred to as *Dao De Jing*.

3 Zhuang Zi, *Chuang tzu: The Inner Chapters,* trans., Angus Graham (London: Allen & Unwin, 1981), 46.

4 Ibid., 30.

5 Ibid., 38.

6 Ibid., 38.

7 Ibid., 26.

8 Ibid., 26.

9 Ibid., 37.

10 Ibid, 29.

11 Ibid.

12 Ibid., 42.

13 Ibid., 59.

14 Ibid.

15 Han Fei Zi, *The Complete Work of Han Fei Tzu,* trans., W. K. Liao (London: Arthur Probsthain, 1959).

16 Ibid., 167-206.

17 Ibid., 207-227.

18 Ibid., Chapter 29.

19 Zhuang Zi, *Chuang tzu*, Chapter 13, "The Tao of the Sovereign."

20 Ibid.

21 Han Fei Zi, *The Complete Work of Han Fei Tzu,*"Chapter 6, "Commentaries on Lao Tsu's Teachings."

22 Ibid.

23 Cf. Sun Tsu, *The Art of War,* trans., Samuel B. Grifitth (Oxford: Oxford University Press 1963); also Lionel Giles, *The Art of War by Sun Tzu* (Edition: ELPN Press, 2009).

24 *Dao De Jing*, Poem 76.

25 Ibid., 41.

26 Ibid., 36.

27 *Dao De Jing*, Poem 43 "Dao seng I" (The Way Begot One).

28 *Dao De Jing*,Poem 79 "Ho Ta Yuan" (How can you think).

29 *Dao De Jing*, Poem 78 "Tien hsia you je" (Nothing is weaker than water).

30 *Dao De Jing*, Poem 76 "Jen Chin Sheng Yeh" (Alive, a man is supple).

31 *Dao De Jing*, Poem 57 "I cheng chuh Kuo" (Govern the Realm).

32 Sun Zi, *The Art of War "L. A. Giles Version,* p. 35."

33 *Dao De Jing*, Poem 68 "Shan Wei shih Che" (A skillful soldier).

34 *Dao De Jing*, Poem 69 "Yung Ping Yu Yen" (The Strategists).

35 *Dao De Jing*, Poem 30.

36 Sun Tsu, *The Art of War*, 141-143.

37 *Dao De Jing*, Poem 32.

Chapter 10

Contribution and Challenge of Mīmāṃsā to the Dream of a Global Hermeneutics

Francis X. Clooney
Professor, Harvard Divinity School, Harvard University, Cambridge

If we ambition an interreligious and cross-cultural hermeneutics suited to today's global context, at stake is, or should be, the very idea of a globally relevant interpretive frame that is not simply another project of Western thinking, increasingly in English, about the wider world. The challenge then is to come up with a variety of *locally grounded*-yet-*globally open* hermeneutics, accessible outside their home cultures and context. At stake are widely relevant modes of interpretation that arise outside the West and achieve global reach, as global actors and agents of (re)interpretation, not merely as content for familiar and dominant Western systems. We *want* them to be universal, after all. Yet we are also tempted to borrow from them in a piecemeal fashion, and out of context. We need to seek intelligibility without colonizing, without merely cannibalizing their hermeneutics in the course of applying a Western hermeneutic repeatedly. The tension is clear: even when the principles are, or seem to, be universal, all hermeneutic systems are still local, grounded in particular texts and traditions of interpretation. We are required to learn from a truly different hermeneutics without merely saluting difference. We cannot settle either for the merely particular or for the seemingly universal; we must rather seek an intermediate ground. To create the space for hermeneutic systems from outside the West requires that we do the requisite study, ideally in the languages of non-Western cultures, and that we resist the modern overlay of all cultures such as obliterates their particularity with the West's seemingly general (concealed) particularities.

Even if we are all "reading texts," we can diversify, unsettle what reading means by learning from a variety of systems of interpretation which, even if we will write (about) them in English, are allowed to intrude vigorously onto that English language discourse. This is the point of thinking interculturally about hermeneutics. Gaining dexterity regarding these other, often ancient hermeneutical systems entails necessarily the educational work of forming religious and philosophical intellectuals versed in more than one cultural system of hermeneutics, possessed of intelligible access to multiple interpretive frames, without falling into the error of blandly over-generalizing on the very topic of "global hermeneutics."

This essay emphasizes three points. First, the way forward in the quest for globally relevant hermeneutical systems involves attending very closely to these alternative systems, in particular by studying their particular hermeneutic practices. Expression and style are key, and not just content, and the specific natures of given texts are what allow us to move from the particular to the universal. Second, the Vedic Mīmāṃsā tradition of interpretation – Veda-tarka, Vedic reasoning, Vedic India's quintessential hermeneutic tradition – is an obvious case of an indigenous Indian hermeneutic system that is substantive enough to stand on its own in a global context, if indeed we take it up as a whole and study it patiently. Third, we need the services of a text that makes Mīmāṃsā available to us without compromising its detail, style, and complexity, and for this purpose, the *Jaiminīyanyāyamala* (*Garland of Jaimini's Reasons*; henceforth, Garland) of Mādhava Ācārya (1297-1388) is ideal. More on this text below.

On Mīmāṃsā

First, a little background is in order. Mīmāṃsā is self-described in *Mīmāṃsā Sūtras* I.1.1 as "inquiry into dharma;" the word itself may be elaborated as "the desire and effort to know in proper measure," " the effort to intense reflection," or "enquiry, theoretical discussion (sometimes as opposed to practice)."[1] The cases and problems arising are from the originally chosen set of ritual acts and ritual texts noted by Jaimini (300-200 BCE) in the *Mīmāṃsā Sūtras*, 907 cases (adhikaraṇas) set forth in 2644 sūtras. While Mīmāṃsā analyses are grounded in the details of Vedic rituals and the texts governing those rituals, it does not, except on very particular points, offer useful guidance on how actually to do rituals, nor even an idealized description of the Vedic canon of texts. It focuses rather on the difficult cases where it is uncertain how to read and apply one or another text in its proper ritual context, and accordingly understand the web of sacrifices and their texts properly read. It did so for the sake of clarity regarding principles about performance and, it seems, for the sake of the purest, simplest understanding of the rules governing and therefore facilitating ritual and textual coherence and synergy. In the course of their deliberations, the Mīmāṃsā thinkers took care to state the strongest positions on either side of the matter, and decide for one interpretation and reading, for the ultimately most convincing reasons in support of what was already know to be settled practice.

The laconicity of Jaimini and the lack of clear markers in the Sūtras make it impossible to map precisely what the *Sūtras* are about, but we can recognize the traditional themes distinctive to each adhyāya as summarized in the explanatory *Vistara* that accompanies the *Jaiminīya Nyāya Mālā* (*The Garland of Jaimini's Reasons*, henceforth the Garland) of Mādhava (1297-1388):[2] the authority in the form of injunctions (*vidhi*), commendatory statements (*arthavāda*), etc. (Adhyāya I), the distinction (*bheda*) among actions, sacrifices, gifts, etc. (Adhyāya II), the accessory status (*śeṣatva*) of the fore-sacrifices, etc., as for the sake of the new and full moon sacrifices, etc. (Adhyāya III); decisions regarding which actions are done for the sake of the ritual (*kratu-artha*), and which are for the sake of the person (*puruṣa-artha*), as ritual performer or more generally in his ordinary life (Adhyāya IV), constraint in terms of order (*krama*), etc., even if this is mentioned and not explicitly enjoined (Adhyāya V), the fact that there is ritual eligibility and competence (*adhikāra*) for the agent but not of those ineligible due to various deficiencies, plus other cases related to ritual eligibility and competence (Adhyāya VI), transfer (*atideśa*) of details from an amply described ritual to one merely sketched or named, by explicit statements and by statements inferred with reference to the names of various sacrifices, etc. (Adhyāya VII), special cases of transfer, according to which mode of procedure is followed, which deities or materials substituted, etc. (Adhyāya VIII), there is modification of rites (*ūha*) in their adapted forms, by the changing of the name of deities receiving the offering, materials offered, etc. (Adhyāya IX), there is the cancellation (*bādha*) of no longer relevant details in adapted rites, as when the threshing cannot be applied to gold coins, etc. (Adhyāya X), there is the common performance (*tantra*) of subordinate helps, such as the fore-sacrifices, once but serving multiple rites (Adhyāya XI), the incidental help (*prasaṅga*) of subordinate rites, such as the fore-sacrifices, brought in to help the primary animal rite, but also contributing to related rites (Adhyāya XII) While in every case there is some justification for these identified categories, only three adhyāyas (I, III, IV) clearly announce their theme.

For the sake of brevity, allow me to generalize some features of the Mīmāṃsā way of thinking. Mīmāṃsā's practice of heremeneutics is deeply rooted in the vedic context, and not interestingly separable. This is, in a true sense, Vedic tarka. Its measures of authority are rooted in the Vedic, intensely committed to the instructions of that body of texts, and perhaps even so specific to the Veda that generalization becomes a greater problem. Mīmāṃsā's reasoning is material and non-abstract. While some of the commentators do at times branch off into more arcane linguistic, grammatical, and epistemological issues, such ventures are exceptional when seen against the background of the entire set of cases. The Sūtras are dedicated to an "on the ground" approach. It offers examples, over and over again, of disciplined rules for reading texts. It is attentive to direct and explicit meanings, but also patient in sorting through layers of meaning that are deeper and more complexly related to sentences, whole statements, and contexts. Everywhere it discerns intent, and aims to get at the purer, simpler purpose of any statement or action; yet it does so without relying on the hypothesis of an author whose mind must be read in order to get at the meaning of what he or she wrote. When Jaimini does generalize some hermeneutical principles, he does so only in the most laconic of ways, as this important sūtra, buried deep in the third Adhyāya, indicates:

> Śrutiliṅgavākyaprakaraṇasthānasamākhyānāṃ samavāye pāradaurbalyam arthaviprakarṣāt
>
> As for direct assertion, indirect meaning, statement, context, place, and name: when [more than one] pertain in the same instance, the posterior is weaker than the prior, because more remote from the final purpose. (III.3.14)

These are the six measures of authority (pramāṇa) which stand in relations of precedence and confirmation with respect to one another, and which, once mapped properly, communicate the meaning and use of all disputed Vedic texts.

Accepting that the Veda is self-interpreting, Mīmāṃsā emphasizes act, not theory nor essences. Text and rite go together, are not separable. The specific view of ritual – act and word – practiced in Mīmāṃsā fosters a comprehensive relatedness in which all elements are implicated in the same whole. In addition, the system is resolutely decentered. Thus, in both detail and by cases, Mīmāṃsā is therefore also resistant to generalization, even if it is also clear that the Sūtras stand above and apart from the array of Vedic texts and rituals. It is more than ritual details and words, yet cannot stand apart from them. The particular and universal inseparably together, the universal thought through practically, as needed, with respect to distinctions that will help identify all the more clearly what meanings are to be gleaned for the sake of getting the required next action straight. This thwarts efforts to identify some principles which replace the rest. Its judgments set forth competing measures of authority, and detect hierarchies among statements and within them, as is needed in cases where measures of authority compete.

Despite these interesting points, it would be a mistake to imagine Mīmāṃsā to be an innovative system, capacious in its adaptiveness and or even embrace of new cases. On the contrary, the Mīmāṃsā is strikingly conservative. The Sūtras of Jaimini early on set the boundaries for Mīmāṃsā consideration, even if there was sufficient fluidity in the wording of the sūtras that Śabara's great task was to identify the cases that prompted the discussions. Thereafter the Mīmāṃsā worked within that set of cases, certain revisions and differences enunciated particularly by Kumārila Bhāṭṭa notwithstanding. Much of the reflection occurring in Mīmāṃsā looks inward, attentive to its own set of internal questions. Its debates were never primarily conformed to questions arising from sources other than the rituals. While the case studies and the included texts and practices do have "real world" reference, and while the very distinction between the Vedic and ordinary or worldly realms is not simple and is debated in the *Sūtras*, one does not find, in the major portion of the *Sūtras*, any effort to make Mīmāṃsā relevant to wider Indian intellectual discourses, religious or philosophical. While there are insights to be learned from Mīmāṃsā that may be of great help in the reading of any text, or any practical endeavor, its distinctive wisdom, in its depth and as a whole, is barred to all but those willing to go inside the tradition, and work through its cases.[3]

On the Garland

It is easy to appeal to "Mīmāṃsā," but the study of it is notoriously difficult. Not only is it a very large system encoded in over 2700 sūtras, but its "system" such as it is, is almost entirely comprised of cases which must be considered one by one. Mīmāṃsā resists generalization or utilization for the sake of examples useful in another, alien hermeneutic system. While select borrowing from Mīmāṃsā is a fair enough endeavor if understood for what it is, it does not meet the primary need of the integral appropriation of a system which as a whole can be seen to offer an alternative to any modern Western theorizing of the issues of interpretation. The Sūtras are larger than any of the other classic sūtra texts of ancient India, and serve as a placeholder and mnemonic for ritual cases and texts known to the teachers of the sūtras, but not given in them; the commentarial tradition, partially as a result of the vast energy and scope of the Sūtras, and partially due to their obscurity, grows and grows to immensity; and as time passed, we must conjecture that fewer people practiced or understood the rituals and ritual texts at issue in the Mīmāṃsā cases.

Given how difficult it is to use, draw on, the massive literature of Mīmāṃsā, there are considerable advantages then in turning to Mādhava's Garland.[4] In this text, he offers approximately 1500 ślokas (henceforth verses) to cover the cases of Jaimini, encapsulating and highlighting the essential nuances of each. His work, which might be thought of as intended for "advanced beginners" (much as the *Summa Theologiae* of Thomas

Aquinas too was for beginners), brilliant in economy of expression, and also in its discrimination regarding what it leaves out, by its omissions estimating the relative value of what is found in the tradition. At the beginning of his work, Mādhava notes that Mīmāṃsā had become an ocean of learning too broad and deep, inaccessible to beginners. He needed to pay attention to the commentators, and yet, by his own design, reduce their expansive teaching very selectively to the essence of each argument, constrained within the self-imposed format of one or two ślokas. Thus then Mādhava, for the sake of reducing the tradition to the minimal form that he judges still to be faithful to that tradition, also excludes what he considers to be extraneous knowledge, not required by the cases.

The Garland models the Mīmāṃsā religious reasoning, such as eschews mythology and cosmology, discourse about God, and much of what we think of as philosophy. Along the way, Mādhava casts aside most of the interesting philosophical and grammatical issues, articulated particularly by Kumārila in response to the criticisms of contemporary intellectuals such as the grammarians and logicians, Buddhists and even Vedāntins. Turning in, writing for an orthodox elite, Mādhava succeeds in opening up with supreme lucidity the standard Mīmāṃsā issues, now in proportion and without undue attention to the small, *ad extra* portion of Mīmāṃsā. Mādhava might then be taken to be a summarizer, digester, abbreviator, but we do well to honor his Garland as a more substantive project that is asking, over and over again, what is the core, most important, true flowering of the text, the display of the garland (*mālā*) of reasons? It is concrete, specific, and it focuses on "the ratio." At its core, we might say, is this search for the best possible reason for why certain texts are read as they are read, actions performed in one way and not another.

In this way he also offers "the stuff" of a hermeneutic education, presenting 900+ cases to be worked through, setting up and – by making it all available – ulitmately demanding a process of slow learning and study. The Garland is a perfection of Mīmāṃsā, comparable only to the Sūtras themselves which – as incredibly successful and productive as they were – can hardly be seen as regular or adequate and lucid as one might imagine. It potentially opens up, challenges, the ordinary hermeneutics by which we interpret the world; it is "a remedy for the remedy" of the well-meant hermeneutic solutions we often propose, even with the best of intentions, when picking and choosing from other traditions, calling them to witness to the points made by privileged figures in the West.

Reading the Garland

Mīmāṃsā is a substantive system of interpretation such as can, if rendered accessible in its wholeness and integrity by a text like the Garland, hold its own in a global context, as a hermeneutical system genuinely from outside the

West. There are problems, of course, regarding whether it can be sufficiently distinguished from its own Vedic context as to be useful in the global context or even, simply, on other parts of the globe. But before returning at the end of this essay to that key issue, I must first emulate Mādhava by thinking through examples. While Mādhava's great economy means that we do not need to learn the rituals and read widely in ritual corpus or in the works of his predecessors, we *do* need to read *his* text, if we are truly to understand Mīmāṃsā and, later on, make the case for Mīmāṃsā's global relevance.[5] If Mīmāṃsā is all about concrete and material learning, we can hardly treat it only on an abstract level. This again is why the Garland is the premiere text that opens the tradition to us. Consider again III.3.14, a sūtra that lays forth an entire hermeneutics in just a few words: "As for direct assertion, indirect meaning, statement, context, place, and name: when [more than one] pertain in the same instance, the posterior is weaker than the prior, because more remote from the final purpose."[6] The sūtra offers the real estimate of authoritative ways of knowing in the Mīmāṃsā tradition, in a very compact form the six measures of authority. Mādhava, following Jaimini and the lengthy intervening commentaries, unpacks and spells out the meaning of this dense sūtra by a series of six cases. He summarizes the competiton – direct assertion outranking indirect meaning, indirect meaning outranking statement, statement outranking context, context outranking place, and place outranking name – not in an original way, but with a great precision that balances respect for detail with posing as succinctly as possible the reason for preference for one measure of authority over the other, in each case.

The principles at issue in what follow are not entirely foreign to us. Even by the fact of translation I have already made connections to broader and non-technical contexts:

> Śruti – direct assertion: what is explicitly stated in a text; liṅga, indirect meaning: what is not explicit but can easily be inferred from what is explicit; vākya, statement: what the whole of a sentence or group of sentences intimately tied to a ritual action tells us; prakaraṇa, context: not simply words, sentences, and paragraphs near to one another on a page, but the set of interacting words and deeds collected by the "need" of the various things said or actions proposed for one another, to be complete or completed; textually, a broader category than statement; sthāna, krama,[7] place, sequence: with reference to proximity of statements or actions to one another, and too the order of names, actions within the description of a ritual; samākhyā, names: as indicative of where things belong, often grouped under one category identified by the name.

The actual verses' spelling out can be done without attention to extra-textual contexts, and without attempting to read the minds of authors; everything one needs is right there, in the text. Conversely, the six measures are spelled out not thematically (as is done in other Mīmāṃsā texts) but only by way of examples, which only irregularly use the very terms that are ostensibly in balance. Every text is possessed, we can say, of the basic measures announced by Jaimini, "direct assertion, indirect meaning, statement, context, place, and nàme," and in terms of these, the meaning of the text and its proper use can be spelled out.

Let us see how Mādhava presents these six measures of authority. I give his verses with minimal commentary, so that the reader can assess what is communicated and what is left unsaid and taken for granted by Mādhava.[8] First, illustrating the greater strength of direct assertion with respect to indirect meaning, etc., a mantra mentioning Indra is used at a rite where Agni is the primary deity. But this use of the mantra is not strong enough to multiply deities or to draw in Indra (= Śakra) as the deity in place of Agni, the presumed deity of the installation of the altar:

> Regarding "The fire altar is to be set up, with the verse to Indra:" is there option here between Agni and Indra, | Or combination, or just Śakra alone, or Agni alone? ||
>
> There is option, because of direct assertion and indirect meaning. There is combination by repetition of the quality. | Because "direct assertion is in accord with its potency," here it is Śakra, due to indirect meaning. ||
>
> The potency is expressed and direct assertion is fast. Indirect meaning infers direct assertion. | Thereby arises an understanding with no further need, by direct assertion, and it is established as regarding just Agni. || (case 7)
>
> Second, illustrating the greater strength of indirect meaning with respect to statement, etc., the fact that the parts of a longer mantra inviting the deity to sit on a prepared seat cohere in one statement does not outweigh the force of indirect meaning, by which those parts apply individually to parts of the action of preparing, inviting, etc.:
>
> The first half of the mantra is "Your seat" and the latter portion is "sit on it." Does all of it pertain | To preparing the seat and arranging it,9 or is each part just for the stipulated half? ||
>
> Because of the word "it," all is one statement, so it should be the former ("all"). Since indirect meaning | Is nearest to direct assertion, statement is thus barred, and so they are used respectively (in regard to each "half"). ||

In this example statement is barred, but not due to "by the verse to Indra." | Because [the barred words] would have no purpose after such barring, there would be an undesirable lack of authority.(8) ||

Third, illustrating the greater strength of statement with respect to context, etc., the contextual pressure to use a whole mantra with respect to a whole action is outweighed by the content of the statement, which apportions parts of the mantra to parts of the action:

When it says, "This oblation is to be oblated for Agni and Soma," | Should "After cutting this" be accessory to all of it, or not? ||

From context, it should be accessory to all. Not so. (Arguing from) context requires three (steps) | Whereas (arguing from) statement requires only two. So, it should be in accord with the latter, as stronger than context. || (9)

Fourth, illustrating the greater strength of context with respect to sequence, etc., the mutual need of the dice-playing, etc., for one another outweighs the proximity of those actions, in the sequence of description, to the inaugural anointing sacrifice:

Are the dice-playing, etc., that occur at the Rājasūya in the "inaugural anointing sacrifice" | Accessory just to that, or for the sake of all? Accessory just to that, because near to it. ||

Because carried forward in accord with the Rājasūya's manner, they are accessory to all. | That the inaugural anointing sacrifice needs these has to be conjectured, and stronger than that is evident context. || (10)

Fifth, illustrating the greater strength of sequence with respect to name, the order of actions in the prescriptive texts outweighs the fact that the purification mantra appears in a textual section pertaining to the cake-rite purification:

Is the mantra, "Be pure" subsidiary to the "cake-rite purification" | Or to the purity of the buttered-offering vessel? Let it be the former, due to the name. ||

"Cake-rite's" may be interpreted in accord with its root form or its strengthened form.10 | Because [the name is] not mentioned in proximity, the former would have to be construed. But the latter is already construed, due to sequence. || (11)

So, the mantra more quickly relates to the purity of the buttered-offering vessel. Sixth, in this last of the cases alone Mādhava makes no reference to a guiding text. He simply takes up the very idea that this calculus of barring: direct assertion bars indirect meaning, and indirect meaning bars statement, etc. Barring is not itself a violation of the Veda. Mādhava distinguishes the mistaken interpretations arising here – such as are barred – from the treatment of the topic later on in the Sūtras:

> Is barring not proper, or is it? It is proper regarding neither what is established nor what is not; |
> One not begun, the other a fact. Of that regarding which there is intent, let there be barring. ||
> In the Tenth Book, there is barring of what is potential according to authoritative knowing. But here, there is barring |
> Of what is only seemingly potential. Therefore, the barring is of what is not yet established. || (12)

Much more can be said on the details of texts at issue here, and Mādhava does little more than mention them in a most compact fashion. He is interested in the competing realms of authority of the six measures of authority, and focuses on matters of precedence, wherein lies the point of such cases. We can readily see the intense calculus set forth here, such as lays out six measures of knowledge not abstractly, but as in relation to one another. Every one of these cases is made specific by Mādhava's reference to the disputed text that Śabara had suggested. The six measures of authority, listed by Jaimini, are not given in a list by Mādhava, and are meant to be worked out case by case, in practice. This is even if the principles are surely meant to be useful regarding other cases and in that practical sense tend to generalization. There is sufficient complexity here, and detail, such that the cases cannot be subsumed into an ancient or contemporary Western hermeneutics.

The six measures of authority together suffice, in the Mīmāṃsā view expounded here by Mādhava, in providing in every case an adequate reading of the Vedic texts and corresponding rites. There is no appeal to the intentions of an author; this is no before, above, or outside the text. Intentionality, if it may be called that, remains solidly that of the words as they stand before us, and as connected to the actions of which they speak, to which they are connected. Still more notable, and problematic for us today, will be the seeming confidence that the reader's subjective interests and inclinations do not matter; indeed, the Garland in part educates the reader, purifying her or him of any such subjective claims. Nor indeed does historical consciousness come into play. The text contains every clue that is needed, clues evident to the discerning reader.[11]

Yet all of this is subtle and implicit, and the reader may miss it. These six measures of authority are imbedded deep within the Third Adhyāya of the Sūtras, and even that Third Adhyāya seemingly has another agenda, as Mādhava states at its beginning:

> In the Second Adhyāya, the division of actions was completed. Regarding those divided actions, |
> This matter of the relationship of accessory and that to which it is accessory needs to be taken up next, hence it is here considered. ||

The measures of authority are stated only in the middle of III.3. They are given presumably in order to facilitate the calculation of dependent relations among the accessories in relation to what which they depend on, but are not given priority over the cases in which they can be glimpsed in practice. Neither is it a good practice for us to abstract them from III.3 and debate them apart from the cases in which they are expressed. So, in the long run, we are still drawn deeper into the larger patterns of the Sūtras which, like many a classical system, do not patiently tolerate those who would extract the part without learning the whole.[12]

From the Garland to Global Hermeneutics?

I have highlighted Mīmāṃsā as a particularly well-known hermeneutical system that should not be ignored and that cannot be deemed merely a version of some already-global, Western hermeneutical system. In arguing for Mīmāṃsā's potential global role, I have highlighted the Garland not because it offers a new or distinctive version of Mīmāṃsā positions on philosophical or hermeneutical issues, but because its brevity makes it feasible to contemplate apprehending the whole of the Mīmāṃsā system, not just a few sections of it.

But if the Garland makes it possible to pay serious attention to Mīmāṃsā, then much work lies ahead of us if it is to be Mīdrawn into the global hermeneutical conversation. The first work is of course to study the text, case after case. After that, further progress can be made by way of small-scale and focused comparisons that draw Mīmāṃsā gradually into the wider world audience of hermeneutical studies. Here we can begin with already existing scholarly works that in important ways raise the issue of Mīmāṃsā and hermeneutics, or Mīmāṃsā hermeneutics; while this essay has focused entirely on the Garland as the text which in practical terms makes the whole of the Mīmāṃsā available, no single approach can be the sole approach, and readers may prefer to avail themselves of other scholarly resources. Yet it is the case that few scholars have attempted to take seriously the vast majority of the text such as occurs after the First Adhyāya.[13]

For parallels to Mīmāṃsā in general and the Garland in particular, as text and occasion for study, we may look for religious texts that share a similar commitment to condensation, a negotiation of meaning by way of a language of rules, and an investigation of large interpretive issues in and not apart from the details of ritual practice – all within the bounds of a set of standard examples. Thus we might very appropriately turn to the Jewish Rabbinic tradition, which is likely to offer us apt comparisons that illumine Mīmāṃsā's analogous form of legal reasoning. Jacob Neusner nuances what kind of philosophy the Mishnah is, so densely connected as it is with the details of pluriform material religion:

> While the Mishnah may be properly read as philosophy formed out of arguments set forth through lists and the hierarchization of the things that are listed, the document certainly does not make abstract philosophical points or ordinarily express its principles in explicit generalizations. All points concerning classification, for example, are made through talk of pots and pans, of menstruation and dead creeping things, of ordinary water which, because of the circumstance of its collection and location, possesses extraordinary power. The compositions of the Mishnah speak of the commonplace corpse and ubiquitous diseased person; of genitalia and excrement, toilet seats and the flux of penises, of stems of pomegranates and stalks of leeks; of rain and earth; of wood, metal, glass and hide. And these are treated not as symbols or even as examples but are made to carry the full weight of discourse. I cannot imagine less fertile ground for the seed of abstract theorizing on the nature of things. The Mishnah therefore provides an extreme example of how practical logic and applied reason come to expression and are worked out solely through the nitty-gritty of ordinary and everyday life. Its mode of speech – the way it speaks, not only what it says – is testimony to its conception that within the everyday are contained the highest and most abstract truths not merely of wisdom but of knowledge, in our language, natural philosophy or science.[14]

He speaks later again to the way that material realities can be philosophized without being rendered isolated entities which we seek to understand in terms of their essences:

> What the sages of the Mishnah accomplished was the recasting of facts supplied by or derived from Scripture. They re-formed the facts into problems exemplary of principles. When people reread the facts about concrete things and find them exemplary of abstract principles, the concrete things lose their practicality altogether. What now matters is relationship, not material reality. What is at stake here is the classification of things in relation to one another, not the consideration of the thing on its own."[15]

Such analogies with rabbinic reading and reasoning are invitations to think different about philosophy, hermeneutics, and then too Mīmāṃsā.

Learning from readers of Mishnah shows how modern readers, willing to engage in reading practices that take precedence over theory, can similarly approach Mīmāṃsā texts such as the Garland.

The Christian tradition too may have such resources, particularly from the premodern era. Attention to the construction of church creeds and the initial work in fashioning medieval summas of theology and sentence collections as pedagogical tools will be productive. So, too, we can usefully attend to early modern catechisms with respect to their distillative and pedagogical purposes, and their difficult balance between the presumed lack of advanced knowledge on the part of the reader and the necessary advanced knowledge of the catechism-writer, will help us to understand the strategies for the codification of knowledge, complex and argued wholes reduced to the most economical, brief form.

As for more philosophical parallels, I suggest a perhaps surprising parallel: the structures of writing and learning evident in Wittgenstein's *Philosophical Investigations* compel the reader to read in a certain way. I propose such a comparison not because I think that Wittgenstein is a kind of Western Mīmāṃsaka or that Mādhava might gain respectability by being allowed to stand next to Wittgenstein, but because the pertinent texts, *Philosophical Investigations* and the Garland, demand a similarly "surface reading" that excludes abstraction, generalization, and improvement by methodological and thematic summation. Wittgenstein's writing, understood in its literary mode, is a good parallel that reinforces similar expectations regarding the process of slow learning and the deferral of theoretical reflection.[16] I quote the recent work of Maria McGinn on the *Philosophical Investigations* to indicate the kind of reflection on Wittgenstein that would resonate well with the work of reading the Garland properly:

> [U]nderstanding Wittgenstein's method and its connection with the form of the text is the key to understanding the Investigations... Wittgenstein himself emphasizes over and over again that it is a method or a style of thought, rather than doctrines that characterizes his later philosophy. It is, moreover, his insistence that his philosophical aims do not involve him in putting forward 'any kind of theory' (PI 109) that makes the question of method, and of how to read his remarks, such a difficult one, for it suggests that we cannot approach the book in the usual way, with a view to finding and extracting the views which are expressed in it.[17]

We need to resist the temptation to impose a higher order of system upon Wittgenstein's seeming disorder – which keeps falling short of thematic order – by organizing and thematizing his work. It is the process of learning in the particular that matters and must be honored, a particular kind of grammatical investigation of the kind that, as grouped, comprise the Philosophical Investigations. And so, "These investigations of how a part of our language works are invariably subtle and complex, and how Wittgenstein uses them as a means to unravel philosophical problems can only properly be understood by *looking at how his method works in practice*."[18] Accordingly, working through the examples is not an accidental feature of the work:

> By using these techniques [Wittgenstein] attempts, not a systematization of the rules that govern our use of words, but an evocation of the distinctive patterns of use that characterize our employment of them; it is by making ourselves aware of these distinctive patterns of use that we clarify the grammar of our concepts. The purpose of Wittgenstein's evocation of the details of our practice of using the different expressions of our language is twofold. On the one hand, he uses it to make us aware of the clash between our philosophically reflective idea of how a concept works and the way it actually functions, and on the other, he uses it to draw our attention to the profound differences in the patterns of use that characterize the different regions of our language.[19]

Close reading, doing, and not talking-about: this is, to be sure, a different path into the work of hermeneutics. But a commitment to close reading is perhaps the best way to understand Mīmāṃsā properly and find a place for it in the global hermeneutical conversation.

Yet we must not be too optimistic. The very specificity and thoroughness that make the Garland so very interesting must also prompt legitimate doubts regarding whether a system so inward-looking, fundamentally tradition-oriented, and case-grounded can really be transported beyond its seemingly fixed set of cases. An answer to this question has to do with whether the hard work required can be done in the modern West and on the global scene; whether there are scholars in sufficient number ready for that work; and whether by even the hardest labor there is a serious prospect of a global appreciation of Mīmāṃsā. At first glance, there seems to be little chance that this difficult discourse, still largely in Sanskrit and often difficult to understand in translation, will flourish as a universally accepted global discourse, or come to prominence in the wider expanse of Asia or Africa or the Americas. After all, the costs of learning may be thought to outweigh the benefits.[20]

But once we see what Mīmāṃsā is about what is possible, the very fact of Mīmāṃsā's imposing intellectual edifice can stand as a stern reminder of the limits of the universality of any powerful, popular hermeneutic arising in the West. Until proven otherwise, it is simply *not* the case that the hermeneutical systems we regularly draw on and use globally – from Plato and Aristotle and Augustine to Gadamer and Ricoeur and Derrida – are global simply because they are intellectually more sophisticated or more compelling. The global dominance of the West, the heritage of colonialism, and (by way of translation) the availability of European hermeneutical systems in English are indispensable conditions for the globality of the West's systems. Once this is admitted, alternative systems such as Mīmāṃsā can stand as a reminder and a rebuke to apparent globlisms that are more tribal than inclusive, easier rather than more substantive.

Notes

1 Jean-Marie Verpoorten, *Mīmāṃsā Literature* (Wiesbaden: Otto Harrassowitz, 1987), 1. See also Francis X. Clooney, *Thinking Ritually: Retrieving the Pūrva Mīmāṃsā of Jaimini* (Vienna: Institut für Indologie der Universität Wien, 1990); "Mīmāṃsā as Introspective Literature and as Philosophy," Springer Encyclopedia of Indian Religions. Springer Publishing: forthcoming; and "Reading into the Mīmāṃsā Tradition by Way of the *Jaminīya Nyāya Mālā*," under preparation.

2 Verses 13-24 in the Vistara. I have used throughout Mādhavācārya, *Jaiminīyanyāyamālāvistara or Pūrvamīmāṃsādhikaraṇamālā*. Edited by Pandit Sivadatta. Pune: Anandasrama Press, 1892. Translations are my own.

3 For a fuller version of this account of Mīmāṃsā literature, see Verpoorten, and my "Mīmāṃsā as Introspective Literature and as Philosophy."

4 The Garland is dependent on the Śāstradīpikā and intent upon finishing Pārthasārathi's work of distilling the Mīmāṃsā intellectual tradition back to a perfected version of the Sūtras. On Mādhava's further distillation of Pārthasārathi's work, see my "Reading into the Mīmāṃsā Tradition."

5 Mīmāṃsā has of course been studied by modern scholars, both in India and the West. Yet, too often it is noticed merely in terms of its possible contributions to philosophy on specific points of epistemology, theory of language, etc. It is too often quoted piecemeal for the sake of use within some other hermeneutic system, be it Western or Vedānta. One reason for this may be historical. The sometimes heated rhetoric of Mīmāṃsā and Vedānta on particular issues has often been misinterpreted so as to suggest that Mīmāṃsā is a mere ritualism superseded by Vedānta. In that situation, Mīmāṃsā has little chance of being taken seriously as a complete hermeneutical system. Only when it is more properly and integrally understood, will Mīmāṃsā be revealed as a quintessentially Indian and exceedingly subtle hermeneutical system. The Garland is one of the best texts enabling us to gain this overview and proper understanding.

6 For an alternative manner of introduction the pramāṇas as measures of authoritative knowledge, see Kṛṣṇa Yajvan, *Mīmāṃsā Paribhāṣa*. Translated and annotated by Swami Mādhavananda. Mayavati: Advaita Ashrama, 1987.

7 Jaimini's sūtras III.3.14 mentions *sthāna* (place) in fifth place, whereas the Garland refers rather to *krama* (order).

8 For a succinct and valuable explanation of the cases, see James Benson's translation of Mahadeva Vedāntin's *Mīmāṃsānyāyasamgraha: A Compendium of the Principles of Mīmāṃsā*. Wiesbaden: Harrassowitz Verlag, 2010, 414-417. While this is a later text, it is

most helpful, and my introduction to each set of verses is indebted to Mahādeva's – and Benson's – succinct summation of the cases.

9 The seat is *sadana*, and the arranging is *sādana*.

10 Its root form just indicates the cake; its strengthened form connected it by name to the cake rite.

11 The Garland does not propose any mythic telling of an authorless or eternal Veda. It simply puts it this way, in I.1 case 7, "Do Vedic statements have no authority or not? They have no authority, | Since there is a need for a specific connectedness (of words), because we rule out the notion of not needing it. || Regarding the Veda, like the world, no specific connectedness for the meaning of the statement | Can be grasped. Hence, the statement is authoritative, having no need. ||"

12 But the real test still lies in further such experiments, that is, in the further cases thought to apply the apparatus of the interlocking measures of authority. Here, for instance is the very next case, 13, appearing at III.3.15-16:

When it says, "Just three [offerings] at the sānha [one-day] rite, twelve at the [multiple-day] ahīna rite," | Should there be twelve [offerings] at the jyotiṣṭoma sacrifice or at the [group-of-days] ahargaṇa rite? || Due to context let it be the former; it being ahīna is not contradicted. | Rather, because of root meaning, it is not in any way hīna [lacking, hīna]. Then let it be optional. || Rather, the name "ahīna" is distinct from "sānha," so let ["ahīna"] be conventionally understood [as a name, ahīna] and applied to the ahargaṇa rite. | Because of the genitive case, the fact of "twelves" is to be taken away from its [jyotiṣṭoma] context. ||

On the kinds of rites, see Benson, 417. For Mādhava, what matters is assessing what the name (ahīna) means here, taken in a root (not-lacking) sense or conventional sense (the rite named "ahīna"), and which turns out to be the simplest explanation: taking ahīna conventionally as the name for a group of rites, and thus tantamount to the similarly signifying ahargaṇa rite. The reasoning is intense, and stated as minimally as possible – and followed by approximately another six hundred cases, between here and the end of the last adhyāya.

13 While this essay has narrowly focused on the Garland, there are numerous resources available for other approaches to the study of Mīmāṃsā in relation to hermeneutics. See for instance: Purusottama Bilimoria, "Authorless voice, tradition and authority in the Mīmāṃsā: reflections in cross-cultural hermeneutics" *Sambhasa* 16, 1995, 137-160; Francis X. Clooney, *Thinking Ritually: Retrieving the Pūrva Mīmāṃsā of Jaimini.* Vienna: Institut für Indologie der Universität Wien, 1990; "Why the Veda has No Author: Language as Ritual in Early Mīmāṃsā and Post-Modern Theology," *Journal of the American Academy of Religion* 55 (1987), 659-684; "Dharmamatra Karma: A Reevaluation of the Pūrva Mīmāṃsā SŪtras 2.1.9-12 with Śabara Bhasya," *Journal of Oriental Research* [Madras] (1989), 157-168; "What's a God? The Quest for the Right Understanding of devata in Brahmanical Ritual Theory (Mīmāṃsā,)" *International Journal of Hindu Studies* I.2 (1997) 337-385; "Pragmatism and Anti-Essentialism In the Construction of Dharma in Mīmāṃsā Sūtras 7.1.1-12," *Journal of Indian Philosophy* 32.5 (2004), 751-768; Francis X. D'Sa, *śabdaprāmāṇyam in śabara and Kumārila: towards a study of the Mīmāṃsā experience of language*. Vienna: Institut für Indologie der Universität Wien, 1980; Vincent Eltschinger, *Can the Veda speak?: Dharmakīrti against Mīmāṃṣā exegetics and Vedic authority: an annotated translation of PVSV 164,24-176,16.* Wien: Verlag der Österreichischen Akademie der Wissenschaften, 2012; Elisa Freschi, "Structuring the Chaos: Bhāṭṭa Mīmāṃsā Hermeneutics as Depicted in

Rāmānujācārya's 'śāstraprameyapariccheda:' Critical Edition and Annotated Translation of the Fourth Section." *East and West.*Vol. 58, No. 1/4 (December 2008), 157-184; Othmar Gächter, *Hermeneutics and language in Pūrva Mīmāṃsā: A Study in Śābara Bhāṣya.* Delhi: Motilal Banarsidass, 1983; Daya Krishna, "Mīmāṃsā before Jaimini: Some Problems in the Interpretation of *sruti* in the Indian Tradition," JICPR 9.3 (1992), 103-112; Daya Krishna, "Is the Doctrine of Arthavāda Compatible with the Idea of Śruti?" and "The Mīmāṃsāka vs. the Yājñika" in *Contrary Thinking: Selected Essays of Daya Krishna*, Edited by Nalini Bhushan, Jay L. Garfield, and Daniel Raveh.New York: Oxford University Press, 2011, respectively 219-227, and 228-244; Kunio Harikai, *The Hermeneutics of Classical India.The Study of Arthavāda and Mantra of the Mīmāṃsā School.* Kyoto 1990 (In Japanese); Kunio Harikai, "The Mīmāṃsā Interpretation of the Particle hi in the Brāhmaṇa Literature: Is Anumāṇa Possible in the Veda?" in *Expanding and Merging Horizons: Contributions to South Asian and Cross-Cultural Studies in Commemoration of Wilhelm Halbfass.* Karin Preisendanz, editor. (Beiträge zur Kultur- und Geistesgeschichte Asiens 53). Wien: Verlag der Österreichischen Akademie der Wissenschaften 2007; V. N. Jha, "Rules for interpretations of scriptural texts."*Philosophical Concepts Relevant to Sciences in Indian Tradition. History of Science Philosophy and Culture in Indian Civilization* III.5. Pranab Kumar Sen, Editor. New Delhi: Munshiram Manoharlal Publishers, 789-792.

14 Jacob Neusner, *Judaism as Philosophy: The Method and Message of the Mishnah.* Columbia: University of South Carolina Press, 1991, 55.

15 Ibid., 76.

16 I discuss more amply the illuminating parallels with Rabbinic reading and with the project of Wittgenstein's *Philosophical Investigations* in my "Reading into the Mīmāṃsā Tradition," though still in an introductory manner.

17 Maria McGinn, *Wittgenstein and the Philosophical Investigations.* New York: Routledge, 1997, 10.

18 Ibid., 13.

19 Ibid., 14.

20 We might also ask: Even if Mīmāṃsā makes sense as an indigenous Indian hermeneutics, why would it be of interest to Nigerians, for examples, or the Japanese? A good question, but note that we do not ordinarily ask this question about Gadamer or Ricoeur.

Chapter 11

The Dialectic of Non-dual Intuition of the Absolute
A Study of Śūnyatā of Nāgārjuna in Mūlamādhyamikakārikā

Stephen Chundamthadam
Jnana-Deepa Vidyapeeth, Pune

Nāgārjuna,[1] a philosopher, and Buddhist monk who lived in the second centaury[2] is well known for his famous work *Mūlamādhyamikakārikā*[3] (Fundamental Verses on the Middle Way) in which he gives a scholarly presentation of the topic *śūnyatā*. In propounding *śūnyavādā*, Nāgārjuna rejected the substantialist views of *dharma* upheld by the Buddhist *Abhidharma*[4] texts but accepted the teachings of the *Prajñāpāramitā*[5] (Perfection of Wisdom). The *Abhidharma* tradition, represented by *Sarvāstivāda*[6] School (asserting everything that exists) continued the early Buddhist practice of analysing and contemplating the *dharma,* the momentary factors and the arising and dissipation of existence. Nāgārjuna through the doctrine of *śūnyatā* argued that *abhidharma* tradition's teachings with regard to reality is not philosophically viable.

Nāgārjuna in his *Mūlamādhyamikakārikā* presented the concept of *śūnyatā* of *Prajñāpāramitās* in a logically convincing way. He elaborately dealt with the metaphysics, the path of liberation and religious teachings of the *Prajñāpāramitā* texts. He was of the opinion that the deepest spiritual experience is the recognition that all things are empty. Chandrakirti who was the prominent philosopher of *Prāsaṅgika* School of *Mādhyamika* says, "The holy master Nāgārjuna, having the method of *Prajñāpāramitā* as known without misconception, out of compassion in order to enlighten others composed the *Mūlamādhyamikakārikā.*"[7] Nāgārjuna in his philosophical discussions on *śūnyatā* responded to two of the prominent Buddhist traditions of his time i.e., the *Abhidhamma* and *Prajñāpāramitā* traditions. He reinterpreted the real intent of the teachings of the Buddha in a logically convincing manner.

The Term Śūnyatā and its Development

The term *śūnyatā* has various interpretations in Buddhist history. These interpretations made sense only within a particular religious context and any attempt to extract them from a particular religious context would cause a loss of their original meaning. The word '*śūnyatā*' is derived from the root '*svi,*' which means "to swell, to expand." 'Emptiness,' 'openness,' 'voidness,' 'non substantiality,' and 'relativity' are some of the other meanings attributed to *śūnyatā*. Following the teachings of *Prajñāpāramitāsūtras*, Nāgārjuna in *Mūlamādhyamikakārikā* repeatedly emphasised *śūnyatā* as the most distinctive feature of the whole of reality. Because nothing could be clearly said about reality, thinkers of his time used the term *śūnyatā* to refer to reality. Nāgārjuna says, "You do not know the purpose of *śūnyatā*; *śūnyatā* is not used for the sake of *śūnyatā*,"[8] but for guiding the mind to reality. The term *śūnyatā* is used in the *Nikāyas*[9] to show the impermanence of phenomena and lack of self. Through meditation or descriptive analysis monks tried to remove mental and emotional disturbances due to attachment to objects. In order to express non attachment as a requirement for liberation *Nikāyas* in the early stage used terms like 'empty,' 'impermanent' etc., but *Prajñāpāramitāsūtras* used *śūnyatā* to denote the same phenomena extending its scope to everything.[10] All *dhammas* are impermanent, all *dhammas* are without self, and all *dhammas* are emptiness. The centrality of the teachings of Buddha is emptiness, which was faithfully followed by the Abhidharma[11] school of Buddhism.

The Abhidharma School used the term *śūnyatā* with a different meaning. They claim that though entities like tables or any sentient beings appear to be real in their own right, in reality they are only conceptual constructs. "These conceptual constructs are empty of any ultimate significance, are ultimately valueless and are not worthy of attachment."[12] After the death of Buddha, as years passed by, his disciples and followers have developed erroneous views: things are causeless; they have false causes; they are annihilated, or are eternal. They could not understand the real intent of Buddha's teachings and started giving various interpretations merely based on the letters.[13] There was a need for clarity and appropriate interpretation of Buddha's ideas. Nāgārjuna, by reinterpreting the concept *śūnyatā* in *Mūlamādhyamikakārikā*, laid a strong philosophical foundation to the teachings of *Prajñāpāramitā* School.

Nāgārjuna and Mādhyamika School of Thought

The Mādhyamika School belongs to the Mahāyāna[14] tradition of Buddhism. Nāgārjuna himself and Aryadeva, his famous disciple, belong to the early period of Mādhyamikas in the history of Buddhism in India. Based on the central theme i.e., voidness (*śūnyatā*), Nāgārjuna developed the philosophy of the 'middle path' in terms of dependent origination (*pratityasamutpāda*), no self (*anātma-niṣvabhāva*) and voidness (*śūnyatā*). Though Nāgārjuna developed his philosophy as a critical response to the Theravada tradition of *Sarvāstivādins* and Abhidharma philosophers, his views were also critical response to the Indian realists such as Sāṅkhya and Vaiśeṣikā and the Indian school of logic,[15] Naiyayikas. His use of *prasaṅga* (*reductio ad absurdum*) is the application of reasoning (*tarka*) method found in *Nyāyasūtra.*[16] Nāgārjuna employed reasoning as a tool to reach the transcendental truth.

Empirical Truth and Transcendental Truth

Nāgārjuna in his *Mūlamādhyamikakārikā*, which is the best example of his highly developed philosophical thinking, argued that Buddha taught two truths, the truth of worldly convention (*loka saṃvṛti*), and the truth of ultimate reality (*paramārthataḥ*). Conventional reality merges into the ultimate reality. Nāgārjuna, by employing reason as the tool to deal with the conventional reality, was trying to give a solid philosophical foundation to the Buddha's teaching.

Though there were references to the problem of two truths in the *Āgamas* and *Nikāyas*, the distinction was not very clear. Texts like *Scripture on the Wisdom of the Benevolent King* and *The Scripture on Cessation,* in the *Prajñāpāramitā sutras* the term 'two truths' is mentioned.[17] It was Nāgārjuna, who for the first time, deeply reflected upon the two truths and formulated them as central philosophical doctrine. Nāgārjuna writes in *Mūlamādhyamikakārikā*, "The teaching of the *Dharma* by the various Buddhas is based on two truths; namely, the relative (worldly) truth and the absolute (supreme) truth."[18] The worldly truth and the absolute truth can be understood as experiences and ideas of the empirical world and of the transcendent world. Gadjin Nagao in his work, *The Foundational Standpoint of Madhyamika Philosophy* writes,

> The world of ordinary, everyday consciousness is here referred to as the worldly, which includes not only the biological world but also the human world of culture and society. The higher transcendent world is regarded as a religious, numinous world, and ultimate meaning is established as a negation of the everyday world, beyond it and transcendent to it.[19]

How are these two worlds interconnected? The higher truth is beyond the grasp of ordinary people. Such people are to be instructed in the level of lower truth with a view to guiding them through the higher truth i.e., *śūnyatā*. Following the example of his master the Buddha, Nāgārjuna out of compassion, adopted the technique of 'excellence in the choice of methods,' or 'skill in means' (*upāyakauśala*)[20] to instruct people of different levels of intellectual capability. Nāgārjuna writes in *Mūlamādhyamikakārikā*,

> A wrongly conceived śūnyatā can ruin a slow–witted person.
> It is like a badly seized snake or a wrongly executed incantation.
> Thus, the wise one (i.e., the Buddha) once resolved not to teach about the dharma thinking that the slow–witted might wrongly conceive it.[21]

Nāgārjuna was of the opinion that the slow–witted must be taught the lower truth because the higher truth is harmful to such people. However, if properly instructed the lower truth may lead a person to higher truth. Nāgārjuna's attempt was to articulate clearly the absolute truth with the support of the empirical truth. According to R D Gunaratne,

> He was not only demolishing saṃvṛti of the early Buddhist and establishing the paramārtha of the Mādhyamika, but was also incorporating the saṃvṛti in the paramārtha verses themselves. That is to say, he was making the Kārikā (Mūlamādhyamikakārikā) a 'living' embodiment or the practical example of the position, the paramārtha captures and incorporates the saṃvṛti.[22]

Though the focus of the *kārikā* is the transcendental truth, it incorporates the empirical truth. Empirical truth[23] is the starting point of Nāgārjuna's journey towards the transcendental truth. There is a progressive realization of the one to the other; it is a continuum culminating in the transcendental truth. So, both are not at the same level but at two different levels of reality. According to Richard King, "The distinction between two truths is semantic and not ontological… Nāgārjuna accepted the practical distinction between the two, but this is essentially pragmatic and should not be taken to be a 'real' distinction."[24] Semantic distinction between the two truths requires different tools to arrive at the final truth. Reason alone is incapable of reaching the final goal i.e., emptiness (*śūnyatā*) so he made use of the doctrine of dependent origination (*pratityasamutpāda*) for the journey towards the absolute truth.

Emptiness is a Qualified Term

Nāgārjuna uses emptiness always as a relational term; it is emptiness of something. He uses the term with adjectival implications. "Emptiness' is always the emptiness of something; or emptiness is always the predicate of something."[25] For Nāgārjuna the ultimate reality is emptiness (*śūnyatā*). Nāgārjuna does not make any general statement with regard to emptiness. He clearly wanted that emptiness is not something in general, but emptiness is always of something. Karika says,

> One should not say he is void or non-void, both or neither.
> But one may use terms for (such) designation.[26]

Nāgārjuna wanted to express ideas and concepts clearly and distinctly so he used designations. By stating things concretely, he was refuting or referring to things with the logical and rational backing. When he says, "All this is empty," and not "All is empty"[27] the term *this* is used with a special meaning to avoid generalization. "All this is empty" is not the same as saying "All is empty." Nowhere in *Kārikā* have we come across a statement like "All is empty." However, it is worth noting that even when Nāgārjuna makes such a universalized statement, he retains 'this' in order to eliminate the absolutist claim.

When a Mādhyamika philosopher makes a statement, 'table is empty,' the spontaneous question would be "empty of what? The answer is "empty of inherent existence, or self nature, or, in the *essence*."[28] The assertion that the table is empty means to say that it lacks essence. When we say that a table lacks essence, it does not mean that the table is non-existent. The existence of the table as it is depends on the perceiver and his pre-understanding, which he inherited from his culture and society.[29] That means if furniture like table had not evolved in our culture, it would have been described as merely five objects: four quite useful sticks and a slab of stick wood. It says that the table depends for its existence on its parts, on its causes, on its material and so forth. Apart from these, there is no table. So, we can say that the table is an object of space and time chosen by us as the referent of a single name. It is not an entity existing on its own. That independent character is precisely what it lacks. That is why it is empty, relative, and dependent.

Beings are without self-nature, beings and entities exist based on dependent co-arising. From a phenomenal point of view, beings and entities are relatively real but absolutely unreal. Therefore, reality is emptiness. Emptiness does not depend on philosophical conception. "Emptiness is the exhaustion of all philosophical views."[30]

Dialectic as a Critique of Reason

Dialectic is a technique used in refuting any of the doctrines. In Western Philosophy, Zeno is considered the first one, who made use of dialectic.[31] T. R. V. Murti is of the opinion that Buddha was the first philosopher in India to discover the dialectic. Buddha refused to answer certain metaphysical questions such as whether or not the world has a beginning or an end in time and whether or not someone exists after death. Murti argues that Buddha did not answer these questions because he knew that they could not be answered at all. Thus, Buddha's expression was his critique of his reason, which trades always in opposites. Thereby Buddha's silence was the first Buddhist use of dialectic.[32]

According to T. R. V. Murti,

> Dialectic is self-conscious spiritual movement; it is necessarily a critique of reason. This is not possible without the consciousness of the opposition of the thesis and the anti thesis. There must be at least two viewpoints or patterns of interpretations diametrically opposed to each other. A dilemma is not a critic, for that is a temporary predicament having reference to a particular situation. The dialectic is a universal conflict affecting every sphere of things.[33]

Though it is not so common in science,[34] dialectic is extensively used in philosophy. Philosophy identifies a pattern or a concept with a view to universalizing it. Once universalized it becomes an idea of reason.[35] In philosophy, sense experience supported by reason is necessary to prove or to disprove a hypothesis then the hypothesis can be made a universal idea. Therefore, our conclusion is this: dialectic, which trades reason in opposites, is implicit in philosophy. Moreover, Nāgārjuna makes use of this dialectic to lead human beings to *śūnyatā*.

Nāgārjuna's Dialectic

Nāgārjuna makes use of dialectic as a tool to reach the final goal. Murti understands Nāgārjuna's dialectic as "a movement from the relativity of buddhi (intellect) which is phenomenal to the non dual intuition of the absolute, from *dṛṣṭi* (dogmatism) to *prajnā* (intuitive knowledge of the absolute)."[36] Nāgārjuna's dialectic tries to remove the conflict inherent in reason by rejecting both the opposites taken singly or in combination. Nāgārjuna is convinced that the conjunctive or the disjunctive synthesis of the opposites is but another view. Reason or intuition can be effectively used only when there is no independent or self-existing principle (MMK 24.14). Therefore, Nāgārjuna's rejection of all views is the rejection of the competence of reason to comprehend reality. Moreover, the rejection is not based on any positive grounds or the acceptance of another view. It is solely based on the inner contradiction implicit in each view.

According to Murti:

The dialectic is a passage, a movement, from concept to concept; it is at once creative of newer, more comprehensive, and higher concepts. It is a negative and a positive function of Reason. It presses each concept (e.g. Being), squeezes out all its implications, as it were; and at this stage it becomes indistinguishable from its very opposite (Non-Being). But through this negation there arises a new concept. And as this concept has been engendered by its opposite, it is richer in content, and includes the previous one. Negation is not total annulment but comprehension without abstraction.[37]

Nāgārjuna heavily depends on reason in his progress towards the absolute, and at the end, he even despises reason. Nāgārjuna adopted the methods of formal reasoning from the *Tirthikas* and utilized them to expound *dharma*. In the *Kārikas*the three 'laws of thought' of western logic are not denied. Furthermore, two of them are explicitly affirmed. The principle of contradiction is the most effectively used argument by Nāgārjuna since he relies heavily on dichotomies. This principle is expressed in two places:

> Therefore cessation of a real existing entity is not possible;
> And certainly both an existing entity and a non-existing entity cannot be possible in the same case.[38] (trans. F. Streng, Eptiness, 1967 p. 192)
> And a real-nonreal producer does not produce in a real-nonreal manner.
> For, indeed, how can "real" and "non-real," which are mutually contradictory, occur in one place?[39] (trans. F. Streng, Eptiness, 1967 p. 193)

The law of Excluded middle also is used clearly in some places:

> A goer does not go, a non-goer does not go; what third one
> other than goer and non goer goes?[40] (trans. Kenneth K. Inada, *Nagarjuna*, 1970)
> A goer does not stand still, and a non-goer does not stand still;
> what third one other than goer and non goer stands still?[41] (trans. Kenneth K. Inada, *Nagarjuna*, 1970)

With regard to the third law of identity, it remains neither affirmed nor denied by Nāgārjuna. Nonetheless, unity and multiplicity are mentioned in a non-logical sense in many places:

> Others do not occur in an other and does not occur in a non-other;
> and when otherness does not occur, there is neither an other nor an identity.[42] (trans. Kenneth K. Inada, *Nagarjuna*, 1970)

Nāgārjuna made use of the tetralemma (*catuṣkoṭi*) which was prevalent in the Buddhist tradition before him.Tetralemmas are the best examples of the use of reason and it is clear reference to the use of three laws of thought in Nāgārjuna's philosophy.

Language and Meaning

Some of the schools of Indian thought accepted correspondence between words and objects as the basis of meaning. If words do not correspond to objects, they are unreliable and false. They are reliable and true, if they correspond to the objects. In Indian philosophy, there are two different views with regard to the nature of objects to which words refer. The Nyāya School holds the view that a word refers to an individual, the class residing in the individual and its configuration or form. The Mimamsa School argues that a word refers to a genus and only indirectly to a particular. Still, they all hold the referential theory of meaning which claims that the meaning of a word is the extra-linguistic object for which it stands. A word is meaningful only if it stands for an object, and words that stand for the same object having the same meaning.

Nāgārjuna's emptiness is aimed at refuting the popular theory of meaning. To Nāgārjuna, "words and names are unreal or empty; no word has a meaning by itself. The meaning of a term is not the same as the object for which the term stands, but is dependent upon conditions and circumstances."[43] It means to say that if the conditions were different, the meaning of the word would be different and would even vanish. From the standpoint of the worldly truth, where words seem to denote certain objects, there seems to be a 'man' and a 'place or state,'*nirvana*. Therefore, the contention is clear: meaning of a term is dependent upon the conditions or circumstances. So, if the context or condition changes, the meaning of the word changes. Then language is a mere instrument or tool. Nāgārjuna claims that metaphysical systems are simply fabrications based on a misconceived notion about the role of language in relation to the world.[44]

According to the teaching of Nāgārjuna on emptiness, it is wrong to hold the referential theory of meaning. Moreover, it is wrong to have the contextual view of meaning also.[45] His analysis does not aim at showing that the meaning of the words is derived from the "relationship which one linguistic unit has with other linguistic units." Nevertheless, it shows that no legitimate relationship between linguistic units can be established intelligently. "Our language, according to Nāgārjuna, appears to have its 'legitimate' or 'right' use or function when it is seen from the conventional point of view." From the conventional point of view, the agent for give and take is the 'reason.' "But if we really examine the nature of its ordinary use and function, we will find that it involves contradiction or absurdity."[46] If that is the case, there is no sense in defining the meaning of a word as its 'use.'

Nāgārjuna is not against reason. He is indeed committed to the laws of rational argument and criticism. He never suggests any mystical ways to reach the final stage i.e. emptiness. He is of the opinion that rational arguments can help one to abandon error and to acquire right knowledge. The conventional world, according to Nāgārjuna is completely riddled with contradictions. Our pre-theoretical and pre-philosophical conceptions of the world and reality are full of contradictions and incoherence. Nāgārjuna believed that it is the task of *Mūlamādhyamikakārikā* to present them coherent with a view to helping people to reach the final goal.

Skillful Means and Wisdom

Nāgārjuna's aim of writing *Kārikā* was with a desire to guide people to liberation through skilful means and wisdom, not to explain or describe reality. Buddhist doctrine on wisdom is abundant, but always includes skilful means. "The attainment of Buddhahood must come about as a combination of these two inseparable elements. If at the stage of attainment we differentiate the Dharma body of ultimate meaning from the perceptible form body of worldly convention, wisdom belongs to the realm of ultimate meaning and skilful means to worldly convention."[47] The royal road, the great path from practice to attainment, progresses from worldly convention to ultimate meaning. Therefore, it is this path which helps the human beings to realize Buddhahood. The progression from practice to attainment is an entirely human endeavour; it is merely a worldly convention.

Role of Reason in *Mūlamādhyamikakārikā*

Nāgārjuna makes use of reason extensively in explaining conventional reality and so he did not negate the role of reason. In chapters 1 –24 of MMK, with the help of reason he analyses different concepts with a view to explaining the ultimate reality. In fact, what Nāgārjuna attempts to do is to clear away the metaphysical problem of reality as conceptual confusions. The ultimate role of reason, according to Nāgārjuna is to find out that every entity or phenomena is dependently originating. If everything is dependently originating, then everything is empty. He uses the term *paśyati,* which means 'perceives'[48] several times in the *Kārikā*. Nāgārjuna claims, "not to perceive (*na paśyati*) is self nature or substance (*svabhāva*) or permanent existence (*bhāva, astitva*). What he claims to perceive (*paśyati*) is dependently arisen phenomena as well as dependent arising."[49] Such perceptions are not the results of a special intuition but they are the results of the absence of ignorance created by one's dispositions. In MMK Nāgārjuna writes:

> Whatever is dependently co-arisen
> That is explained to be emptiness.

That, being a dependent designation
Is itself the middle way.
Something that is not dependently arisen,
Such a thing does not exist.
Therefore a non empty thing
Does not exist.[50]

Once we understand that things are dependently originating, the next step we get to know is that the dependently arising is emptiness. "To say of something that it is dependently co arisen is to say that it is empty. To say of something that it is empty is another way of saying that it is arisen dependently."[51] Reason ultimately has to leadto this state.

If things are dependently arising, then how do the dependently arisen things get identity? The identity of any dependently arisen thing depends upon verbal conventions. To say of a thing that it is dependently arisen is to say that it is nothing more than being the referent of a word. That means a thing is a tangible part of the infinite spatiotemporal causal relationship."To say of a thing that its identity is a merely verbal fact about it is to say that it is empty. To view emptiness in this way is to see it neither as entity nor as unreal – it is to see it as conventionally real."[52]

Conclusion

Nāgārjuna was faithful to the compassionate master in expounding the concept of *śūnyatā*. "Emptiness is proclaimed by the victorious one as the refutation of all viewpoints; But those who hold 'emptiness' as a viewpoint have called these incurable." MMK13.8. Nāgārjuna, in *Mūlamādhyamikakārikā* attempted to give a philosophical explanation to the concept emptiness, which his master refused to do. Emptiness cannot be understood with the help of reason alone. The role of reason is twofold i.e., to reveal that things are dependently co-arising and in that process to show the path to the ultimate reality. Reason is very much operative in the conventional realm and its primary duty is to reveal that things are dependently co-arising including the four noble truths. "Whoever perceives dependent arising also perceives suffering, its arising, its ceasing, and the path (leading to its ceasing)." (MMK 24.40) Nāgārjuna, in *Mūlamādhyamikakārikā* argues that logically consistent argument could lead one to the abandonment of error and to knowledge. Though the conventional truth does not have any bearing in the transcendental realm, the absolute truth is not possible without the conventional truth.

For Nāgārjuna *śūnyatā* is a creative tool in discovering new and creative frontiers for philosophy. As far as *śūnyatā* is concerned, Nāgārjuna's was not a blind leap into the unknown but he faithfully followed the *Prajñāpāramitā* line of thinking. *Śūnyatā*, according to Mādhyamika philosophical discourse receives a distinctive meaning in the Buddhist thought as it is substantiated in *Mūlamādhyamikakārikā*. Unlike other thinkers of his time, Nāgārjuna realized that the problems related to the absolute truth could not be solved by intellectual reasoning alone but it required an intuitive approach. In this attempt instead of offering a new solution to the problems in philosophy, he made a radical critique of the existing philosophical systems. He redefined the limitations of language in revealing the ultimate reality *i.e., śūnyatā*. In this attempt he presented *śūnyatā* as dependent co-arising as a solution to the problem of extremes.It is true that he laid a solid foundation to the concept of *śūnyatā* but he had to take resort to intuition. Intuition has its field of activity in the transcendental realm. Therefore, we have to accept that Nāgārjuna's attempt to give a philosophical foundation to *śūnyatā*, when approached from the perspective of the absolute is yet to be made logically convincing.

Notes

1 Nāgārjuna (2nd century C E), according to tradition was born in South India and received brahminical education in religious and secular subjects. Later in the Himalayas, he mastered *Tripiṭaka* and obtained *Mahāyāna Sutras, Vaipulya Sutras,* etc. He propounded the doctrine of emptiness (*śūnyatā*) and is traditionally regarded as the founder of the *Mādhyamika* ("Middle Way") school, an important tradition of *Mahāyāna* Buddhist philosophy.

2 There are different opinions about the time of Nāgārjuna, especially that of Chinese. Fa – hua – chuan – chi says Nāgārjuna lived at the end of the fifth century CE. Another Chinese author Hui – Yuan is of the opinion that Nāgārjuna lived in the ninth century CE. Although, there are different opinions, we accept the account given by Kumārajīva who claims that Nāgārjuna is believed to have lived between 150 – 250 CE. For further details, refer T.R.V. Murti, *The Central Philosophy of Buddhism* (London: George Allen and Unwin, 1955), 83, 91-93.

3 Murti attributes the authorship of five more books to Nāgārjuna other than *Mūlamādhyamikakārikā*. They are *Śūnyatā–saptati, Yukti – ṣaṣṭika, Vigrahavyavartinī, Vaidalya – sūtraprakaraṇa*, and *Vyavahāra – siddhi*. Other texts attributed to Nāgārjuna are *Ratnāvali, Catuḥ – stava, Pratītya – samutpāda – hṛdaya, Mahāyāna – viṃsaka, Bhāva – samkrānti – śāstra, Prajñā – daṇda*, and *Suhṛllekha*. There is no common agreement among the scholars regarding the authenticity of this attribution. Based on the content and style of these works we can arrive at the conclusion that these works are from the same author. The authorship of *Mūlamādhyamikakārikā* is accepted by all. Murti, *The Central Philosophy of Buddhism*, 88-91.

4 *Abhidharmapiṭaka* is the title given to the third collection of the Buddhist canonical books. Both historically and logically, *Abhidharmma* represents the Dharma. Traditionally it is mentioned after the *Vinaya* and *Sutta Piṭaka.*

5 *Prajñāpāramitās* are the earliest of the *Mahāyāna* literature dated around 100 BCE.

6 *Sarvāstivāda* School of Buddhism argues that the world is composed of 75 *dharmas*, which exist throughout the three periods of time, i.e., past, present and future. Nāgārjuna's *śūnyavādā* was a reaction to this proposal. See *The Encyclopedia of Religions*, s.v. "Nāgārjuna."

7 Richard H. Robinson, *Early Mādhyamika in India and China* (Madison: The University of Wisconsin, 1967), 62.

8 Herschel K.J, "Nāgārjuna's Philosophy," *The Living Word* (January-February 1987): 31.

9 *Nikāyas* is a term used to refer to the collection of Buddhist scriptures. The origin of this literature goes back to the second century after the death of Buddha. It appears in *Dīgha Nikāya, Majjhima Nikāya,* etc.

10 *The Encyclopedia of Religions*, s.v. "*Śūnyam* and *Śūnyatā.*"

11 *Abhidharmika* text is believed to have been composed about 300 BCE.

12 *Routledge Encyclopedia of Philosophy*, 1998, s.v. "Buddhist Concept of Emptiness."

13 Robinson, *Early Mādhyamikain India and China*, 66.

14 *Mādhyamika* literally means 'the middle way,' which comes in the Mahāyāna Buddhism. The Mahāyāna tradition does not identify Buddha with a historical person. Therefore, when Mahāyāna Buddhists or Mādhyamikas refer to Buddha, it means a symbolic representation of the ultimate reality *Dharma kāya.*

15 The history of Indian Logic can be divided into ancient, medieval, and modern periods. Akṣapāda Gautama who wrote *Nyāyasūtras* was the prominent figure in the Ancient period (650 BCE – 100 CE). Dignāga who wrote *Pramāṇasamuccaya* heads the medieval period. Gaṅgeśa's *Tattva Cintṇāmaṇi* is the most important work in the modern period beginning from 900 CE. A number of commentaries were written on these important works. Nāgārjuna's *Vigrahavyāvartini* is a response to the challenges posed by Naiyayikas, the major pillar of Indian logic. *Encyclopedia of Indian Heritage*, 2002, s.v. "Indian Logic."

16 *Routledge Encyclopediaof Philosophy*, 1998, s.v. "Buddhism, Mādhyamika: India and Tibet."

17 In the early commentaries also like *Extensive Abhidharma Commentary* and later *Treatise on the Perfection of Truth,* these two truths are discussed.

18 *dve satye samupāśritya buddhānām dharmadeśanā /*

lokasaṃvṛtisatyaṃ ca satyaṃ ca paramārthataḥ //

Kenneth K. Inada, *Nāgārjuna: A Translation of his Mulamādhyamikakarika with an Introductory Essay* (Tokyo: The Hokseido Press, 1970), 24: 8. Hereafter we shall refer to this classical text as MMK.

19 Gadjin Nagao, *The Foundational Standpoint of Mādhyamika Philosophy* (New York: State University Press of New York, 1989), 23.

20 L. Stafford Betty, "Nāgārjuna's Masterpiece – Logical, Mystical, Both or Neither?"*Philosophy East and West*, vol. 33, no. 2 (April 1983).

21 *Vināśayati durdṛṣta śūnyatā mandamedhasaṃ /*

Sarpo yathā durgṛhito vidyā va duṣprsādhitā //

Ataśca pratyudāvṛttaṃ cittaṃ deśayituṃ muneḥ /

Dharmaṃ matvāsya dharmasya mandairduravagāhatāṃ //MMK 24: 11-12.

22 R D. Gunaratne, "Understanding Nāgārjuna's Catuṣkoṭi" *Philosophy East and West*, vol. 36, no. 3 (July 1986): 231.

23 *vyavahāramanāsritya paramārtho na deśyate /*
paramārthamanāgamya nirvāṇaṃ nādhigamyate // MMK 24: 10.

24 Richard King, "Śūnyatā And Ajāti: Absolutism and The Philosophies of Nāgārjuna and Gaudapada" *Journal of Indian Philosophy*, vol. 17, no. 4, (December 1989).

25 Frederic J. Streng, *Emptiness in Religious Meaning* (Nashville:Abingdon Press, 1967), 59.

26 *Śūnyamiti na vaktavyama śūnyamiti va bhavet /*

Ubhayaṃ nobhayaṃ ceti prajnñaptyarthaṃ tu kathyate // *MMK*: 22:11.

27 David J. Kalupahana, *Nāgārjuna: The Philosophy of The Middle Way* (Albany: State University Press of New York, 1986), 86.

28 Jay L. Garfield, "Dependent Arising and Emptiness of Emptiness: Why Did Nāgārjuna Start with Causation" *Philosophy East and West*, vol. 44, no. 2 (April 1994): 220.

29 Ibid., 220.

30 Chadrakirti, *Prasannapāda*, vs. 248-49.

31 Zeno invented irrefutable arguments against motion, change, and the void. At that point, it meant that he was fully aware of the implications and absurdities of 'becoming.' In the *Parmenides* of Plato, we find the systematic beginnings of the dialectic. There Plato exposes the contradictions involved in the notions of 'one' and 'many,' 'being' and 'becoming.' However, there is no attempt to go beyond these opposites.

32 Richard P. Hayes, "Nāgārjuna's Appeal," *Journal of Indian Philosophy*, vol. 22, no. 4 (December 1994).

33 Murti, *The Central Philosophyof Buddhism*, 124.

34 In science when there are conflicting hypotheses, they can be settled by an appeal to sense experience. Science is experimentation with things presented to us by sense.

35 Murti, *The Central Philosophyof Buddhism*, 125.

36 For Nāgārjuna absolute is the non dual intuition (*Prajñāpāramitā*) The term 'absolute' is used here the way Murti has used in his work *The Central Philosophy of Buddhism*, 301.

37 Murti, *The Central Philosophy of Buddhism of Buddhism*, 127-28.

38 *sataśca tāvadbhāvasya nirodho nopapadyate /*

ekatve na hi bhāvaśca nābhāvaścopapadyate // MMK: 7: 30.

39 *Kārakaḥ sadasadbhūtaḥ sadasatkurute na tat /*

Parasparavirudhaṃ hi saccāsaccaikataḥ kutaḥ // MMK: 8:7.

40 *Gantā na gacchati tavadagantā naiva gacchati /*

Anyo ganturagantuśca kastṛtīyo hi gacchati // MMK: 2:8.

41 *Gantā na tiṣṭhati tāvadagantā naiva tiṣṭhati /*

Anyo ganturagantuśca kastṛtīyo tha tiṣṭhati // MMK: 2:15.

42 *Nanayasmin vidyate nyatvamananyasmin na vidyate /*

Avidyāmane cānyatve nāstyanyadvā tadeva vā // MMK: 14:7.

43 Hsueh-hi Cheng, "Nāgārjuna, Kant and Wittgenstein: The San-Lun Mādhyamika Exposition of Emptiness" *Religious Studies* vol. 17 (1981).

44 Wittgenstein in the Western Philosophical tradition was of the opinion that looking for the meaning of a word is not the same as looking for an object or a non-lingual referent. The meaning of the word lies in the context. For him metaphysical systems are only fabrications.

45 According to Wittgenstein, the contextual view of meaning is right, not the referential view. For him the meaning of a word is in its use in the language. Wittgenstein claimed, "don't ask for the meaning, ask for the use." For him philosophy should not be the

explanation and description of the actual phenomena, but ought to be the description of the actual phenomena of language.

46 Cheng, "Nāgārjuna, Kantand Wittgenstein," 82.

47 Nagao, *The Foundational Standpoint of Mādhyamika Philosophy*, 24.

48 Nāgārjuna uses the term more or less in the same sense as Buddha used it in the "*Discourse to Katyayana.*"

49 Kalupahana, *Nāgārjuna*, 82.

50 *Yah pratītyasamutpāda śūnyatāṃ tāṃ pracakṣmahe /*
Sā prajñaptirupādāya pratipatsaiva madhyamā //
Apratītya samutpanno dharmaḥ kaścinna vidyate /
Yasmāttasmādaśūnyo hi dharmaḥ kaścinna vidyate // MMK: 28: 18-19.

51 Garfield, "Dependent Arising and Emptiness of Emptiness," 229.

52 Ibid.

Chapter 12

The Liberative Hermeneutics of Dr. Ambedkar

Noel Sheth
Professor Emeritus, Jnana-Deepa Vidyapeeth, Pune

There are two forms of Buddhism: Hīnayāna, of which only the Theravāda school is living, and Mahāyāna, in which there are many schools existing. The original texts of Theravāda are in Pāli, while the original Mahāyāna texts in India were in Sanskrit.

Although the Theravāda canon came to be more or less closed by the fifth century CE, the Mahāyāna canon remained open for a much longer time. Mahāyānists believed in the principle that whatever is well-spoken (*subhāṣita*) is uttered by the Buddha (*Buddhabhāṣita*).[1] Christianity also has a similar dictum, viz., *Omne verum, a quocumque dicatur*, *a Spiritu sancto est* ("Whatever is true, by whomsoever it may be uttered, is from the Holy Spirit").[2] But, unlike Christianity, Mahāyāna took whatever was well-spoken to have scriptural value. Hence, it did not arrive at the conclusion that revelation was final and complete: Scripture itself could progress and evolve in accordance with the needs of the time.

While the Mahāsaṅghikas (a now extinct Buddhist group) were for the literal meaning of the Scriptures, thus considering interpretation unnecessary, the Mahāyānists believed that truth was beyond letters. Theravāda took an intermediary position, recognizing the need for interpretation. According to the Theravādins, we must endeavour to understand the Buddha's discourses (*suttas*) in the right way while interpreting them according to the letter or suggestion (*vyañjana*). It is necessary to conform to both the letter (*attha*) and the spirit (*dhamma*).[3] The *Nettippakaraṇa* and *Peṭakopadesa* present the Theravāda method and principles of exegesis. All interpretations must agree with the established tradition: it is not just *sola scriptura*.

It is in Mahāyāna, however, that there was an increased tendency to emphasize the eternal truth (*dharma*) rather than the literal content of the Buddha's message (*buddhavacana*). The Buddha tells Mahāmati not to be attached to the words of the canonical texts, for truth is beyond letters. The texts sometimes deviate from their straightforward course in order to adapt themselves to the understanding and varied dispositions of people. Hence, one should conform to the meaning and not to the letter.[4] Those who are attached to the letter do not know the truth; in their ignorance, they grasp the fingertip that points to the moon: they cling to the words, which are only the fingertip pointing to the reality (*tattva*).[5] The emphasis was on direct experience and freedom from words. In the sixth century CE, the Chinese developed the eschatological theory of the "Latter Age of the *Dharma*" (*mo-fa*; Japanese *mappō*). This theory led to the idea of reinterpreting Scripture in terms of the changing circumstances, paying more attention to the needs of the times than to the intention of the original author or compiler.[6] This was indeed a remarkable anticipation of the hermeneutics of our day – mind you, this was as early as the 6th century CE.

Not being interested in historical criticism, the Buddhists do not distinguish much between the teaching of the Buddha and that of his disciples, both of which are enshrined in Scripture. Yet, paradoxically, precisely because they are less interested in history, they are freer to make history in accordance with the signs of the times: they are less bound by a historically conditioned Norm of the past.

A literal, fundamentalist interpretation leads one to reject other understandings and Scriptures, and thus fosters fundamentalism. Even the more conservative Theravāda does not stick merely to a literal interpretation. Mahāyāna goes further and relativizes the importance and significance of Scripture. There is a greater realization of the cultural limitations and incompleteness of Scripture, so much so that the canon itself remained somewhat open, not fixed for all time. Such an attitude also frees oneself from the compulsion of somehow extracting a solution from Scripture for every modern problem that confronts us. Scripture, then, is not such a rigid Norm for Buddhism as it has been for the Semitic religions. The Buddhist, therefore, can be less dogmatic, and more tolerant towards other Scriptures and traditions.

However, one should not conclude that the Buddha and the Buddhist Scripture have no authority. Many a time both the *Dharma* (the religion) and the Buddha are extolled, and an appeal is made to their authority. In fact, the norm for accepting or rejecting a doctrine or practice is to see whether it conforms or not with the *suttas* (doctrine) and the *vinaya* (rules of the Order) set forth in

Scripture.[7] The true *Dharma* is beyond the range of reason and must be learnt from the Buddha (*Tathāgata*).[8] The tradition of religious disputations (*rtags-gsal*), which now survives in Tibetan Buddhism, has become a stereotyped discussion conducted entirely with quotations from canonical works,[9] thus showing again the importance given to the canonical texts. Still, in the light of what has been said above, the Buddha and the Scriptures are not accorded the same type of authority, as is the case in the Semitic religions.[10]

The Background of Dr. Ambedkar

Some may not agree fully with the novelist Anaïs Nin's statement, namely, "We do not see things as they are, we see them as we are."[11] Still there is more than a grain of truth in this assertion, since our perspectives and views tend to be influenced by our background. In Hermeneutics, this constitutes our horizon. I shall therefore first outline the social background of Ambedkar that made him see the Hindu and the Buddhist Theravāda Scriptures from a particular perspective.

Dr. Bhimrao Ramji Ambedkar was born in 1891 as a Mahar, traditionally an outcaste Hindu group, but he passed away in 1956 as a Buddhist. As a child, Ambedkar experienced many humiliations of the rigid caste system: he was thrashed for drinking water from a public water source, the village barber refused to cut his hair, and in school the teachers did not want to be polluted by coming in contact with his notebooks or his person, so that water was poured into his mouth without touching him.[12] In spite of all odds, Ambedkar rose to become a highly accomplished person, earning a doctorate from Columbia University, New York, and another doctorate from the University of London. Later in his life, he started and edited newspapers, founded and taught in colleges, and held high offices. Yet he was frequently subjected to ill-treatment by caste Hindus: he was evicted from his rented house, beaten up and received death threats. He realized that the only way for low-castes and outcastes to better their lot was a mass movement of social revolution.[13]

Ambedkar emphasized that, according to the Buddha, "worth and not birth was the measure of man."[14] He launched a scathing attack against the caste system that dehumanized the low castes and especially the outcastes, who were called untouchables.[15] Ambedkar strongly disagreed with Gandhi on the subject of class and caste.[16] Although he felt that inter-caste marriage was an effective way of abolishing caste, he thought that this would not take place unless the authority of the Hindu sacred texts is itself questioned and denied for it was these sacred texts that taught the caste system.[17] He wanted that the so-called untouchables be treated with equal human dignity as anyone else. He led various types of mass marches to gain access to drinking water from wells that were prohibited to untouchables, and to gain entry into temples that were out of bounds to them. He held mass meetings to conscientize the untouchables, started and edited newspapers to promote their cause and founded colleges for their education. He even founded a political party.[18] When he became a Theravāda Buddhist in 1956, in a period of thirty-six hours half a million people had converted to Buddhism under his leadership.[19]

Ambedkar's Interpretation of a Ṛgvedic Hymn

One of the basic requirements for authentic textual hermeneutics is that one should know the language of the text very well. Ambedkar acknowledges that he does not have mastery over the Sanskrit language, even though he is interpreting Sanskrit texts of the Hindu Scriptures. However, he feels that, after spending fifteen years in studying the texts in English, he has some degree of competence to deal with the subject of caste. In hermeneutical terms, on the one hand, there is some distanciation of the original Sanskrit texts, which acquire semantic autonomy from the original composers or authors and the culture of those times; and, on the other hand, there is a distance between the present-day reader and the ancient Sanskrit texts, but Ambedkar feels that he can bridge the distance and put himself into the world of these texts to some extent at least, so that some fusion of horizons results. Still, he adds, "It may well turn out that this attempt of mine is only an illustration of the proverbial fool rushing in where angels fear to tread. But I take refuge in the belief that even the fool has a duty to perform, namely, to do his bit if the angel has gone to sleep or is unwilling to proclaim the truth."[20] He feels very strongly about the unjust oppression of the lower castes and outcastes and so he gives a clarion call for their liberation, particularly because the "angels," i.e., the upper castes, do not speak up.

Ambedkar deals with the topic of caste in three different volumes, so he literally speaks volumes about it. For our purposes, however, I shall merely outline his critical interpretation of the well-known hymn of the *Ṛg-veda* (10.90) called the *Puruṣa-sūkta* (the Hymn of the Cosmic Person), which deals with cosmogony through the Cosmic Person's self-sacrifice. Ambedkar pays particular attention to verses 11 and 12 which state that the Brahmins (the priestly class, who are on the highest rung of the ladder of the caste system) sprang from the Cosmic Person's mouth, the (lower) Kṣatriyas[21] (the warrior class) originated from his arms, the (still lower) Vaiśyas (or business class) from his thighs, and the (lowest) Śūdras (or menials) sprang from his feet. Ambedkar maintains that the hymn makes the existing hierarchical gradation of the classes, i.e., an actual, existential situation, into a law, a *de jure* case, of an ideal society. Although class discrimination actually exists in many societies, no other society in the world has made it a sacrosanct, unchangeable creed of "an ascending scale of reverence and a descending scale of contempt."[22] The hymn mentions the origin of animals from the Cosmic Person but, then, instead of moving on to the generation of human beings, it straightway launches into the origin of the classes. Furthermore, no other part of the *Ṛg-veda* speaks of the origin of the classes; all origins of human beings in other parts of the *Ṛg-veda* do not make any gradation among human beings. In some other passages, the *Ṛg-veda* mentions different occupations to earn one's livelihood, e.g., in *Ṛg-veda* 1.113.6. However, unlike these other passages which refer to a categorization of different types of work, the *Puruṣa-sūkta* alters the system of classification of *work* into a rigid and unchangeable system of unequal *workers* who cannot change their occupation.[23] The *Puruṣa-sūkta* could very well have asserted that all the four classes originated from the different mouths of the Cosmic Person, since the Cosmic Person has a thousand heads (10.90.1); in this way, all the classes would have been equal. Moreover, according to Ambedkar, such a manner of origination would have been known to the composer of the *Puruṣa-sūkta* since it is found in the *Viṣṇu-purāṇa* which describes the production of the four Vedas from the four mouths of the god Brahmā (*Viṣṇu-purāṇa* 1.5.54-57). Instead, however, the *Puruṣa-sūkta* chose to bring in a hierarchy, pointing out that the Śūdras emanated from the feet, the lowliest, and the most despicable part of the human body.[24]

Ambedkar points out that the elsewhere in the *Ṛg-veda* only three classes are found, without any mention of the Śūdras. Moreover, *Śatapatha-brāhmaṇa* (2.1.4.11) and the *Taittirīya-brāhmaṇa* (3.12.9.2) describe the generation of only three classes, and not the Śūdras. Therefore, Ambedkar concludes that the mention of four classes by the *Puruṣa-sūkta* clearly indicates that it is later than the other hymns and later than these two Brāhmaṇa texts.[25] A further confirmation of this is that, according to scholars, the language of the *Puruṣa-sūkta* is much later than the rest of the *Ṛg-veda*. He also proposes additional arguments to show that the hymn is a later interpolation, later even than parts of the *Śatapatha* and the *Taittirīya Brāhmaṇas*. Moreover, Ambedkar draws our attention to the fact that, whereas the rest of the hymn is in a narrative form, verses 11 and 12, on the contrary, do not have a narrative structure but have a form of a question and answer (What was his mouth? What arms had he? What are said to have been his thighs and feet? The Brahmin was his mouth [and so forth]). This question and answer style disrupts the narrative form. The reason is that the author of the hymn wanted to insert a new topic and that, too, in an emphatic manner. Hence, not only is the hymn a later addition, but these verses 11 and 12 are much later even than the hymn. He suggests that the hymn, or at least these two verses, were a "forgery" by Brahmins in order to give scriptural support to their class prejudices.[26]

Ambedkar's, more generalized, conclusion is that the *Puruṣa-sūkta* is a "fabrication" of the Brahmins. He rejects the belief that the Hindu Scriptures are infallible and hence not subject to amendment. He emphasizes that the Hindu Scriptures contain "fabrications which are political in their motive, partisan in their composition and fraudulent in their purpose."[27] Moreover, the Brahmins bestowed on this idea of hierarchy of classes the seal of unquestionable sacredness, so that it could never be altered.[28]

Before I go further, however, I would like in fairness to draw our attention to the fact that we do find statements in Hindu texts that rise above class discrimination. For example, *Bhagavad-gītā* 5.18 asserts that the wise look equally on a Brahmin endowed with wisdom and good breeding, on a cow, an elephant, and even a dog or an outcaste.

Although Ambedkar explicitly accuses the author of caste prejudice, we can see that the text is due to cultural conditioning.[29] In his social zeal for emancipating the low castes and outcastes, Ambedkar occasionally makes statements that are palpably wrong. For instance, he claims that the author of the *Puruṣa-sūkta* should have been aware of a method of explaining creation as emanating from different mouths, as mentioned in the *Viṣṇu-purāṇa*. But the latter text is several centuries later, and the author of the *Puruṣa-sūkta* cannot be expected to know this view of the *Viṣṇu-purāṇa*. However, I do agree with Dr. Ambedkar that just because a text is found in the Scripture, this fact does not make it sacrosanct and valid for all times and seasons. In other words, Scriptures too can be culturally conditioned, biased, or mistaken, and this is the case with the Christian Scriptures too.

Ambedkar's Hermeneutics of Theravāda Pāli Texts

Having spelt out one example of Ambedkar's critique of a Hindu Scriptural text, I now move on to his hermeneutics of Buddhist Pāli texts. Unlike in the case of Sanskrit texts, Ambedkar did have a good mastery over Pāli. This is attested by the fact that he wrote a Pāli Grammar.

The eight-fold path is interpreted not so much as leading to spiritual liberation (*nibbāna*), as is traditionally the case in Buddhism, but as the road "to remove all injustice and inhumanity that man does to man." Charity (*dāna*) is meant to "remove the suffering of the needy and the poor and to promote general good;" compassion (*karuṇā*) aims at "the relief of poverty and suffering wherever it exists."[30] Traditionally, compassion, one of the four important virtues cultivated through a meditational practice called the four Brahma-vihāras (Sublime States),[31] does not have a social justice or a social concern thrust to it. But Ambedkar reinterprets these traditional spiritual practices in terms of social justice.[32]

Hermeneutics tells us that the reader plays a decisive role in the interpretation of the text, which has a semantic autonomy, i.e., it is not inextricably attached to the original author or the context in which it appears, or the original addresses of the text. The text has a *sensus plenior*, a fuller meaning, not originally intended by the author. However, the semantic autonomy of the text is not absolute; reader and text must enter into a "conversation" and the reader's interpretations should resonate in some way with the text.

Discovering the fuller meaning in a number of texts, Ambedkar unfolds their social implications and, in doing so, he is also following the earlier Buddhist hermeneutic approach.

There is ample support in the Pāli Buddhist Scripture for Ambedkar's criticism of the caste system. The Buddha challenged the caste claims of Brahmins, proposed arguments against the caste system and asserted that all humans were equal. He denied that caste was based on birth and gave an ethical reinterpretation of the caste system: a Brahmin is anyone who is wise and virtuous; an outcaste is anyone who is wicked.[33] Hence, Ambedkar's clarion call for emancipation from caste is very much in agreement with the Theravāda Buddhist Scripture's attitude towards caste.

On the other hand, Ambedkar does not accept some of the fundamental teachings of Buddhism. Although one can find deeper meaning in a myth and one does not have to take a religious text literally since it could have symbolic significance, still one might accept Ambedkar's assertion that the Buddha could not have decided to go forth from the householder's life into the life of a wandering mendicant, due to his having seen for the *first* time, at the adult age of 29, a person who was ill, an aged person and a corpse. But he also wonders whether the formulation of the Four Noble Truths, one of the cardinal doctrines of Buddhism, is a later addition by the monks and not part of the Buddha's authentic doctrine. He thinks that these noble truths are pessimistic and do not offer hope to human beings, for everything is sorrow. In his judgement "this formula cuts at the root of Buddhism" and constitutes "a great stumbling block in the way of non-Buddhists accepting the gospel of Buddhism."[34] In his presentation of the Buddha's First Sermon, Ambedkar narrates that the Buddha declares that the kernel of the Buddhist religion (*dhamma*) is human beings and the relation of human beings to other human beings. And this was the Buddha's first postulate [= truth].[35] This is very different from the scriptural formulation of the first noble truth which states that there is suffering. In the scripture the second noble truth states that the cause or condition of suffering is ignorance and craving but, for Ambedkar, the second postulate affirms that there is suffering and poverty among humans and the removal of this suffering is the only goal of Buddhism; nothing else is Buddhism (*dhamma*).[36] He asserts that, according to the Buddha, the root-cause of all suffering in the world was the continuous "conflict between classes" and he was determined to find an answer to such oppositions.[37] In another passage Ambedkar mentions greed as the cause of lack of contentment, i.e., suffering, but he quickly gives greed a social twist by emphasizing that the Buddha censured covetousness because it results in "blows and wounds, strife, contradiction and retorts; quarrelling, slander and lies. That this is the correct analysis of class struggle there can be no doubt. That is why the Buddha insisted upon the control of greed and craving."[38] For Ambedkar, human suffering seems to be almost exclusively due to social reasons: suffering is due to "man's inequity to man."[39]

Similarly, Ambedkar rejects the Buddhist theory of rebirth, in the sense of "transmigration," i.e., just as a light from one lamp does not transmigrate when another lamp is lit or a verse does not transmigrate from a teacher to a student who is taught that verse, so too there is no rebirth in the sense of transmigration.[40] According to him, the Buddha's religion "had nothing to do with life after death."[41] Ambedkar finds it contradictory that Buddhism did not believe in a soul,[42] and yet believed in *karman* (results of past deeds) and rebirth.[43] According to him, the Buddha believed in the rebirth only of the body, i.e., of the four material elements of which the body is composed, viz., earth, water, fire and air. However, since these elements that are reborn are not necessarily from the same dead body,[44] it was "most improbable" that the Buddha believed in the rebirth of the same sentient being.[45] Furthermore, the Buddha's understanding of the law of *karman* was quite different from that of Hinduism, not only because Buddhism denied the existence of the soul,[46] but also because, for the Buddha, *karman* had its effect only on the present life, and not on future life. The Buddha did not teach such a doctrine of *karman* having an effect on future life; it was introduced into Buddhism later on by someone who wanted to make Buddhism similar to Hinduism or who was ignorant of the correct Buddhist understanding. Another, and more pernicious, reason for this "inhuman and absurd doctrine" was "to enable the state or the society to escape responsibility for the condition of the poor and the lowly."[47] The Hindu Brahminic *karman* theory was meant "to sap the spirit of revolt completely": especially the Śūdras and women of all classes, the two most demeaned groups, were kept ignorant and brainwashed into becoming innocent supporters of Brahmanism; Brahmins, Kṣatriyas and Vaiśyas connived together to keep them oppressed.[48] In other words, for Ambedkar, the theory of *karman* and rebirth was invented in order to attribute the cause of the suffering of the untouchables, the women and the poor to misdeeds in their past lives; however, the real reason for their suffering was due to the exploitation by so-called higher classes through an unjust social system. Ambedkar holds that the Buddha rejected the existence of the soul, its rebirth, the Hindu theory of *karman*, and the salvation of the soul; the Buddha rejected the fatalistic understanding of *karman*, interpreting it in a scientific way, and thus putting "new wine in old bottle."[49]

Traditionally, monks (*bhikkhu*)[50] lived a monastic life, largely away from society. However, for Ambedkar, the monk's role is double: to pursue his own spiritual progress and, at the same time, to compassionately serve people by giving them guidance. A monk should not withdraw from the world: "a Bhikkhu who is indifferent to the woes of mankind, however perfect in self-culture, is not at all a Bhikkhu."[51] Hence, in this respect too Ambedkar departs from tradition and gives a social orientation to the monk's life.

Other Buddhists from other countries in Asia have also reinterpreted traditional Buddhist doctrines and practices and given them a social thrust.[52] However, although they did meet with some opposition, they have generally not been accused of starting a new sect or tradition. But some Buddhists have charged that Ambedkar's challenging some fundamental doctrines of Buddhism, such as the Four Noble Truths and the doctrine of *karman*, puts him outside the pale of orthodox Buddhism, and makes him the promulgator of Ambedkarism[53] or a new "vehicle" (Navayāna), in addition to Hīnayāna (the Lesser Vehicle) and Mahāyāna (the Great Vehicle) and an offshoot of the latter, Vajrayāna (the Diamond or Thunderbolt Vehicle). There is more than a grain of truth in such criticism. On the one hand, we sympathize with Ambedkar's wanting to make the Buddhist Scripture relevant to the oppressed peoples: *karman* and rebirth only rubbed salt on the wounds of the untouchables, blaming the very victims for their own present state of suffering, when, in reality, it was the Brahmins who had, down the centuries, heaped untold sufferings on the backs of low castes and outcastes. This, indeed, was Ambedkar's hermeneutic horizon. On the other hand, although the Buddhist scholar Bhadant Anand Kausalyayan maintained that Ambedkar's Buddhism was a "new orientation but not a distortion" of traditional Buddhism, since all the fundamentals of Buddhism were present in it,[54] in my humble opinion, Ambedkar does, in fact, originate a new form of Buddhism. But there is no problem in this. After all, just as in the case of many other religions, Buddhism has developed into many forms, some of which are no more extant; moreover, even among the living versions there are such diverse varieties as the very radically different Theravāda and Mahāyāna; and, even within Mahāyāna, there is a whole gamut of widely differing schools, such as the schools of Tibetan Buddhism, Chinese Buddhism and Japanese Buddhism, each with a number of sub-schools.

Ambedkar proposes three principles to distinguish what the Buddha actually taught from later accretions in the Buddhist Theravāda Scripture: (1) whatever is rational and logical, (2) whatever contributed to society's benefit, and (3) whatever is stated with certitude are from the Buddha.[55] Of these three, the most important was whatever promoted the uplift of society and, more particularly, of the downtrodden in India and elsewhere. This was the ultimate hermeneutic key that he used to interpret what he considered to be true Buddhism.[56]

Although traditional Buddhism did not lack social concern, and in fact, one can point to a number of passages in the Buddhist Scriptures that anticipate many a modern application of the principles of justice (e.g. bonuses), yet, in practice, traditional Buddhism paid attention to meditation and a spirituality that shunned the world. Ambedkar, however, reads the Buddhist texts with the new lens of social justice, making them relevant to the oppressed classes.

Even so, instead of totally rejecting doctrines which are fundamental to the Buddhist tradition and thus inviting strong criticism from some scholars and traditionalists, Ambedkar could have utilized the Buddhist hermeneutic theory of the two types of truth, conventional truth and absolute truth. In this way he could have advocated his important liberative views without antagonizing the traditionalists and scholars, and ending up giving birth to a new school of Buddhism.

Conclusion

Like the Christian Liberation Theologians, Ambedkar too was prophetic and openly and strongly denounced institutions as well as persons. But both were concerned with alleviating suffering, especially of the poor and the downtrodden. They both propagated a paradigm shift from a traditional otherworldly concept of liberation to a this-worldly liberation, or rather, blended the two in varying degrees. This approach is actually supported to some extent by the Scriptures and other original sources of both the religions. The religious and the secular are not watertight compartments, but influence and strengthen each other.

Some Christian Liberation Theologians advocated violent means in order to achieve the goal of social justice. Ambedkar, on the other hand, even though he used language that bordered on the acerbic and led protest marches, always took a physically non-violent approach.

Both Ambedkar and the Christian Liberation Theologians emphasize orthopraxis, rather than orthodoxy: the stress is on action and less on abstract speculation. Christian Liberation Theology is often linked with the political ideology and the economic analysis of Marxism, but this is not the case with Ambedkar.

On a more metaphysical plane, in Christianity the person has intrinsic worth: the person is a child of God, with an immortal soul. But in Theravāda each one is not a soul or substance, but only a series of discreet momentary aggregates and yet can still be an object of social concern and compassion. I may add that, in Mahāyāna, the person does not exist even for one moment and yet the ideal is to delay one's salvation for the sake of persons who do not really exist. Hence, the motivation for social concern differs not only between Buddhism and Christianity, but also between the two Buddhist traditions of Theraṿāda and Mahāyāna. Although traditionally Christianity has shown greater social concern than Buddhism, yet it has been more violent and intolerant than Buddhism.

Notes

1 *Sikṣāsamuccaya*, 1.2, p. 12. Unless otherwise stated, all references to the Buddhist Sanskrit texts cited by me are to the Darbhanga ed. published by the Mithila Institute.

2 This saying from Peter Lombard (*Patrologia Latina,* ed. J. P. Migne, 191, 1651), and cited by Thomas Aquinas (*Summa Theologiae* P.Ia-IIæ, q.109, a.1, Videtur quod 1) owes its origin to an earlier version ("*Quidquid....verum a quoqumque dicitur, a sancto dictiur Spiritu.*"), attributed by Aquinas and others to Ambrose (*Patrologia Latina*, 17, 245) but actually from the pen of an unknown author, whom Erasmus called Ambrosiaster: see St. Thomas Aquinas, *Summa Theologiae*, gen. ed. Thomas Gilby, O. P., 60 vols.; vol. 30 (1a2æ. 106-114): ed. and tr. Cornelius Ernst, O. P. (Oxford: Blackfriars; London: Eyre and Spottiswoode; New York: McGraw-Hill, 1972), p. 68, n. 3.

3 *Aṅguttaranikāya*, pt I, 2.4.10, p. 66. Note that, unless otherwise stated, all references to the Pāli texts cited by me are to the Nalanda ed. published by the Government of Bihar.

4 *Saddharmalankāvatārasūtra*, at 3.85, pp. 78-79.

5 *Saddharmalankāvatārasūtra*, at 3.85, p. 79 and 6.3, p. 91.

6 *The Encyclopedia of Religion*, s.v. "Buddhist Literature: Exegesis and Hermeneutics."

7 *Mahāparinibbānasutta*, in *Dīghanikāya*, pt II, 3.18, pp. 96-97.

8 *Saddharmapuṇḍarīkasūtra*, at 2.37, p. 27.

9 R. A. Stein, *Tibetan Civilization*, tr. J. E. Stapleton Driver (Stanford: Stanford University Press, 1972), pp. 160-163.

10 For a comparison between the authority of the Buddha and that of Christ, see Chai-Shin Yu, *Early Buddhism and Christianity: A Comparative Study of the Founders' Authority, the Community, and the Discipline* (Delhi: Motilal Banarsidass, 1981), esp. Chs. 1 and 7.

11 Anais Nin, *Seduction of the Minotaur* (Denver: Allan Swallow, 1961), p. 124. Incidentally, even though she says that the words are Talmudic, these words are not found in the Talmud: see Jonathan Kadane Crane and Joseph Born Kadane, "Seeing Things: The Internet, the Talmud and Anais Nin," RRJ 11, 2 _f11_342-345 10/21/08 10:11 PM.

12 Dhananjay Keer, *Dr. Ambedkar: Life and Mission*, 3rd ed. (Bombay: Popular Prakashan 1971), pp. 12-15.

13 Christopher S. Queen, "Dr. Ambedkar and the Hermeneutics of Buddhist Liberation," in *Engaged Buddhism: Buddhist Liberation Movements in Asia*, ed. Christopher S. Queen and Sallie B. King (Albany, New York: State University of New York Press, 1996), p. 49.

14 B. R. Ambedkar, *Dr. Babasaheb Ambedkar: Writings and Speeches*, comp. by Vasant Moon, vol. 11, *The Buddha and His Dhamma* (Bombay: Siddharth College Publication, 1957: 5th ed. Bombay: Education Department, Govt. of Maharashtra, for Dr. Babasaheb Ambedkar Source Material Committee, Reprinted, 1992), p. 306 (III.IV.2.5). Ambedkar numbered the books, parts, sections and paragraphs of his *The Buddha and His Dhamma.* Since, the pagination of this important work differs in different editions, I also give the reference in parenthesis, after the page number(s) of the edition I am using, e.g., (III. IV.2.5), whenever this work is cited; and, for the sake of brevity, the book will be cited henceforth only by its well-known title, without mentioning its vol. number (11) in his collected works.

15 The current prevalent and accepted term is *dalit*, derived from the Sanskrit *dalita*, which means 'split,' 'cracked,' 'broken,' 'crushed,' 'downtrodden.' However, the Sanskrit verbal root *dal*, not only means 'to split' etc., but also means 'to expand or bloom open (as a

flower).' Hence, for *dalits*, the term not only signifies their oppressed condition, but also evokes the unfolding and even bursting forth of their creative energies in order to create a new and just society.

16 B. R. Ambedkar, *Dr. Babasaheb Ambedkar: Writings and Speeches*, comp. by Vasant Moon, vol. 1 (Bombay: Education Department 1974; Bombay: Education Department, Government of Maharashtra, for Dr. Babasaheb Ambedkar Source Material Committee, Reprinted, 1989), pp. 15-17, 27-96; B. R. Ambedkar, *Dr. Babasaheb Ambedkar: Writings and Speeches*, comp. by Vasant Moon, vol. 9 (Bombay: Education Department, Government of Maharashtra, for Dr. Babasaheb Ambedkar Source Material Committee, 1991), pp. 274-297.

17 Ambedkar, *Writings and Speeches*, vol. 1, pp. 67-69.

18 Mohan Dass Namishray, *Caste and Race: Comparative Study of BR* [sic] *Ambedkar and Martin Luther King* (Jaipur and New Delhi: Rawat Publications, in association with Motilal Bhimraj Charity Trust, 2003), pp. 115-118.

19 Christopher, S. Queen, "Dr. Ambedkar and the Hermeneutics of Buddhist Liberation," in *Engaged Buddhism: Buddhist Liberation Movements in Asia,* ed. by Christopher S. Queen and Sallie B. King (Albany: State University of New York Press, 1996), pp. 54-55.

20 Ambedkar, *Dr. Babasaheb Ambedkar: Writings and Speeches*, vol. 7 (Bombay: Education Department, Government of Maharashtra, 1990), Preface, p. 11.

21 In v. 12 of the hymn the word used is Rājanya.

22 Ambedkar, *Writings and Speeches*, vol. 7, p. 26.

23 Ambedkar, *Writings and Speeches*, vol. 7, pp. 27-30.

24 Ambedkar, *Writings and Speeches*, vol. 7, pp. 33-34.

25 Ambedkar, *Writings and Speeches*, vol. 7, pp. 133-134.

26 Ambedkar, *Writings and Speeches*, vol. 7, pp. 134-138.

27 Ambedkar, *Writings and Speeches*, vol. 7, Preface, p. 14.

28 Ambedkar, *Writings and Speeches*, vol. 7, p. 31.

29 We also have examples of cultural conditioning in other Scriptures, for instance, abstention from blood as essential for Christians (Acts 15.20, 28-29): this was due to their Semitic background.

30 Ambedkar, *Buddha and His Dhamma*, p. 129 (II.II.6.5-6).

31 For a brief explanation of the concept and practice of the four Brahma-vihāras, particularly on *mettā* (loving kindness) and *karuṇā* (compassion),see Noel Sheth, S.J., "Christian and Buddhist Altruistic Love,"*Gregorianum* 87:4 (2006): 815-820.

32 Other Buddhists in different Asian countries also reinterpret traditional Buddhist doctrines, giving them a social orientation: see Noel Sheth, S.J., "Contemporary Buddhist Activism for Social Justice in Asia," in *Social Action as Mission: Prophetic Interventions in Human Promotion and Integrity of Creation,* ed. by Joy Thomas SVD and Victor Sagayam Zackarias SVD (Mumbai: St Pauls, 2013), pp. 125-152.

33 Noel Sheth, S.J., "The Buddha's Attitude to Caste,"*Negations* 1:4 (October-December 1982): 23-26.

34 Ambedkar, *Buddha and His Dhamma*, Introduction.

35 Ambedkar, *Buddha and His Dhamma*, p. 121 (II.II.2.15-16).

36 Ambedkar, *Buddha and His Dhamma*, p. 121 (II.II.2.17).

37 Ambedkar, *Buddha and His Dhamma*, pp. 57-58 (I.II.6.8).

38 Ambedkar, *Buddha and His Dhamma*, pp. 239-240 (III.III.4.7-14).

39 Ambedkar, *Buddha and His Dhamma*, p. 284 (III.V.2.16).

40 Ambedkar, *Buddha and His Dhamma*, pp. 348-349 (IV.II.IV.1-29).

41 Ambedkar, *Buddha and His Dhamma*, p. 121 (II.II.2.14).

42 This refers to living Buddhist traditions. There were Buddhist schools that believed in some sort of soul or person (*pudgala*), but these schools have ceased to exist: see Leonard Priestley, *Pudgalavāda Buddhism: The Reality of the Indeterminate Self* (Toronto: Centre for South Asian Studies, University of Toronto, 1999).

43 Ambedkar, *Buddha and His Dhamma*, Introduction; p. 343 (IV.II.II.3.15-16).

44 Ambedkar, *Buddha and His Dhamma*, pp. 330 and 332 (IV.II.I.2.7-14, 40-41).

45 Ambedkar, *Buddha and His Dhamma*, p. 333 (IV.II.I.3.2-5).

46 It should be emphatically noted that, although Hinduism believes in a soul, there is no real rebirth of the soul, since, unlike in Christianity, the soul is eternal, without beginning and end. It is only due to its ignorance that the soul is said to be reborn; what is really reborn is not the soul, but the subtle body (*sūkṣma-śarīra*).

47 Ambedkar, *Buddha and His Dhamma*, pp. 337-344; 348-349 (IV.II.II.1 – IV.II.II.3; IV.II.IV.1-29): see esp. pp. 337-338 (IV.II.II.1.8-23); pp. 338, 340-341(IV.II.II.2.3, 23-24, 29-32); pp. 343-344 (IV.II.II.3.15-23); pp. 348-349 (IV.II.IV.1-29).

48 Ambedkar, *Buddha and His Dhamma*, pp. 91-92 (I.V.3.39-44).

49 Ambedkar, *Buddha and His Dhamma*, pp. 103-104 (I.VII.1-2).

50 Literally, it means 'beggar,' but refers to a monk since, in the early years of the Order, they used to go begging; Ambedkar speaks only of monks because the Order of nuns ceased to exist in Theravāda long ago.

51 Ambedkar, *Buddha and His Dhamma*, pp. 434-435 (V.II.4.16-22).

52 See Noel Sheth, S.J., "Contemporary Buddhist Activism for Social Justice in Asia," in *Social Action as Mission: Prophetic Interventions in Human Promotion and Integrity of Creation*, ed. by Joy Thomas SVD and Victor Sagayam Zackarias SVD, Mumbai: St Pauls, 2013, pp. 125-152.

53 An Indian periodical, the *Maha Bodhi*, and a Burmese journal, *The Light of Dhamma*, are cited to this effect by Keer, *Ambedkar: Life and Mission*, pp. 521-523.

54 Joanna Rogers Macy and Eleanor Zelliot, "Tradition and Innovation in Contemporary Indian Buddhism," in A. K. Narain, ed. *Studies in the History of Buddhism*, 2nd ed. (Delhi: B. R. Publishing Corporation, 2000), pp. 134-135.

55 Ambedkar, *Buddha and His Dhamma*, pp. 350-351 (IV.II.5.1-16, esp. 11-16).

56 Queen, "Ambedkar and the Hermeneutics of Buddhist Liberation," p. 59.

Chapter 13

Quest for Identity and Liberation
A Dalit Hermeneutical Reading

Selvaraj Arulnathan
Indian Social Institute, Bangalore

Emancipation of a community from its oppression and subordination solely depends upon the consciousness of its existential reality and in which direction the community as a collective entity moves, because one's consciousness determines the course of one's action. It can be either liberative or submissive. Dalit emancipation is determined by the type of consciousness that the community constructs. It is collective as their subordination is also collective. Their collective subordination is an identity issue beyond any ego and it has to be dealt with collectively. If someone suffers because he/she belongs to an ethnic group, a social group, a religious group, a regional group or any other category, it becomes a social problem, which demands collective action. Hence, construction of subordinated consciousness is as well a collective task, a shared responsibility for constructing positive identity. Thus, the identity of a group depends upon its level of consciousness, submissive, aggressive, or assertive.

Subordinated people of a given social and historical situation engage in creating their identity through constantly and collectively constructing their consciousness. There is a dialectical relationship between their life world and the process of consciousness building. It is in this process that a community aspires for its liberation. It again is determined by how the community understands, interprets, and engages for action for liberation. I would like to call this as the process of hermeneutizing the collective experience of a community. This paper presents how Dalit community constructs its collective and liberative identity in and through its historical, social, political, cultural contexts and how hermeneutic reading of Dalit experience becomes important in the formation for its liberation.

Clarification of Concepts

It is important to clarify some of the concepts used here like Hermeneutics, Dalit identity, Consciousness, etc. as they assume specific meanings pertaining to Dalit liberative discourse.

Hermeneutics

Hermeneutical tradition belongs to the subjectivist strand in social thought in that the rational is seen as an attribute and construct of the subject. It consciously foregrounds the subject into the social and historical situation to construct knowledge. Thus, the subject becomes the central figure and agent in generating knowledge and meaning to human situatedness/reality. Etymologically *Hermeneutics* means the science of understanding and interpretation.[1]

Hermeneutic tradition rejects the positivist idea that there is a single method of arriving at knowledge for both the natural and social sciences. The social world is a universe of *meaning(s)* which demands an approach specific to its object, and hermeneutics comes to its aid by interpreting what motivates others (*introspection*), 'understanding' in terms of human inter-relatedness.[2] What happens in this process is that the interpreter shares the inner experience of the thinking, speaking or acting of the object.[3] Thus, hermeneutics remains firmly anchored in the subjectivist epistemology on which all actor-oriented theories are based.[4] Because of this understanding, hermeneutics rejects *a priori* knowledge as Dilthey advocates. He rejects the idea of an *a priori* rationality of the subject.[5] Hermeneutics is thus a path-breaking movement[6], 'a movement from vagueness to clarity,' which anchors its axis in the existing realities and how the subject approaches such a reality in and through one's experience with the reality.

Dalit identity

The word "Dalit" has its roots both in Indian and Hebrew languages. *Dalit* in Sanskrit is both a noun and an adjective. As a noun, *Dalit is* used for all three genders, masculine, feminine, and neuter. Etymologically the term is derived from the Sanskrit root '*dal'* meaning to crack, open, split, oppressed, subjugated, and broken.

Dalit is a self-designation for a group of people formerly treated as untouchables. It has gained, in recent years so much attention and international recognition. It also bears existential significance and political importance. It bears witness to Dalit uprising and mobility as a politically motivated group determined to change their position in the social hierarchy. It at once creates an existential anger in and capacity to organize and agitate for their rights. It creates in them assertive consciousness which is fore-grounded in/for Dalit emancipation. Hence, today it gains meaning and importance in philosophical discourse.

Construction of Dalit Consciousness

Dalit identity is determined by the level of Dalit consciousness the community develops. However, consciousness itself is understood and interpreted variously within philosophy.

According to Descartes, *consciousness is the essence of the mind* and any material entity is separable into distinct parts.[7] The Danish philosopher and psychologist Jorgensen has discussed consciousness in some detail. He writes about "person-identification," i.e., identification with another person, and distinguishes between *emotive* and *conative* forms. The former refers to the catching effect of emotional states and expressions, and the latter refers to situations where persons act together to reach the samegoal.[8] According to Lycan, "consciousness has to do with the internal or subjective character of experience, paradigmatically sense experience. It is also conceptual problem, not merely an empirical one."[9] Wuthnow, a leading Psychologist defines consciousness "as the ongoing process of that which needs to be recognized as not simply a psychological phenomenon, but as a process linked in important ways to the functioning of society."[10] The Study Week of Vatican Academy of Science gives a more amenable definition as "consciousness intends that it strictly designates the psycho physiological concept of perceptual capacity, of awareness of perception, and the ability to act and react accordingly."[11] All the above definitions reveal most aspects of consciousness, but none of them is comprehensive.

Based on the above enumerations, I consider that human consciousness arises from brain organization, and is developed in each of us. Most of our interpretations in our life take place unconsciously, automatically evolved over millennia. For example, when Barrack Obama says about his grandma, "a woman who once confessed her fear of black men who passed by her on the street, and who on more than one occasion has uttered racial or ethnic stereotypes that made me cringe" is a typical example of how we interpret things and events form opinions and make judgments unconsciously.

Karl Marx looks at consciousness as the production of social relations in the economic, social, and political realms. For him, social existence determines the construction of one's consciousness.

> In the social production of their existence, people inevitably enter into definite relations, which are independent of their will, namely relations of production appropriate to a given stage in the development of their material forces of production. The totality of these relations of production constitutes the economic structure of a society, the real foundation, on which arises a legal and political superstructure and to which correspond definite forms of social consciousness… It is not the consciousness of men that determines their existence, but their social existence that determines their consciousness."[12]

I look at the construction of consciousness just the opposite. I adduce that the construction of one's consciousness determines their social existence. Thus, constructing consciousness is an ongoing process. It is an activity of perception, reflection, and evaluation. It is a continuous process and realization in time, space, and event continuum. In the usual sense, social existence determines the consciousness of people as Marx opines, but as far the subordinated people as Dalits are concerned, the consciousness of the people of their subordinated conditions determines their existence. It is a kind of intense and continuous sensibility of resistance against their subjugated status of life.

Three Types of Consciousness Construing Dalit Identity

From the above perspective of construction of consciousness, my investigation reveals that there are three types of consciousness operative in Dalit life world. They are,

Untouchable Consciousness

This type makes a Dalit (subjective self) feels that he/she is intrinsically inferior to the dominant caste people (objective other). S/he feels that it is his/her fate to be born in this particular community, and to suffer silently the burden of untouchability. The best way to live is to accept the given without any question or resistance. The dominant self is real and complete; the subordinated self is incomplete and deficient.

SC Consciousness

The second type is *SC consciousness*. In this model, Dalits feel that they are inferior to the dominant caste people. The difference in this is the state becomes his/her dominant other. Under this mindset, they depend on the state and believe the state will liberate them. What they forget is that those who represent the state (the policy makers and the people in power) are from the dominant caste and they represent the dominant social order, not the subaltern people.

Dalit Consciousness

The third type of consciousness is *Dalit consciousness*. In this model, the Dalit feels that s/he has an esteemed self like any other. Their condition is not a real one but imposed upon them. Both the society and the state are the cause for it and they must fight it out. For this, they rely on their personal and community strength and unity. They become their own. Social protest becomes the means to achieve their emancipation.

From the foregoing discussion, one can infer that the construction of the consciousness of the subaltern people involves two important factors: Primarily the consciousness of the subaltern people is not something innate, but is constructed both historically and culturally[13] and they have to take active part in eliminating submissive elements.

Philosophical Understadning of Hermeneutics

Wilhelm Dilthey

Wilhelm Dilthey (1833-1911), a contemporary of Nietzsche brought the focus of hermeneutics within the context of history. By dismantling the idea that meaning is sourced from the transcendental self as that of the German idealists, Dilthey turned to human experience as the foreground for engaging any meaningful understanding and interpretation. Human thought, he held is not structured from any *a priori* categories of understanding as Kant believed to be, but arises out of one's experience in the world from within social history. According to him the human self and its understanding of the world is an historical and social construction.[14] Therefore, there is no way to any transcendental understanding of phenomena beyond the frontiers of one's historically conditioned/situated hermeneutic circle.[15]

Martin Heidegger

Pursuing the hermeneutical endeavor of Dilthey, Martin Heidegger, and Hans-Georg Gadamer developed the science of hermeneutics in philosophy. For Heidegger, the kernel of hermeneutics is a movement from the as-structure to the fore-structure. The interpretation becomes primordial, only when the fore-structure (hermeneutical situation) consisting of fore-having, the fore-sight and fore-conception.'[16] In *Being and Time*, Heidegger claims that the understanding of a situation is directly mediated by a fore-knowledge, or sensitivity to situations, that is comprised by the understander's life-world. Heidegger reaches his conclusion by contending that as a necessary part of human "being-in-the-world" (*Dasein*), things are perceived according to how they are encountered and used in one's everyday routines and tasks. It is historical in that understanding builds from the fore-knowledge accumulated from experience. Heidegger brings hermeneutics from a theory of interpretation to a theory of existential understanding. He 'de-psychologizes' hermeneutics by dissociating it from the empathetic perception of other beings. Understanding now appears as a *no-longer-conscious* component of *Dasein*; it is embedded within the context of specific situations and plans, with, in effect, finite computational resources.

Gadamer

Gadamer clarifies that understanding is not an orientation of the subject towards a given external object (not objectivism or referentialism that gives meaning) but "understanding belongs to the being of that which is understood.'[17] For Gadamer, understanding is bound and embedded in history because understanding deploys the knower's *effective-history*, personal experience, and cultural traditions, to assimilate new experiences. Drawing on the Hiedeggerian concept of 'being-in-the-world' Gadamer asserts that human existence is thoroughly and inescapably historical; it is in-the-world. Differentia in interpretation is possible because we 'belong' to different cultures and through conversation, communication there arise a '*fusion of horizons*'[18] that foster the backdrop of any '*communion*.' The fusion of horizons is the space for the departure from our individuality towards a sense of common or 'shared understanding.' Meaning emerges as the text and the interpreter engage in a dialogue, in what Gadamer calls *'hermeneutical conversation*.' The result of such conversation or communion is the possibility of an intersection of the horizon of the author and the horizon of the interpreter. Thus the meaning of a text is not confined to just author's intention or the reader's understanding of it, it projects the possibility of multiple fusions of horizons. Thus interpretation of reality or a text is the differential of sensibilities that includes the psychological, historical, social, cultural and religious and 'linguistic'enterprises[19].

Ludwig Wittgenstein, Ferdinand de Saussure, and Jacques Derrida

In the philosophic-historical continuum of the discussion of hermeneutics, Ludwig Wittgenstein, Ferdinand de Saussure, Jacques Derrida and others do have their seminal contribution. For Wittgenstein, interpretation of linguistic meaning is not a matter of any 'private' affair, for language is a social phenomenon, acquiring its meaning lies in social interaction. Saussure contends that language is structural and the meaning of a text in language is a matter of social convention and belongs to a domain of 'relationship in differences.' Derrida widely known for the idea of deconstruction contends that interpretation of meaning or understanding is revealed by decoding the 'differentia in relation' in the face of the simultaneous presence of the other texts/words.

Hermeneutical Situated and Socially Directed

From the above enumerations, we can say that

(i) As humans we are *necessarily interpretative* (Heidegger) that is to say that the mode of our being is fundamentally hermeneutical,

(ii) our interpretations are from the situatedness in the world in the sense that our *understanding is rooted in the historical cultural social context* (Dilthey, Saussure) in which s/he belongs and, finally

(iii) the mode of being hermeneutical is not fore closed or concealed by the conditionality of one's boundary of a tradition but hermeneutical engagement foster a 'pathway' of towards being-in-the-world (human) by mode ofhermeneutical conversation (Gadamer) in the sense that our interpretations of the world are both *relationally communitarian* and *directional*.

Guided by the above discussion on hermeneutics, we may reinstate the fact that, to *be Human is to be Hermeneutical and to be Hermeneutical is to be socially constructed.*

Black Theology Rooted in Black Experience

To get a sense of trans-cultural understanding of hermeneutics, black reality in the US is the most suited one. Applying hermeneutics in Black Theology, Diana L. Hayes takes the inspiration from James Cone, the noted Black theologian who states that theology is not possible unless one gets to the depth of one's life. According to him, there is no truth for and about black people, which does not emerge out of the context of their experience. It is an investigation of the mind into the raw materials of our pilgrimage, telling the story of "how we got over." For theology to be black, it must reflect upon what it means to be black. Black Theology must uncover the structures and forms of the black experience, because the categories of interpretation must arise out of the thought forms of the black experience itself.[20] He again posits that black experience, black symbols, metaphors, narratives, etc. against the dominant white culture.[21]

Dalit Hermeneutics

The fundamental social reality of India is the existence of caste system and the practice of untouchability premised upon hierarchical social structure. This is the situatedness, the foreground against which, we need to understand and interpret Dalit reality, the '*fusion of horizons' directed towards a specific social particular.*[22] It is against this social situation that Dalit liberation needs to be historically situated and socially engaged.

Dalit Existence as Excluded

Dalit experience/existence is marked by exclusion and discrimination. Anand Telteumbde, a noted Dalit activist and writer speaks about the Dalit existence in the global economic context thus, "in social terms however, all Dalits, irrespective of their economic standing, still suffer oppression. This social oppression varies from the crudest variety of untouchability, still being practised in rural areas, to the sophisticated forms of discrimination encountered even in modern sectors of urban areas. Although the statistics indicate that Dalits have made a significant progress on almost all parameters during the five post-independence decades, the relative distance between them and non-Dalits seems to have remained the same or increased."[23] I too have undertaken some field survey to collect Dalit experience and life stories. From my field survey, the following dimensions of Dalit experience were shared, some of which I would to present here.

Being a Dalit: A Dirty Thing?

Jeya Subramanian, a social activist and educator from Madurai, Tamilnadu, experienced *social exclusion* both in her neighborhood as a child and in the educational institutions. She would cringe at the revelation of her identity in the college as SC student. Her peers would look at her as if she was a 'dirty thing' 'thrown' in their midst. Jakkian experienced the worst form of exclusion when he was forced to introduce himself as the son of a cobbler in the college. Helocates his Dalit existence in its social ambience that denies his physical, psychical, socio-economic, intellectual, and even moral space by which the dominant world ghettoizes his Dalitness within the caste wall.

Denial of the Basic Things for a Human Being

Yesumarian, a Jesuit priest identifies three major areas where Dalits have been discriminated against. First is the denial of land. Land has been the hallmark of a person's identity in Indian context. Dalit lands have been unjustly appropriated by the dominant forces for centuries including the DC land accorded by the British regime. Uma Shankar, an Indian Administrative Officer from the Dalit community opines that land owning is self-esteem. Since Dalits in general are landless laborers, discrimination against them is very high. Second is the denial of education. Education has been a rarity for Dalits from the beginning of Indian education system. Dalits have been grossly denied of their share in education especially when education is considered as the vehicle for mobility and social change. Third isthe denial of housing. Dalits donot have proper housing as poverty and landlessness have been coupled with total and cumulative deprivation. Yesumarian reflects on this phenomenon and attributes this stagnation to caste system. According to him, "as far as Indian social set up is concerned, religion is like a shirt, but caste is like skin. I can change from Ezhumalai to Anthonisamy, but in no way has this changed the life of Dalits."

Caste Perversion as the Root

Caste in India is taken as the symbol of power and domination. If thus caste is considered as the expression of power, it reduces the out castes to total powerlessness. Selvaraj explains this idea about how the dominant caste people treat the Dalits: "We should keep these people like this; we should talk to them in this manner only; then only we will get respect; then only others will look up to us; then only they will have the feeling that we are everything for them." This is the given; this is the social ethos in which Dalits have to realize, evolve and exercise their selfhood. This implies Dalit identity.

Untouchability is the Primordial Experience

"I knew my caste (as untouchable) before I knew my name and its meaning. Our people are not known by their names but by their caste and sub-caste. Our caste name becomes synonymous to our name. Our name is not so important for the dominant caste people, but calling us by our caste makes the dominant caste people feel superior. If at all there is anything real about us is our identity as outcaste," said Selvaraj Arulnathan, when he was interviewed by Amnesty International in Paris; he further remarked that caste is omnipresent and omnipotent in India.

Thus, the identity issue in India is located in the "self-other asymmetrical and vertical relationship ruled by "domination-subordination" discourse. Jakkian brings out very strongly the norm between the Dalit and the caste identity. He says, "It is our enemy who decides how we should be and also our character is formed by them. It is also the surrounding that forms our character.....Untouchability has been the fundamental experience."

Mud, Wood and Cow Dung: More Valuable than a Dalit?

T. K. John, Professor of Theology, Delhi traces the root of the problem in the Hindu social order and traces the locus of Dalit self thus, "I think in Indian society mud, wood, cow dung, rock all these are more appreciated than Dalits. Mud, you want for brick, you touch it no problem; rock also a Brahmin has touched and anybody can touch it no problem; sleep over it, use it for a building and any of these materials is rated higher than Dalits in the Hindu consciousness." This is the core value attached to Dalits by the Hindu social order, which goes with them wherever they go, whichever religion they embrace, and whatever they do and achieve.

While caste has its origin in Hindu religion, it has not spared other religious people. The discriminatory practice against which Dalits left Hinduism and embraced religions like Christianity were greatly disappointed, as it has become the core value of even Christianity in India. Vanitha, a CSI Christian girl who worked in a CSI Christian orphanage clearly sees the contradiction between Christian teachings and practice. She narrates her story with anger, disappointment, and dissent.

> I worked as a helper in R. S. Mangalam in a CSI church run orphanage. I didn't like the job; they did not give me a job for my qualification but for my caste. Instead of giving me the warden job which would fit into my qualification, they sent me to clean the children, and wash their clothes while a person with less qualification was given the warden job. Since the bishop is from Nadar community, he would give better jobs only to someone from his own community.

Systemic caste operation creates a cumulative deprivation, which impairs Dalits of their legitimate right like education, economic independence, and social recognition. This is the situation of the Dalits in India. What we have accounted is only the tip of the iceberg. The facts are the evidences that the given consciousness of the Dalits is one of submissive consciousness ascribed to them by the dominant discourse. This is the Dalit experience in the socio-economic, educational, religious, and cultural levels.

Hermeneutics of Dalit Exclusion

The philosophical analysis of the existential foreground of subjugated people's life-experience calls for hermeneutical interpretation of what is to be a subjugated people (Dalit) as the one who has suffered cultural thrown-away-ness at all levels both in the public as well as in the private spheres. At the innermost personal-individual level a culturally subjugated person (and generation of oppression-suffered) imbibe a deep sense of alone-ness in spite of being or living in the 'social crowd' for s/he is thrown into and outside, within the alienating crowd of the oppressive totality. It is an experience of psychological alienation caused by multiple and networking forms. He/she is forced to live in alone-ness due to social pressure and suspicion and cultural prejudices and power-mind-sets. At the social level, it is an experience of multi-layered discrimination, a deep sense of outcasteness. This is what I do mean here in a philosophical sense, an experience (not just feeling or emotion) of thrown-away-ness. Buddhist terminology for this experience is '*dukkha*' against which Ambedkar crusaded his life to 'annihilation' of such *dukkha*, a sense of *dukkhanirodha*. The experience of thrown-away-ness or forsakenness is the ontological pre-conditioning, the starting point of a phenomenological inquiry.

Dalit Exclusion as Cultural Reproduction

Caste mentality, as endowed, philosophically construed, and culturally imbibed comes to stay alive and determine the common Indian perceptions by its repetitive modes of re-production. In analyzing the reason for the reproduction of Casteism, Ambedkar distinctly clarifies that casteism is continuously reproduced by the social practice of endogamy that is, marrying within the caste fold. In other words, Casteism as form of cultural Darwinism is re-imposed by rituals and social customs and habituations explicit in Indian cultural and religious practices. The modern inventions of caste-named/based associations are but an offshoot of such caste naming to the individuals.[24] The factuality of injustice and inequality institutionalized through the dominant cultures block the way to liberation of both the oppressor as to support the emancipation of the oppressed. An unjust society is not born but reproduced continuously by every single representative of the dominant culture and mindset. It is a refusal to be human. Primarily it is not the dehumanization of the subjugated people, but the *inhumanization* of the subjugating oppressor.[25]

The Epistemological Exclusion

The epistemological exclusion is a sense of denial of truth affirmation. It is a sense of denial of the possibilities of understanding the world from his/her own specificity of life-experience; the subjugated people are at loss, surrounded by dominant paradigms of truth claims (epistemic regimes) whose social function is to maintain the supremacy of dominant world-views or philosophical positions. It is but a sort of mystification of consciousness by myths of 'truths.' What is called truth is what 'I' (dominant culture-person) say. This is what Foucault describes as knowledge as (political) power and such political power determines the scope of what is knowledge in the given epoch. We can call this the epistemic- thrown-away-ness. To exemplify epistemic-thrown-away-ness one can invoke the views of Ben Mijuskovic who maintains that all acts of consciousness and conduct are inevitably motivated by the wish to escape or evade thrown-ness.[26]

Consequently, epistemological thrown-away-ness is the prism through which subjugated people are bound to perceive and evaluate reality. At the same time, s/he would be able to transcend such prism through the mediation of 'struggle.' The words of Ambedkar are pertinent here: "We must stand on our own feet and fight as best we can for our rights. So, carry on your agitation and organize your forces. Power and prestige will come to you through struggle."[27]

Moral Sense of Exclusion

The moral sense of exclusion is but a sense of a denial of values to the affirmation of one's existence. It is enforcement of the morality of the dominant paradigms of social practices. According to De Balzac, of all varieties of thrown-away-ness is foundational an ethical thrown-away-ness and it is most terrifying and dangerous to human community. As so understood, the ethical thrown-away-ness includes the thrown-away-ness inherent in the justification of slavery of the Dalits and the self-imposed, sanctified, and authoritarian freedom of the dominant. It entails the formidable moral courage on the part of the Dalits to facing one's thrown-away-ness (pain-experience) in its diverse forms and of converting it into ethically constructive attitudes and social actions.

Sartre declares in 'The Flies' that the 'gift' of freedom 'is a sad one, of thrownness and a shame."[28] One must choose either freedom or subjugation. A critical Dalit chooses freedom and then shudders at the realization that he is condemned to be "alone, alone … all Alone until death."[29]

Reconstruction of Dalit Hermeneutics as Liberative Consciousness

The ontological condition of being excluded amidst cultural reproductive repression is not and cannot be an end in itself. What has been textually and contextually (cultural) made true can also be culturally reconstructed to be proved false and illegitimate. That is what is meant by evolving a *hermeneutics of a social philosophy of liberation with special reference to Dalit culture*, a human project in a world of humane community. It is situated both in a culture of pain experience, a strong sense of social exclusion due to caste perceptions in the caste worldview of Indian society and in a movement of a protest experience towards affirmation of its identity through liberative possibilities. The exclusion that lies within all choices does not stop with oneself, however on the contrary, man's anguished responsibility includes everyone else in the sense that s/he is obligated to fashion himself, lucidly and courageously as possible, to be a model for all others.[30] Such, for Sartre, is the awesome thrown-away-ness of freedom and responsibility that burdens everyone. This is very much true in the life of subjugated people. In spite of the discriminations that s/he faced throughout his or her life, s/he takes up the responsibility to prochoice freedom, a choice that s/he makes in the face of overwhelmed thrownness, not only for himself, but also to construct the essence of freedom of the entire society. Thus, the moral exclusion of the Dalits within caste culture is replaced by a specific choice of an ethics of emancipation of the entire system or social order. In the Ambedkar paradigm, it is an egalitarian project coupled with a sense of secularism, democracy, liberty, fraternity, and dignity of the human person. I suggest the following as the mode of constructing liberative consciousness, which gain momentum in today's emancipatory Dalit discourse.

Metaphysics of Identity Rejected by Subordinated Consciousness

The experience of the Dalits clearly indicates that they have borrowed identity that has been imposed upon them as metaphysically constructed category. They are imposed upon them as irreversible and incontrovertible to their worldview. Further the subordinated communities were made to feel and consider them as real. The dominant discourse was successful in this venture by destroying most of their historical and cultural resources. On the contrary, their life situations reveal that there is nothing metaphysical about their identity, their place in the society, as the dominant world does not have any such constructs to itself. Hence, it becomes evident that such categories were gradually constructed by human agents and imposed upon one section of the people whom it dumped as untouchables. This benefits the dominant self to remain in their domination. Experience also tells them that the subordinated communities cannot empower themselves as long as they believe in such a priori constructions of their identities. These a priori constructions must be deconstructed and contested to create non-metaphysical categories in the physical, socio-political, economic, and cultural contexts.

Historically Constructed Subordinated Consciousness

Subordinated Consciousness is constructed in and through history especially when the subordinated people become aware of their history in which they enjoyed freedom and equality. This has been the concrete historical evidence of Dalit history. This history unfolding itself empowers the subordinated communities to fight aggressively for their equality with others as in the past. Hence, their consciousness is continuously constructed in and trough the history of their social struggle.

Subordinated Consciousness Constructed through the Discourse of Domination vs. Subordination

The basic experience of Dalits is the domination – subordination world as the given. It becomes their fundamental experience. They donot see a world without this dichotomy of caste vs. outcaste. This domination-subordination dichotomy depersonalizes the subordinated, diminishes their self. On the other hand, it imposes upon the self the dominant culture to be subservient to the dominant self, dominant discourse. As a result, the subordinated self is impoverished, alienated from its life world, culture, and ideological purview. In other words, it lives a borrowed life, possesses a borrowed self, and becomes non-being or negation of being.

Subordinated Consciousness Constructed through Resistance as Mediation for Affirmation

Resistance is the mode by which subordinated self exhibits itself. This is the appropriate way of expressing in a dominant-subordinate social web. When subordination is construed against the will and consents of the subordinated self, it logically and ethically needs to construct itself in the same direction as the dominant self imposes upon the subordinated self. There is no other appropriate way of expressing and realizing its equality and dignity than resistance. A subordinated self can affirm and actualize its being only in and through resistance. By resisting all that is imposed upon the subordinated self, it expresses a sense of selfhood, re-establishes its lost identity, and recaptures its position in the social and cultural milieu. Hence, resistance is the appropriate mode of expression to affirm and retrace the subordinated self towards its empowered self and being. History shows that subordinated people have progressed through resistance expressed in protest movements, demonstrations, and other forms of resistance.

Conclusion

Dalit Hermeneutics thus is primarily derived from Dalit reality both in its existential realm and in their day-today experience of oppression, discrimination, and protest to re-establish their historically lost freedom and selfhood. Hermeneutics, though a western tool to understand and interpret realities in their social, economic, political, cultural and historical contexts, is very much in the helm of Indian social and political philosophical fields. It is even significant to employ such tool to not only investigate Indian philosophical systems and values, but also expose the methodological paucity of Indian intellectual exercise and continue to invent newer tools to understand and expand knowledge generation of subaltern realities in Indian soil that is deeply casteist, cultural fundamentalist and political anarchist. It is in such a context, Hermeneutical tool becomes expedient, even ethical to unravel Indian realities.

Notes

1 Lecture delivered by TA David Weininger in 1999, Accessed from *http://people.bu.edu/wwildman/WeirdWildWeb/courses/wphil/lectures/wphil_theme19.htm* (accessed on January 20, 2014).

2 Kees Van Der Pijl, "Hermeneutics, Weber, Constructivism," in *A Survey of Global Political Economy* (Brighton: University of Sussex: 2009), 88-89.

3 Ibid., 91.

4 Ibid., 92.

5 See Rudolf A. Makkreel and Frithjof Rodi (eds.), *Wilhelm Dilthey Selected Works: Introduction to the Human Sciences* (Princeton: Princeton University Press, 1989), 23.

6 Some famous exponents of hermeneutics in contemporary thought might include Friedrich Schleiermacher, Wilhelm Dilthey, Martin Heidegger, Hans Georg Gadamer and Paul Ricouer.

7 W. G. Lycan, *Consciousness and Experience* (New York: MIT Press, 1996), 1.

8 D. W. Jorgenson, "Capital Theory and Investment Behavior," *The American Economic Review*, vol. 53, no. 2 (1963): 247-259.

9 Lycan, *Consciousness and Experience*, 2.

10 R.Wuthnow, *Meaning and Moral Order: Explorations in Cultural Analysis* (California: University of California Press, 1976), 60.

11 W. R. Uttal, *The Psychobiology of Mind* (New York: John Wiley & Sons Inc., 1978), 7.

12 Karl Marx, *A Contribution to the Critique of Political Economy* (London: International Library Publishing Company, 1859).

13 Selvaraj Arulnathan, "Constructing Subordinated Consciousness: A Dalit-Black Reading," *Satya Nilayam Chennai Journal of Intercultural Philosophy* (October 2012): 67-68.

14 Stanley J. Grenz, *A Premier on Postmodernism* (Cambridge: William B. Eerdmans Publishing Company, 1996), 101.

15 Ibid., 102.

16 Johnson J. Puthenpurackal, *Heidegger through Authentic Totality to Total Authenticity* (Burssels: Leuven University Press, 1987), 240.

17 H. G. Gadamer, *Truth and Method*, trans & ed. Garrett Barden & John Cumming (New York: The Seabury Press, 1984), xix.

18 Ibid., 273, 337, 340-341, 349, 357, 358.

19 Wittgenstein in continuation of Gadamer's hermeneutics sees meaning as linguistically contextual revealed in its uses or what he calls 'language games.'

20 James H. Cone, *God of the Oppressed* (Maryknoll: Orbis, 1997), 16–17.

21 Diana L. Hayes, "James Cone's Hermeneutic of Language and Black Theology," Theological Studies 61 (2000): 612.

22 "Fusion of horizons" (German: *Horizontverschmelzung*) is a dialectical concept which results from the rejection of two alternatives: objectivism, whereby the objectification of the other is premised on the forgetting of oneself; and absolute knowledge, according to which universal history can be articulated within a single horizon. Therefore, it argues that we exist neither in closed horizons, nor within a horizon that is unique.

23 Anand Temtumbde, "Globalization and the Dalits" http://ambedkar.org/research/GLOBALISATIONANDTHEDALITS.pdf (accessed on 20 April, 2014).

24 S. Lourdu Nathan, *Hermeneutics of a Philosophy of Dalit Liberation: Re-Structuring Dalit Wisdom* (un published).

25 Ibid., 52.

26 B. Mijuskovic, *Loneliness in Philosophy* (Assen: Van Gorcum, 1979), 1-38.

27 D. Keer, *Ambedkar: Life and Mission* (Bombay: Popular Prakashan, 1995), 168.

28 J. P. Sartre, "The Flies," in *No Exist and Three other Plays*, trans, S. Gilbert (New York: Random House, Vintage Books, 1995), 123.

29 Ibid., 124-125.

30 Cf. Report of the National Campaign on Dalit Human Rights; Prem Kuman Shinde, *Dalits and Human Rights* (Delhi: Isha Books, 2005).

Chapter 14

The Portrait of Women
A Feminist Hermeneutics of Sangam Literature

I. Josephine Jeyashanthi
Creative Writer and Independent Scholar, Chennai

(Considering the complexity of the use of diacritical marks for Tamil and Sanskrit words used in this essay and its negligible importance for the reader, the author has chosen not to use diacritical marks in her essay – Editor.)

Sangam poetry laid down the foundation for the entire Tamil poetic tradition that has flourished for over two thousand years. It is the root of the massive Tamil literary tree, from which branches have spread in many different directions.The predominantly secular Sangam poems influenced the later religious works of Jain, Buddhist, Shaivite, and Vaishnavite poets. The universality of emotions, which are revealed through the natural elements of the five landscapes, has made the poetry timeless, and for all cultures. Max Muller has rightly observed that "Tamil is one of the highly cultivated of languages and possesses the richest store of indigenous literature."[1]

Scholars differ on the period of the Sangam books, but many agree that they are between 300 BCE and 300 CE. Most of the poems are secular in nature. There are very few references of northern religions in the early anthologies. The poets, both men and women, came from all backgrounds – kings, noble men, learned men, doctors, businessmen, teachers, metal smiths, goldsmiths, cattleherders etc. In addition, there is *Tholkaapiyam*, the ancient text. Parts of it were written before the poems. However, some parts were written later.

The word Sangam is not Tamil. It is not used anywhere in the Sangam literature. It is derived from the Sanskrit word 'samgha,' which means 'academy or fraternity.' It comes from the Buddhist and Jain sanghas that existed in Madurai between sixth and eighth centuries, competing with Hinduism. The word is mentioned for the first time in the eighth century commentary of *Iraiyanaar Akapporul*, by Nakkeerar. In A. K. Ramanujan's words, "This spurious name Sangam (fraternity, community) for the poetry is justified not by history, but by poetic practice."[2]

The Sangam was a college or assembly of Tamil poets held under royal patronage. Tradition has it that three Sangarns lasted for 9,900 years; they were attended by 8,598 poets, and had 197 Pandya kings as patrons. The available Sangam literature in fact was compiled between 300 and 600 CE. However, some portions of this literature date back at least to the second century CE. This literature can be roughly divided into two groups, narrative and didactic. The narrative texts are called *Melkannakku* (Eighteen major works) which comprise eight anthologies and ten idylls. The didactic works are called *Kizhkannakku* (Eighteen minor works).

It is believed that the first of the three Sangams were attended by gods and legendary sages, and most of these works have perished. Of the second, there survives only the early Tamil Grammar, *Tholkaapiyam*. The poets of the third Sangam wrote the 'Eight Anthologies' (*Ettuthogai*). Together the 'Eight Anthologies' make up a very large body of poetic literature, and contain well over 2,000 poems, ascribed to more than 200 authors. The eight anthologies are: (i) *Nattrinai*-400 short poems on love; (ii) *Kurunthogai*-400 smaller love poems; (iii) *Aingurunooru*-500 short erotic poems; (iv) *Pathitruppathu*- a short collection of eight poems in praise of the king of Chera country; (v) *Paripaadal*-twenty-four poems in praise of gods; (vi) *Kalithogai*-l50 love poems; (vii) *Aganaanooru*-400 love-lyrics; and (viii) *Puranaanooru*-400 poems in praise of kings. To them must be added 'The ten songs' (*Pathuppaattu*), containing ten longer poems of similar style but of a rather later date.

Sangam poems are so very interesting to read. They describe love between man and woman, friendships, battles, relationships between mothers and daughters, plants, trees, animals, birds, land, mountains, waterfalls, streams, ponds, oceans, and astronomy. They also different eco systems and the people who live there, their way of life, the structure of their houses, their trades, export and import, the Greek and Roman traders and mercenaries, battles between different Tamil kingdoms, and above all, the king who rules the country.

The Sangam literature is basically of two types – one is *Akam* and the other is *Puram*, The *Akam* poetry talks about inner aspects like Love, marriage, household, relationships, etc., whereas Puram talks about exterior aspects like War, business, social life, etc.

The Sangam landscape (Tamil: *Agatthinai* "inner classification") is the name given to a poetic device that was characteristic of love poetry in classical Tamil Sangam literature. The core of the device was the categorization of poems into different *tiṇai*s or modes, depending on the nature, location, mood, and type of relationship represented by the poem. Each *tiṇai* was closely associated with a particular landscape, and imagery associated with that landscape – its flowers, trees, wildlife, people, climate, and geography – was woven into the poem in such a way as to convey a mood, associated with one aspect of a romantic relationship.

The subtle nuances were placed in the literature based on their origin and landscapes. Love and lifestyle of the people were dependent on the nature of the landforms. The people lived very close with the nature. Those are named *kurinji*, *mullai*, *marudham*, *neidhal*, and *paalai*. *Kurinji* refers to the mountains and adjoining lands. *Mullai* refers to the forests and adjoining lands. *Marudham* refers to the plains and adjoining lands. *Neidhal* refers to the sea and adjoining lands. *Paalai* doesnot have a separate landform, whereas the *Kurinji* and *Mullai* lands dried by drought were referred to as *Paalai*. In fact, these lands are mentioned as '*naduvunilai*,' meaning 'in between.' The term '*Paalai*' was coined later by the commentators.

Status of Women in Sangam Literature

The question of the 'status of women' in any historical period is complicated because the lived experience of all women may not be fully reflected in literature.

The question of 'status of women' also needs to be broken down into more concrete questions about the property rights of women, their access to education, their role in the family, marriage and household practices, the nature of their participation in religious life, etc. The literature needs to be carefully interpreted to clues about the lives of women.

Generally, the Sangam period is glorified as the heroic age and the Sangam Literature speaks about love and war. The perceptions of these poems are that the men were warriors and the women were waiting for their men at home.

The arguments for 'women were treated as equal in sangam' would be in the lines of, women were educated, some women chose their partners, women learnt and performed arts and they were poets etc. However compared to the privileges enjoyed by the men, as could be derived from the literature, the status of women was significantly less. They were educated but only at home, whereas men went out for education and women could perform art only in the confines of their homes mostly.

The role of men and women are clearly defined in a poem according to whichlives of men are defined by their work where as lives of women are defined by men. Though this is a common understanding, this cannot be said to be entirely true as because the Sangam Age presents us with three kinds of women:

(i) Women who belong to royal family;
(ii) Common women who lived in five landscapes: *Kurinji* (hill area), *Mullai* (forest), *Marudham* (field), *Neidhal* (sea), *Paalai* (dessert); and
(iii) Women poets

Grammar for the Life of Women

Tholkaapiyam is supposed to be the master guide for all *Sanga Ilakiyam*. *Tholkaapiyam* throws much light on the social history of the Tamil Country prior to the 5th Century BCE. It reflects an age long and characteristic civilization developed by the Tamil Country before they encountered the Aryans.[3] It describes (not prescribes) the Tamil grammar with three divisions *Ezhuthadhikaram* (The formation of words), *Solladhikaram* (The syntax of language) and the final *Poruladhikaram* that talks about the meaning and thoughts that are conveyed in the literary works. It is here in the last division how a Man and Woman should be and should be portrayed are expounded. Thus, this chapter throws light on how gender was viewed and treated before, during and after *Tholkaapiyam*. Let me quote a few verses with the meaning and try to understand what it signifies.

> Timidity, bashfulness, and credulity
> are the ruling traits in woman (heroine).
>
> – *Kalaviyal* 96, *Tholkaapiyam*.

This has been further stated in few other poems too. Apart from these, the qualities like chastity, good conduct, tenderness, patience, temperance, self-control are supposed to be that of a woman. Even for love and marriage, the grammar book, *Tholkaapiyam* laid rules that portray man superior to the woman.

Tholkaapiyam speaks of ten qualities: Lineage, fortitude, age, physical form, tendency to do something great, inclination to sexual passion, steadfastness, graciousness of demeanor, discerning mind and material endowment, that are supposed to be matched between a couple.

> The hero and heroine united in love,
> There mark a harmony and compatibility in
> Lineage, conduct as behaving such ancestry,
> Fortitude, age physical form,
> Propensity and inclination to sexual passion,

Steadfastness, graciousness of demeanour,
A discerning mind and material endowment.
–*Meipattiyal* 269, *Tholkaapiyam*

This seals the question of whether men and women were treated equally in the ancient Tamil culture. The statement that 'the man being of a superiority standing does not matter' begs the question what if it was the other way round. Obviously, the answer is that it matters but why it matters is left unsaid. Moreover, the fact that it is unsaid reveals that the patriarchal society easily understood the why. It is a general notion that in Sangam age, women were treated equally or respectfully, but the rules laid by *Tholkaapiyam* are clear evidence that women were treated inferior to men.

Sangam age is also glorified for the life of people associated with nature. If the poems are read carefully, we could perceive that women lived very close to the nature. Men usually consider nature as their possession and they believe that it is their right to preserve or destroy. Likewise, in Sangam age women were regarded as possession of men, born to give pleasure and joy to men.

For example, *Kalithogai*, a poem written by Kabilar, describes how men had the mindset of possessing women as an object of pleasure. When the boy grips a girl's hand against her wishes, she asserts her displeasure and distress by saying that 'you can't do this just because you enjoy it.' He appeals to her 'to stop analyzing it and to use her high intellect.' He further justifies,'water is sweet to the thirsty person, but it's not sweet to the water itself' (whatever that may mean!). He also says that it is all right to steal and take a girl who is distressed by a five-headed snake. Later the girl presumes that if such is the situation probably she was united with him in the past birth and hence gives in. Again, the man does not heed to the opinion of the woman and instead bulldozes without any concern for her.

Hey, boy, have you no shame?
You're trying to unite me with you
by gripping my hand,
even if I don't want to.
Girl you know all that.
I don't know about it.
You are like a delicate
vine with clusters of flowers.
I desired your sweet embrace, and
embraced you.
Water is sweet to the thirsty person,
But it's not sweet to the water itself.

In these particular lines, the poem expresses that the meaning of the birth of a woman is to fulfill the desire of the man. Scholars, who discuss the meaning of Sangam poems conveniently avoid this reality and simply adore the Sangam age as a golden period for women.

Worshipping Widowhood

In a poem in *Nattrinai*, the heroine does not fear death, but is scared that she might forget her lover in the next birth. It portrays that a woman once engaged in a relationship with a man considered him as a partner forever including her next birth.

> I am not afraid of death.
> What I fear is if I die, I'll forget my
> Lover when I am born again.
> – Ammoovanar, *Nattrinai* 397

From these kinds of poems, Tamil scholars generally project that love of men and women are very deep that a woman does not want to live after the death of her husband. They see it as a symbol of chastity of a woman, but in reality, woman, even from royal family committed suicide just to avoid the cruel life of widowhood after her husband's death.

In case of death of her husband, the woman had to undergo the cruelty of widowhood, which was referred as '*Kaimai.*' A woman describes in graphic detail, the hardship of '*Kaimai*:' ornaments shed, head shaven and seeds of water lily was eaten as food. The poet feels it is better to die than to live a life like that.

In history, we have read about women committing suicide after a defeat in war due to fear of being raped by enemies. Here we read about women committing suicide immediately after the death of their husbands because they feared going through widowhood. One poem in Kụrunthogai describes how after the death of a male monkey, its mate unable to bear the 'pain of widowhood,' gives off its newly born young one to her clan and jumps off from a tall mountain to die. This is obviously a metaphor but goes to depict the pathetic condition of widowhood. It is to be noted that the woman chose to die in this case not because she could not bear the death of her husband but because she did not want to bear the pain of widowhood that would have been inflicted upon her.

The poem by Perunkoppendu, the queen of King Poothapaandiyan, clearly illustrates the plight of a woman after the death of her husband. She wanted to undergo '*Sati*' after her husband's demise, but poets prevented her. During that time, she expressed her fear of widowhood in the following poem.

All of you noble men! All of you noble men!
You do not let me go, you do not allow me to put
an end to my life! All you noble men with your perverse planning!
I am not a woman to endure eating a ball of boiled rice
squeezed within a hand and left lying overnight on a leaf
without a touch of fine fragrant ghee pale as the seeds
from a curving cucumber striped like a squirrel and split
open with a sword, or to eat food of steamed velai leaves
cooked in tamarind and a paste of white sesame seeds,
nor am I one to sleep, without a mat, upon a bed of stones!
To you the pyre of black branches that has been raised
on the burning ground may well be fearful but to me,
now that my husband with his powerful arms has died,
a lake flowing with water where lotuses
open their luxuriant petals and the fire are the same!

– *Puranaanooru* 246

In general, people take this poem as an example for the unmatchable love of woman for her man as she wants to commit suicide immediately after his death, and they also glorify as a woman of modesty and chastity, but the truth is, this particular poem is an illustration of the cruelty of widowhood faced by women, including royal women.

Women in Sangam Age Economy

From the explanations and illustrations given by the scholars for Sangam poems, one could conclude that the women folk had nothing in their life, except longing, waiting for their heroes; but the truth is entirely different. There were women, who worked hard selling fishes, salt, and weaving.

A pastoral economy existed side by side with agriculture in Sangam Age. In Sangam typology, this eco-region was referred to as Mullai. It can be said that women played a leading, possibly even a dominant role in the pastoral economy. Sangam literature like the Perumpanatruppadai gives a detailed account of women doing dairy farming including churning butter, ghee, and buttermilk and hawking these from door to door, in the other eco-zones like *Marudham* and *Neidhal*.[4]

Although Sangam Literature speaks about the life of working-class women, the literary people are not seriously taking these examples for the role of women in economic upliftment. Onepoem speaks about an '*Ainen*' woman, who does not fear the sound of thunder. Scholars do not take these kinds of poems for reference to describe the courageous aspect of hunting women. Instead, they simply praise worship and glorify the timidity of women, who are expected to live at home, waiting for their heroes from battlefield.

The women of warrior community are called *Moodhin Magalir*. *Mullaippaattu* describes the role of women in battlefield. Young women along with soldiers served as guards with swords. It shows the bravery and participation of women in battlefield. Yet, only the sons of *Moodhin Magalir* are praised by the scholars, who never incline to read the role of women in battlefield.

Women Poet in Sangam Age

There are more than thirty women poets in Sangam Literature. It is quite interesting to know, learn, and understand their lives, which teaches us the real feminism. For example, *Tholkaapiyam* says that, a woman cannot praise her own beauty or express her sexual urge. Velliveethiyaar, a great poet of Sangam Age simply overlooked this grammar for womanhood. She, with all her emotions, expressed the beauty of her body and the sexual urge in her thirteen poems.

Another poet, Avvaiyaar, who was greatly respected for her intelligence by the kings of her period, had the courage to challenge, question, and advise the kings. Her platonic friendship with a king named Athiyamaan is described in her poems without any pretension. She even ordered the king once to supply more toddy to a loyal warrior.

Nakkannaiyaar is another poet, who also, like Velliveethiyaar, expressed her love without any fear; but all these poets remain unmarried. Here arise some questions. Why are the intellectual and creative women poets not married?

According to Alan Dundes, men envy that women are able to give birth to the children. The envy of men on the procreative quality of women explicitly flood myth creations, where it is projected as men give birth or create life. Even in Bible, Eve is given birth from the rib of Adam.[5] We could see the same tendency in Sangam Literature.

The daughters of the King Paari, Angavai and Sangavai, who are praised even today for their poem, were taken by Kabilar, a poet and a friend of Paari, from places to places, kings to kings, were not married by anyone.

Unfortunately, these aspects in Sangam poems are simply ignored and overlooked by the scholars as well as learners. The life of women poets and the philosophy that lies in their poems are typical examples of the fact that intelligent women were not accommodated in the normal or regular life. Most of the women poets remained unwedded as they were challenging the common notion of Sangam society about women.

There are no references to female-infanticide or explicit dismissal about the birth of a girl child in Sangam literature. However, the pride of having or giving birth to a male child has been depicted in many occasions. The words of women who had given birth to male children are considered so powerful and it was believed that it would come true. Man appreciates woman who had given him a son to carry on his legacies.

Forgotten Female Bonding

Apart from the protagonist, other characters do exist: The foster mother, friend of the female protagonist, and the other woman, known as *Paratthai*.

The foster mother (*Sevili*) and the friend (*Thozhi*) of the woman play a very important role in the life of protagonists, for they were quite knowledgeable. However, there is no mention about their love life or wedded life. The researchers of Sangam Literature do not throw light on the social status of foster mother and the heroine.

The relationship between the heroine and her friend is simultaneously democratic and emotional since they mutually address each other as "friend" and also as a "mother."

The heroine expresses her love only to herself, as the Sangam concept of "*karpu*" (chastity) prevents explicit statements of love by women, and in those circumstances, the female companion is transformed into a vehicle to convey the depth of the love and the pangs.

In moments of the hero's absence, the heroine suffers a love-laden psycho-dermatological affliction known as pasalai during which her eyes lose their lustre, and her bangles wither loose during the "miserable evenings' and "loneliness" (*Kurunthogai*, 46). In fact, the world remains apathetic to the grief of the beloved. Her love-ridden condition is sadly misunderstood as an evil possession, and her family members perform rites of exorcism on the heroine. During such testing moments it is her friend who states that rites like that of sacrificing a goat or "offering special platters of grain" may not easily placate her except the presence of "the right one, her lover" (*Kurunthogai*, 263).

The litmus test of the depth of the relationship is evident when the heroine agonizes over her friend's concern for her, much more than her beloved's absence thus.

In *Kurunthogai* (224), the heroine laments that it is worse thinking about hero, who is far away, and it is much worse to think about her friend's grief for her. Such unshakable bonds are consequences of the union of the two female souls that remain closely fused despite the oddest of circumstances. This female bonding, which is sporadic in today's modern world, is not discussed as the greatness of women in Sangam Age in Academic or Research area.

The other woman, known as *Paratthai* (Concubine), whom the *Thalaivan* (Hero) visits for pleasure is otherwise neglected and the hero is not bothered about her emotions, feelings or situation of her life. The illustrations of the life condition of *Paratthai* in Sangam are never considered as the dark area of the period. It was also glorified for the heroism of men and patience for women at home. The fact that the *Paratthai* did not have the right to have heir is also simply considered as a norm of the society, and not the plight of women.

Even though the heroine feels worried and jealous, she still talks about her with respect and even refers to her as sister. In a poem (*Aganaanooru*, 16), the emotions of 'the other woman' and how considerately she is treated by Heroine is portrayed. When the son of the heroine is playing, the *Paratthai* thinking no one is around, comes and hugs him affectionately. The heroine witnesses this and embraces her saying 'Don't worry, you are his mother too.' The empathy portrayed is indeed surprising given the situation. This poem gives a lucid picture of the women thinking beyond boundaries. They overlooked their framed life within the narrow walls painted with chastity, timidity, and serenity. Unfortunately, these aspects of women in Sangam do not have place in the modern research.

Notes

1 C. A. Balasubramanian, *Critical Study of Kuruntokai* (Chennai: Paari, 1972), 4.

2 Jan Gonda (ed.), *A History of Indian Literature*, vol. 10 (Wiesbaden: Otto Harrassowitz., 1973), 11.

3 S. Ratnaswami, *A Short History of the Ancient Tamils and their Literature* (Madras: Thaiyalnayaki Veliyeedu, 1979), 44.

4 Sabyasachi Bhattacharya (ed.), *Approaches to History: Essays in Indian Historiography* (New Delhi: Indian Council of Historical Research in association with Primus Books, 2011), 209.

5 Alan Dundes, *Essays in Folklore Theory and Method* (Chennai: Cre-A, 1990), 215.

Contributors

Felix Wilfred, Director, Asian Center of Cross-Cultural Studies. Dr. Wilfred was born in the Indian state of Tamil Nadu pursued his higher studies in Italy and France. After his PhD, he became visiting Professor in Frankfurt, Münster, Nijmegen, Ateneo de Manila and Boston College. From 1977 to 1993 he taught at the St. Paul's Seminary in Tiruchirappalli. From 1993 until his retirement in 2008 he was Professor at the Department of Christian Studies at the University of Madras. He was also a member of the International Theological Commission under the chairmanship of Joseph Cardinal Ratzinger. In 2007, he became the President of the editorial board of the international theological journal *Concilium*. Currently, Wilfred is the Director of the Asian Center of Cross-Cultural Studies (ACCS), which he himself founded. He is a visiting lecturer at the East Asian Pastoral Institute (EAPI) in Manila and member of Statutory Ethical Committee of the Indian Institute of Technology (IIT). In 2011, he joined Trinity College (Dublin) as visiting faculty. His research focuses on intercultural theology and theologies of the Third World, and religious pluralism in Asia.

Nishant Alphonse Irudayadason, Jnana-Deepa Vidyapeeth, Pune. Dr. Irudayadason is a Professor of Philosophy at Jnana-Deepa Vidyapeeth: Pontifical Institute of Philosophy and Religions (JDV), Pune, India. He completed his doctoral studies on Derrida and Ethics at Université Paris-Est and in Insitut catholique de Paris, France. He is currently the Chairperson of the doctoral programme in the Faculty of Philosophy at JDV. His regular courses include Research Methodology, History of Contemporary Philosophy, Ethics, Politics and Hermeneutics. He has presented research papers in many National and International Conferences. He has authored two books and numerous research articles in National and International Journals as well as in edited books. He is a regular contributor to contemporary political analysis in "Light of Truth," a bimonthly published from Kochi, Kerala. His areas of interest include ethics, postmodernity, contemporary western and Indian philosophies. He was the Founder-Director of JDV Centre for Applied Ethics instituted in 2012.

Keith D'Souza, Saint Pius College, Mumbai. Dr. D'Souza teaches Philosophy and Religious Studies at St. Pius College (Mumbai) and is visiting Professor at various other institutions. He has a B.Sc. (Physics) from St. Xavier's College in Mumbai, an M.A. (Philosophy) from the Mumbai University, M.Th. (Systematic Theology) from *Jnana Deepa Vidyapeetha* (Pune). His Ph.D. (Philosophy) is from Marquette University in Wisconsin, USA, with a specialization in narrative hermeneutics. He has published numerous articles in the areas of hermeneutical theory, socio-political philosophy, religious studies and various philosophical themes. He is currently the President of the Association of Christian Philosophers of India (ACPI) and member of the Bombay Philosophical Society. He can be contacted atkeith@jesuits.net.

George Karuvelil is a Jesuit priest belonging to Patna Province, working as formator at Papal Seminary since 1999, and ordinary Professor at the Faculty of Philosophy at Jnana-Deepa Vidyapeeth (JDV), Pune. An accomplished scholar who has published in prestigious National and International Journals such as Journal of Indian Council of Philosophical Research (JICPR), Theological Studies, Zygon: Journal of Religion & Science, besides Church-related publications like Journal of Dharma, and Vidyajyoti; presently he edits *Jnanadeepa: Pune Journal of Religious Studies*.

Kuruvilla Pandikattu, Jnana-Deepa Vidyapeeth, Pune. Dr. Pandikattu is a Professor of Physics, Philosophy and Religion at Jnana-Deepa Vidyapeeth, Pune, India. Currently, he is the Dean of Faculty of Philosophy. He has been actively involved in dialogue between science and religion. Author of more than 36 books and 160 articles, Pandikattu is a Jesuit priest belonging to Dumka-Raiganj Province, India. He has been involved in organising national and international conferences on science-religion dialogue. His main topics of his research are anthropology, eschatology, life-management and transhumanism. He may be contacted at kuru@kuru.in or kuru@jdv.edu.in. Website: www.kuru.in

Brendan Sweetman, Rockhurst University, Kansas City, USA. Dr. Sweetman is a native of Dublin, Ireland, is Professor of Philosophy at Rockhurst University, Kansas City, MO, USA. He is the author or editor of ten books, including *Religion and Science: An Introduction* (Continuum, 2010), *The Vision of Gabriel Marcel* (Rodopi, 2008), *Why Politics Needs Religion: The Place of Religious Arguments in the Public Square* (InterVarsity, 2006), *Contemporary Perspectives on Religious Epistemology* (Oxford U.P., 1992), *A Gabriel Marcel Reader* (St. Augustine's Press, 2011), and, most recently,

Philosophical Thinking and the Religious Context (Bloomsbury, 2013). He has published more than one hundred articles and critical reviews in a variety of journals, collections, and reference works, including *International Philosophical Quarterly*, *American Catholic Philosophical Quarterly*, *Faith and Philosophy*, *Philosophia Christi*, *Philosophical Quarterly*, and *Review of Metaphysics*. A consulting editor and contributor for the *New Catholic Encyclopedia 2014 Supplement*, his books have been translated into several languages.

Jānis Ozoliņš, Australian Catholic University, Melbourne Campus. Dr. Ozoliņš is Professor of Philosophy at Australian Catholic University, Honorary Fellow, Institute of Philosophy and Sociology, University of Latvia. He is a foreign member of the Latvian Academy of Sciences. He is Secretary-General of the World Union of Catholic Philosophical Societies and Vice-President, Asia-Oceania, of the Conférence Mondiale des Institutions Universitaires Catholiques de Philosophie (COMIUCAP). He is Editor of *Res Disputandae* (formerly, *Ethics Education*)*: A Journal for Applied Philosophy and Ethics in the Christian Tradition*. His philosophical interests range broadly over the metaphysics and moral philosophy of Aquinas, classical Confucian philosophy, applied ethics and philosophy of education.

Corina Yoris-Villasana, Andrés Bello Catholic University, Caracas, Venezuela. Dr. Yoris-Villasana has obtained the Bachelor of Arts and Philosophy at the Andrés Bello Catholic University, where she also obtained a PhD in History. Later, she completed the MSc in Logic and Philosophy of Science at the University of Salamanca, where she also completed a PhD in Logic and Philosophy of Science. She has been teaching at Universidad Católica Andrés Bello and her areas of research include Logic, Argument and Political Philosophy. Her thesis in Salamanca titled *Strength and Argumentative Analogy* has won for her Philosophical Research Award in 2010. She is currently the Director of the Master of Philosophy at the Andrés Bello Catholic University and the President of the Venezuelan Society of Philosophy.

Alfredo P. Co, University of Santo Tomas, Manila, Philippines. Dr. Co is an Eminent Professor of Chinese Philosophy and Comparative Philosophy of the Pontifical University of Santo Tomas, Manila, Philippines. He is President of the prestigious Philippine Academy of Philosophical Research and Chair of the Technical Committee for Philosophy of the Philippine Commission on Higher Education. He holds a PhD from the University of Santo Tomas. He holds two postdoctoral doctoral degrees, one from the Chinese University of Hong Kong and the other from the Université de Paris III and Université de Paris IV as a French Government Scholar. He was a Special Fellow of the Pacific Cultural Foundation of Taiwan and of the International Society for Intercultural Studies and Research (India). As well-published scholar, his works have been widely published in prestigious National and International Journals and he also the Editor of *Karunungan*, A Journal of Philosophy. He was the first professor to be honoured with a Festschrift by the quadricentennial Pontifical University of Santo Tomas in 2009.

Francis X. Clooney, Harvard Divinity School, Harvard University. Dr. Clooney is Parkman Professor of Divinity and Professor of Comparative Theology at Harvard Divinity School, Harvard University, and, since 2010, Director of the Center for the Study of World Religions. After earning his doctorate in South Asian languages and civilizations (University of Chicago, 1984), he taught at Boston College for 21 years, until coming to Harvard. In July 2010, he was elected a Fellow of the British Academy, and he has received two honorary doctorates. His primary areas of scholarship are theological commentarial writings in the Sanskrit and Tamil traditions of Hindu India, and the developing field of comparative theology, a discipline distinguished by attentiveness to the dynamics of theological learning deepened through the study of traditions other than one's own. He is the author of numerous articles and books. His latest book, *His Hiding Place Is Darkness: A Hindu-Catholic Theopoetics of Divine Absence* (Stanford University Press, 2013), is an exercise in dramatic theology, exploring the absence of God in accord with the biblical *Song of Songs* and the *Hindu Holy Word of Mouth* (*Tiruvāymōli*). He is a Roman Catholic priest and a member of the Society of Jesus.

Stephen Chundamthadam, Jnana-Deepa Vidapeeth, Pune. Dr. Chundamthadam has obtained his PhD in Advaita Vedanta from University of Madras. He has published several researched articles in scholarly journals and edited works. He teaches Indian Philosophy, Indian Spirituality and World Religions in Jnana-Deepa Vidyapeeth, Pune. He is also a trained specialist in methods of Indian spiritual exercises and Indian martial arts. His areas of research include Indian philosophical and spiritual traditions and World religions. At present, he is the Director of the JDV Centre for Spirituality and Coordinator of MTh in Spirituality in JDV. He is a member of the Society of Jesus belonging to the Jesuit province of Kerala.

Noel Sheth, Saint Xavier's College, Mumbai. Dr. Sheth is President/Rector/Principal Emeritus of Jnana-Deepa Vidyapeeth, Pontifical Institute of Philosophy and Religion, Pune, India, where he was also Professor of Indian Religions and Philosophies. His publications are on the exegesis of Sanskrit and Pāli texts, on Indian religions and on comparative theology and philosophy. A scholar of international repute, he has received many awards, is a member of various international learned societies and administrative bodies, and on the Board of Editors of some international journals. He is an adviser to the

Jesuit General for interreligious relations and member of the Secretariat for Ecumenical and Interreligious Relations of the Society of Jesus.

Selvaraj Arunathan, Director of Indian Social Institute, Bangalore. Dr. Arunathan is a Jesuit priest from Madurai Jesuit province. He is specialized in Dalit and Black Consciousness and has been lecturing on Dalit Identity, Dalit Existence and Dalit Emancipation. He has authored a couple of books, contributed many research articles to National and International Journals. He is a resource person on Social Analysis, Catholic Social Teachings, and Environmental Ethics. At present, he is involved in two important researches: "Implementation of RTE (Right to Education) in Karnataka with Special Reference to SCs and STs" and "A Critical and Analytical Study of the emergence of DICCI (Dalit Indian Chamber of Commerce and Industry)." Formerly, he worked as the Head of the Department of Dalit Studies at Indian Social Institute, New Delhi, and Research Coordinator, ISI Bangalore.

I. Josephine Jeyashanthi (joejesha@gmail.com) is a well-known Tamil writer and novelist. She has been teaching as a Professor of both Tamil Literature and Media Studies in many renowned colleges in India. Many students have used some of her novels as resources for doctoral research. She is one of the pioneers in establishing and succeffuly running Students in Free Enterprise (SIFE) in both Alpha Arts and Science College and in Loyola College, Chennai. As a faculty advisor of SIFE, the student teams led by her secured third place in the international competitions held at Paris in 2006, first among the Asian countires in the New York city in 2007, fouth place in the city of Los Angeles in 2010. Her recent Tamil novel *Sangavai* has won many awards including the prestigious Rengammal memorial award in 2015 and Poet Suganthi Subramaniam memorial award in 2016.